BISHOPS

BISHOPS

The Changing Nature of the Anglican
Episcopate in Mainland Britain

MICHAEL KEULEMANS

Copyright © 2012 by Michael Keulemans.

Library of Congress Control Number: 2011915574
ISBN: Hardcover   978-1-4653-5395-5
                 Softcover   978-1-4653-5394-8
                 Ebook   978-1-4653-5393-1

All rights reserved. No part of this book may be reproduced or transmitted in any form or by any means, electronic or mechanical, including photocopying, recording, or by any information storage and retrieval system, without permission in writing from the copyright owner.

The Scripture quotations contained herein are from the New Revised Standard Version Bible, copyright 1989 by the Division of Christian Education of the National Council of the Churches of Christ in the USA and are used by permission. All rights reserved.

This book was printed in the United States of America.

To order additional copies of this book, contact:
Xlibris Corporation
0-800-644-6988
www.XlibrisPublishing.co.uk
Orders@XlibrisPublishing.co.uk
302352

CONTENTS

ILLUSTRATIONS

FOREWORD

I would like to thank The Revd. Professor Dr. Leslie Francis, the Revd. Canon Jeremy Martineau, Dr. Mandy Robbins and all the members of the Centre for Studies in Rural Ministry at St. Deiniol's Library in Hawarden for their help and encouragement in planning and undertaking the doctoral dissertation upon which this book is based.

My thanks must go to the late Bishop John Robinson of Woolwich and the late Bishop Freddie Temple of Malmesbury, for providing such good models of episcopal oversight early in my career as a Reader and later when I became a member of Church Assembly and then General Synod. My thanks also to Bishop Arthur Bentley-Taylor of the Free Church of England, Bishop David Thomas, the retired Welsh Provincial Assistant Bishop, Bishop Tom Williams, RC Auxiliary Bishop of Liverpool and Bishop Gregory Cameron of St. Asaph in my more recent years as a priest. All four have been generous with their time and given me much encouragement in leading the MV Loach Project and Liverpool Nautical Sixth Form and in starting my parish ministry in Llanwddyn.

I must also thank the Revd. Barrie Williams, the Revd. Andy Jones, Bishop Peter Robinson, Bishop Pelegrino Ronchi and Miss. A. Francis for their help with specific matters of detail.

My thanks go also to those at St. Deiniol's Library, Hawarden, in particular Lindis, Karen and the catering and cleaning staff for their kindness in making my times of research there so comfortable and satisfying. St. Deiniol's is an amazing historical and theological resource.

Thanks too to the staff of my publishers Xlibris, who have tackled this project with helpfulness and competence.

Finally, my sincerest thanks must go to my wife Rosemary, who has borne the burdens of a late academic developer with fortitude and a ready smile. I could not have had greater support anywhere and she has never been too obviously bored by my disjointed jabbering about a subject that so few people know or need to care about.

Needless to say, I alone take responsibility for the accuracy, academic worth and pastoral usefulness of the pages which follow. My hope and prayer is that this book will encourage the development of an Anglican episcopate that is truly Scriptural and effective and will bring glory to God through the lasting growth of the kingdom of Jesus Christ in the hard soil of modern mainland Britain.

Oswestry,
June, 2011.

INTRODUCTION

do bishops really matter to most of Christendom?

ishops are an important and well nigh essential feature of Church
life for by far the largest part of Christendom. In the *UK Christian
Handbook Religious Trends 5 2005/6, 1:3* the statistician Peter Brierley
estimates that in 1990 the Roman Catholics and the Orthodox, the two largest
and most ancient sections of the Christian community, with a total of some
957 million adherents, together comprised some 55% of the world's Christians,
while the Anglican Communion, the Lutherans and a few Methodist Episcopal
groupings merely nudged this already large proportion up to 64%. Thus just
over two thirds of the world's Christians are organised in episcopal fashion,
with the Anglican Communion's 68 million, at 4% of the total, featuring but
slightly in these statistics, however much its Mother Church of Canterbury
might wish to think otherwise.

Non-episcopal Christians, being largely a product of the sixteenth century
Reformation in Western Europe and its myriad mutations and repackagings
since, are but a minority of relative latecomers to the world's ecclesiastical
scene. Yet they should not be too readily dismissed. Through their newer and
freer Charismatic manifestations, they have undoubtedly become a growing,
vibrant and influential element within the Christian body in recent years in
Latin America, Africa and, perhaps not least, in the advanced economies of

the West. At 22% of the world's Christian total in 1990, this clutch of new communities considerably exceeded the 14% of the older and more established Free Church portion. In their spiritual liveliness and willingness to embrace the challenges of a rapidly changing world and yet remain true to the core teachings of Christ, these Charismatic groups are having an increasing impact upon the life of not just their sister Free Churches, but the older and more staid episcopally ordered Churches as well.

The situation in the United Kingdom might seem significantly different, at least at first sight. In the same *UK Christian Handbook Religious Trends 5 2005/6, 2:22-23* Brierley estimates that in 2005 Roman Catholics had 30% of church membership, Anglicans 28% and the Orthodox 5%, making a combined episcopal figure of 63%, almost exactly the same as the global episcopal proportion. However, in the UK, by contrast, the older, established Free Churches totalled 29%, considerably more than their global proportion. This clearly reflects the significant contribution made by the Presbyterians, who being also the legally established Church of Scotland and also strong in Wales and Northern Ireland, comprised some 16% of the UK Christian total.

The newer Charismatic and Pentecostal groupings, despite having a considerable following among the West Indian and African ethnic minorities, actually possessed only 7% of total UK church membership in 1990. For all that, a growing charismatic presence within both the Anglican and Roman Catholic Churches in the UK accounts for at least some of the more exciting and successful attempts to engage with the unchurched masses, such as the Alpha enquirers' courses pioneered at London's Holy Trinity, Brompton. The Charismatic element has also played a major part in the more recent growth of the Cursillo movement, which has done much to revive and energise the Christian lives of countless lay people within the Roman Catholic Church.

It is worth noting three main points in connection with the UK figures. In the first place, they catalogue all four countries of the realm, including Northern Ireland. They show that the largest numbers in both England and Wales are the

Anglicans, while the Presbyterians take the lead in Scotland and the Roman Catholics in Northern Ireland. In three of the home countries, therefore, the largest Churches are episcopal in character.

In the second place, UK Roman Catholic membership has now overtaken the total of Anglican regular worshippers. This reflects the continuing steady decline of Church of England communicants and the weakening social grip of its Establishment position upon the nation. In Wales since 1920, a similarly beneficial though lesser impact of semi-establishment upon the public persona of the Church in Wales has also been wearing off, though at a slower rate than in England. Without the bonus of this social cachet, it is hardly surprising that Anglican memberships in Scotland and Ulster are so much smaller. Yet because of the continuing benefits of this religious inertia in England and Wales, Anglican infant baptisms are still common among non-churchgoers. Indeed, argued upon the basis of baptismal statistics alone, Anglican Church membership in England and Wales would still lift it easily into leading place for the whole UK, leaving the Roman Catholics lagging in second position.

In the third place, in the *UK Christian Handbook Religious Trends 5 2005/6, 8:2-9:18* Brierley shows how the episcopal Churches achieved their 63% proportion of total membership with 56% of the clergy but only 45% of the church buildings. By contrast the mainstream Free Churches had 44% of the church buildings and 36% of the ministers, but only 21% of total church membership. It does therefore appear that despite their increasingly archaic parochial patterns of organisation and their costly burden of historic and architecturally noteworthy buildings, the episcopally governed Churches are nonetheless more efficient than the Free Churches in their use of personnel and plant and the provision of systematic pastoral care, not merely for members of their own worshipping congregations, but also for the wider community beyond.

It is also interesting to note that in mainland Britain, the Anglican Churches have for more than forty years been formally engaged in unity discussions with one or other of the mainline Free Church denominations, in Scotland principally with the Presbyterians and in England and Wales with the Methodists. Time and again talks have stalled over the thorny question of whether these Nonconformist bodies were willing, in Archbishop Geoffrey Fisher's memorable phrase (Purcell, 1969, p. 157) *to take episcopacy into their system.*

The newer and apparently more successful Charismatic groupings such as Vineyard, New Frontiers and King's Church have experienced equal but less public problems in defining the role and character of their own leadership, which appear to boil down in essence to trying to decide how they can best ensure a system of adequate and effective oversight or *episkope* among what are really intended to be loose, fluid and innovative networks of local worshipping Christian fellowships.

what role for bishops?

Despite the ever-increasing number of both diocesan and suffragan posts created in the Church of England over the past century, there has still been little serious thought given to the actual role of the bishop in the Anglican Church. He ordains new clergy, issues licences, confirms the baptised and, sadly too rarely, consecrates a new church building—indeed without his presence, signature and seal, these acts would be considered null and void. Yet the feeling seems to be all too widespread that in its present form our episcopate is not what it should be, that some vital ingredient seems to be missing and that in the selection of new bishops, the assessment of secondary qualities plays a more important part than the attempt to discern if a candidate possesses this special gifting. Quite what constitutes this essential quality still remains something of an open question, but it must surely be high time we tried to find out what it is. In this vital quest we can expect Holy Scripture and nearly two millenia of Christian history to provide us with some useful pointers.

Traditional Catholics cannot conceive of a Church without bishops. It is vital for them to see that bishops are in a clear line of Apostolic succession, maintaining soundness of Apostolic doctrine as much as the more easily recognisable continuity of Apostolic ministry through the laying on of hands down the ages. To them the possible consecration of women as bishops represents a betrayal of both these essentials. Apostolic doctrine, which remains unchanging through the ages, requires a male priest to represent Christ at the sacrament he himself instituted and therefore it follows logically that only a male bishop can ordain the male priests who are to preside at the altar.

Even if all Christendom were somehow to meet together to sanction such an innovation in a sort of grand ecumenical council like Nicaea or Chalcedon— which would today prove to be a ridiculously impossible task institutionally as well as geographically—such an assembly would still find itself flying in the face of both Holy Scripture and Apostolic tradition. For Catholics, a Church with a defective ministry can only result in a Church with deficient sacraments. For that reason alone, some have already gone to Rome and many are now contemplating whether to throw in their lot with the Ordinariate which Pope Benedict so imaginatively established to meet the needs of Anglican Catholic priests and their congregations in 2010.

For Conservative Evangelicals the situation with women bishops is no easier. For some of them, bishops, even while they remain only male, have now become such a constant source of irritation that they would be content to manage entirely without them. It is not hard to see why younger men in particular have got into this negative frame of mind, since they find little evidence of Apostolic qualities in today's episcopate and are often at the sharp end of its open as well as secret antagonism towards both their churches and theological colleges.

Yet in essence the Anglican Evangelical stance should be a great deal more sympathetic towards the episcopalian position than towards the independent. To the Biblical Anglican the evidence of Holy Scripture must always remain paramount, but he has always been more than content to obey the universal tradition of the Christian Church since by doing so he has never actually found himself in direct conflict with the plain teaching of Scripture. The case for having bishops demonstrates no inherent contradiction between tradition and Scripture, but the coming of women bishops would seriously undermine the Biblical principle of male headship in the human family as well as in the family of God's Church. So it happens that for many, like the scattered members of the *Reform* network, this has clearly become a first order issue.

For those whose mindset is more liberal in inclination, and within this group one must realistically include a fair number of *Open Evangelicals* as well as almost all *Affirming Catholics*, bishops occupy a strangely ambivalent role. Openly Liberal bishops, like Tom Butler when he was at Southwark, have proved time and again to be amongst the most authoritarian members of the entire bench. Liberal clergy, by contrast, although vocal in talking up the episcopate as historically essential, tend to view them as a largely administrative class who, although performing a key validating function in choosing and ordaining clergy and chairing committees, have a more obviously decorative attraction by providing a colourful accessory to grace great parochial, diocesan and state celebrations, where, for the most part, they can be relied upon to provide short homilies which will cause offence to none and add immeasurably to the comfort, dignity and acceptability of such occasions.

The *Open Evangelical* hermeneutic, represented by some members of *Fulcrum,* while at least demonstrating outward respect towards Scripture, implies that some of the more plain, irksome and sometimes socially unacceptable commands of the New Testament need to be re-interpreted in the light of the more sophisticated and accommodating society in which we now live. A fair number of modern bishops come from this particular stable, having started off as conservative Evangelicals, but becoming more open to liberal viewpoints as their ecclesiastical careers have progressed and their secular contacts have widened.

Most *Affirming Catholics,* by contrast, make no bones about setting less store by Scripture, since they have tended to acquiesce in nearly all the Biblical agnosticism of the past 150 years and have indeed been actively involved in some of its most recent academic and social manifestations. They tend to be more comfortable with ordering the Church's agenda by the needs of the modern secular state rather than by the demands of a Gospel which they consider to have been modelled to meet the needs of a bygone age.

They nonetheless have a surprisingly rigorous attitude towards worship and an almost pedantic approach towards the words, music and movement of the liturgy. Exuberant mitres, gorgeous vestments and classical gems like a Haydn or Mozart mass are almost *de rigeur* in the London showcases of this charmed circle, but although the ceremonial may be impeccably done, traditional Catholics will say that most of it has long since lost its deeper spiritual significance. The *Affirming Catholic* school of thought has quietly and unobtrusively increased its numbers over the past couple of decades and now has absolute control of both the Scottish and Welsh episcopal benches and probably a slight majority of the English dioceses as well, although in the two English provinces their dominance tends to be obscured by large numbers of suffragan bishops from other viewpoints.

the episcopate is not just an option

This study attempts to look neutrally and analytically at the development of the episcopate in the light of both New Testament evidence and nearly two thousand years of Christian history in an attempt to find out how we arrived at where we are today. The original Church of England ideal of the bishop, so clearly displayed in the 1662 Ordinal, is yet another example of that uniquely Anglican synthesis of Catholic practice and Reformed critique which we see so well expressed in the 1662 Communion service. Its practical, yet deeply theological model of leadership may yet have a pivotal role to play in the remodelling of the diffused body of orthodox Christian believers into some sort of coherent whole.

This is at last coming to be seen as essential if we are to have any realistic chance of acting together effectively in taking on and meeting the challenges of an increasingly anti-Christian age. We must be prepared to make every effort to ensure that the saving and transforming Gospel of Jesus, Son of God incarnate and Divine Rescuer of sinners is communicated effectively to generations bred in an environment totally ignorant of Christian things and out of touch with any branch of the Christian Church.

It seems obvious that in the broadest terms, the Catholics of Christendom, whether Anglican, Roman or Orthodox, hold genuinely to the truth of Holy Scripture and the three historic Creeds, but place an altogether undue emphasis upon the sacraments in the building up and sustaining of the Church and its members. This much is clear from any observation of the content and pattern of their regular public worship.

In a similar fashion, those on the Evangelical side of the fence, whether Anglican, within the Reformed denominations or in the growing Independent sector, seem to place almost their entire emphasis upon the ministry of the Word, in many cases to the virtual exclusion of the Creeds and the sacraments. This too becomes obvious from the content and pattern of their regular public worship.

If there is to be the necessary coming together of all believing Christians into one convincing witness to an unbelieving and cynical world, then we must heed afresh the pressing words of the Lord Jesus as he brings the needs of his disciples before God in his high priestly prayer recorded in John 17:11. There he asks, *Holy Father, protect them in your name that you have given me, so that they may be one, as we are one.*

Later in the prayer in verses 22-23 Jesus explains that this unity among his disciples, for which he is praying, is in fact nothing less than a visible expression of the divine glory which he wants to share with them and with everyone—*I in them and you in me, that they may become completely one, so that the world may know that you have sent me and have loved them . . .* This unity is both the proof of his mission and the testimonial to his truth that we must present to the world. Here is the the Lord's chosen path to effective evangelism.

If this unity that the Lord wishes for us all is ever to become a reality, then it can come about only when Catholics are serious about agreeing to level up the preaching and study of God's written Word to that of the sacraments and Evangelicals admit that it is high time to give the Eucharist a place of honour closer to that of the Word. What we need to rediscover at this crucial moment in Christian history is a careful balance between these two aspects of ministry, the very essence of the despised Anglican *via media* so eminently laid out by Bishop Lancelot Andrewes early in the 17th century. This is a middle way quite unlike what we see in Anglicanism today. It is not a loose or informal gathering of those who believe the bare minimum and look for whatever is the least demanding or challenging, but instead a middle way that represents a generous amalgam of what is the best, the truest and the most in Christian history.

As the main denominations capitulate to the demands of a secular world and increasingly break adrift from their moorings in Holy Scripture and the universal tradition of the Church, orthodox Christian people, from Roman Catholics and Anglicans, through to Independent Evangelicals and Baptists, may in the future find themselves thrown together in common sacrificial witness to Jesus and a shared experience of ecclesiastical loneliness. To satisfy the needs and aspirations of such a varied clientele there can be no hope of achieving a workable unity without the bishop. Indeed, it is within such a unity that the bishop will become once again what he was in the life of the early Church, the teaching spokesman for God, the visible leader and encourager of the local Christian community, the guarantee of its unity of purpose and the authority behind all its ministry and witness. If the whole breadth of opinion within the believing Christian community is to be represented and reflected in its leadership, then such a renewed episcopate becomes an essential—there is no practical alternative.

an overview of the contents

Chapter One discovers the origins of pastoral oversight within the New Testament, and tries to tease out the distinction between the Apostolate instituted by Christ himself and the eldership which developed immediately afterwards. It also examines in detail the linguistic connections behind the interchangeable terms of *episkopos* and *presbuteros* used for this eldership in the Acts of the Apostles and the Epistles and seeks to elucidate from Old Testament Hebrew, Septuagint, Classical and New Testament Greek sources what the original functions and character of this eldership might have been meant to be.

Chapter Two examines in detail what the early Church Fathers had to say about the character and functions of what was by then becoming a separate episcopate, paying particular attention to how analogies were discovered within the Old Testament, how Ignatius of Antioch developed the concept of the local bishop as the focus of Christian unity, how Cyprian of Carthage began to formulate thinking about a bishop's quasi-monarchical role and what procedures appear to have been used to appoint and consecrate new bishops. The chapter then examines some of the ways in which these concepts became affected by the governmental fashions of the later Roman Empire within which they grew and which they themselves came to influence in their turn after Christianity became its official religion under Constantine the Great.

Chapter Three looks at Britain in the early and later Middle Ages, highlighting the special phenomenon of Celtic ministerial organisation and how the English episcopate developed its feudal character both before and after the Norman Conquest. It observes the growing role of bishops as councillors to the monarch and notices in passing the special features and qualities marking the work of two outstanding, but contrasting English mediaeval bishops, Robert Grosseteste of Lincoln and William Wykeham of Winchester, whilst also examining the acute spiritual and temporal tensions that affected those who held such high positions in both Church and State.

Chapter Four investigates the progress of the English Reformation and particularly the important changes to the Ordinal brought about by Thomas Cranmer: how attempts were made both to secure the Apostolic Succession and to remodel the functions and effectiveness of the episcopate around the Scriptural emphasis of teaching the faith; and how these twin aims affected the perceived role of the episcopate within the final shape of the Elizabethan Church settlement. The chapter goes on to examine how the classic Anglican episcopate of the 17th and 18th centuries developed out of this settlement, paying particular regard to the careers of two noteworthy exemplars, Lancelot Andrewes of Winchester and Thomas Wilson of Sodor and Man.

Chapter Five examines how the new Tractarian party developed in the 1830s and 40s within the Church of England, finding itself in competition with a powerful Evangelical minority and with the dominant Latitudinarians, who were themselves being increasingly influenced in a liberal direction by the spread of new scientific ideas. The mechanisms by which Crown episcopal appointments were made under the Palmerston, Disraeli, Gladstone and Salisbury administrations are put beneath the microscope, especially in terms of the competing influences of Queen Victoria, her Prime Ministers and her Archbishops of Canterbury.

Chapter Six turns the spotlight upon the individual backgrounds, qualifications and experience of the English episcopate over the past century. From the data provided by the *Crockford Clerical Directory* it undertakes a statistical analysis of all diocesan bishops at twenty year intervals between 1905 and 2005, classifying them according to their university career and attainments, length of parochial experience, university or theological college teaching and previous ministry as archdeacons or suffragan bishops, as well as their age when first elevated to the bench. These *Crockford* data are augmented wherever possible by other details culled from retrospective editions of *Who was Who*, particularly where they involve intriguing social indicators such as parentage, type of school attended and other aspects of personal information.

Chapter Seven focuses upon the special historical, cultural and linguistic character of the Church in Wales and its divergent organisational characteristics from the Church of England since Disestablishment in 1920, examining in particular the new system it devised for the appointment of its own bishops and parish priests and the generally monochrome form of churchmanship which has developed out of it. Biographical details of members of the bench between 1905 and 2005 are then briefly analysed from *Crockford* and *Who was Who* data in the same way as for English bishops.

Chapter Eight moves the searchlight onto the Scottish Episcopal Church, examining its unique history from Reformation struggles with Presbyterianism to its virtual start from scratch after the refusal of its bishops to take the oath of allegiance to the Hanoverian monarchs. The history of its own particular method of episcopal appointment is examined in detail, as is the international influence of its original electoral procedures in the light of Scotland's key assistance to the fledgling Protestant Episcopal Church in the USA at the end of the 18th century. The holders of episcopal office between 1905 and 2005 are then briefly analysed using the techniques and categories already adopted for English and Welsh diocesans.

Chapter Nine analyses the changing environment of the Church of England since the establishment of Synodical Government in 1970. It examines the ground-breaking 1990 report of the Archbishops' Group on the Episcopate and the operation of the Crown Nomination Committee and seeks to isolate recent trends in views of the episcopal office and the qualities needed for those who aspire to it, looking in particular at the content of the new Ordinal in *Common Worship*. Changing thinking on the episcopate is then briefly evaluated within the Roman Catholic and Orthodox Churches and among other episcopally ordered bodies, especially those with their roots in Anglicanism.

Chapter Ten presents the statistical survey undertaken upon the Anglican episcopate within its context, examining the reasons behind choosing the four dioceses of Bradford, Leicester, Monmouth and Edinburgh to represent the three mainland Anglican Churches. It goes on to stake out the purpose and scope of the questionnaire submitted to all their serving diocesan clergy and half of their key laity, as well as to all English, Scottish and Welsh bishops who retired between 2000 and 2008. It then explains the thinking and methodology behind the common spine of the questionnaire and those extra questions specifically directed to clergy, laity and retired bishops respectively.

This chapter goes on to assess the effectiveness of the chosen survey method. It then moves to collating the wide-ranging statistical results of the questionnaires and attempts to identify those areas where the views, feelings and hopes of laity, clergy and retired bishops most nearly coincide and where their opinions of the episcopal office and its many functions clearly diverge. Preferences in the method of appointment of new bishops are also compared, both between the clergy, laity and retired bishops, and between the three mainland UK Churches.

Chapter Eleven gives the bishops who retired between 2000 and 2008 the opportunity to speak in their own words about their particular perceptions of the episcopate. It concentrates especially upon the satisfactions and the disappointments that they experienced in the course of their work, but also allows them to make more detailed observations upon matters that were covered briefly within the common spine of the questionnaire. Some of these comments prove to be very pithy, as well as informative and revealing.

Chapter Twelve presents the main findings of the survey and attempts to place them within a theological and pastoral context, asking whether existing Anglican appointment procedures are sufficiently open, transparent and democratic in an age that increasingly looks for accountability in the holders of high public office. This chapter also looks for areas in which *episkope* could be exercised more effectively and sensitively. It asks whether existing patterns of diocesan organisation and episcopal ministry remain necessary or viable in the changing social, intellectual, theological and financial environment within which the modern Church must conduct its operations if it is to ensure the greater glory of God through the furtherance of the Gospel and the building of his kingdom.

Chapter Twelve goes on to assert that the sheer size of existing Anglican dioceses in England and Wales has made them a pastoral anachronism. Instead it is suggested that the rural deanery of between 25 and 35 parishes should be upgraded into a mini-diocese so that its clergy and people are able to enjoy regular and accessible oversight and bishops do not find themselves stretched to breaking point. At the same time the appearance of the metropolitan mega-churches and their plants, together with the results of new *Fresh Expressions* ministries are examined to see if they may in time give rise to a totally new brand of bishop, whose function arises naturally out of a developing pastoral situation rather than being imposed upon it by an external straightjacket inherited from the ministerial circumstances and necessities of the far distant Middle Ages.

CHAPTER ONE

The Origins and Purpose of the Episcopate

the significance of the New Testament evidence

It has often been said that in order to give proper consideration to any aspect of Christian theology and practice, there can be no better place to start than within the pages of the New Testament. This must surely apply to the episcopate as much as to anything else. As the Roman Catholic theologian Hans Kung observes so aptly (1968, pp. 17-18):

> *The New Testament writings give us more than just the antecedents and the founding of the history of the Church and ecclesiology . . . . They give us the first decisive phases of a by no means straightforward, indeed complex history of the Church and its self understanding.*

Innumerable scholars, in particular German ones, have spent the past two centuries arguing their case backwards and forwards about the authorship and dating of its separate parts, but even the modern scholar Delbert Burkett

(2002, p. 106) is forced to admit baldly that *by the end of the first century, most of the books that now make up the New Testament had been written and were being collected and read in the churches,* a view widely held by most scholars like F.F. Bruce (1943, p. 12) and Merrill Tenney (1953, p. 401) until around the middle of the 20th century.

More specifically, almost the entire corpus of those New Testament writings relevant to the development of the ordained ministry, notably the three Synoptic Gospels, the Acts of the Apostles, the Pastoral Epistles and 1 Peter, are dated by the German academic Udo Schnelle (1998, pp. 197-423) to before 100 and may therefore be considered to predate the earliest surviving patristic writings, such as Ignatius's *Epistles,* Polycarp's *Epistle to the Philippians* or the allegorical *Shepherd of Hermas,* with the definite exception of only Clement's *Epistle to the Corinthians* and maybe also the *Epistle of Barnabas,* which Burkett (2002, p. 427) reckons could date from as early as 70.

It should therefore be within the pages of the New Testament itself, rather than among the early Fathers of the Church that we begin a search for the roots of the episcopal office, which so quickly became standard practice and thinking for the many Christian communities scattered around the eastern coasts of the Mediterranean Sea which burst into existence as a direct result of the missionary journeys of Peter, Paul, Barnabas, Philip and other early evangelists.

the Apostolate and those who followed after

Perhaps we should begin this investigation by trying to unscramble the relative positions of the Apostles and the new church eldership which they established, especially in the light of the confusion that arose between the two of them over the course of the following centuries. The three Synoptic writers and John all record how the Lord originally called his Twelve Apostles. It is a significant fact that apart from the seminal happenings of Palm Sunday, Good Friday and Easter, all four Evangelists should record this particular event alongside only three others in the entire life of Jesus; the preaching of John the Baptist, the cleansing of the temple and the feeding of the five thousand. This must surely be evidence of the vital importance attached to the call of the Twelve when the first Christians came to compile precise written records of Christ's earthly ministry. Yet these four accounts merely record how Jesus recruited his Apostles: the only function he mentioned to them at this initial stage of their calling was that they should follow him (Luke 5:27).

By contrast there are two accounts only of Jesus actually commissioning his Apostles for the task they were to perform after his Ascension. The fourth Gospel, in the opinion of most scholars probably written towards the very end of the first century, but according to Schnelle (1998, p. 477) maybe as late as 110 to 120, records in chapter 20 how on Easter Night Jesus appeared to ten of them locked up in a house because of their fear of the Jews. Referring to the second part of verse 21, the popular commentator Alan Richardson (1959, p. 211) says:

> The risen Christ commissions his disciples for their task of continuing the mission to the world upon which the Father had sent the Son; that task is to gather mankind into the unity of the Father and the Son which constitutes the Church of Christ; it is nothing less than to restore the unity of mankind, which was lost by Adam's fall at the first creation.

Like most commentators, Richardson chooses not to remark upon the ministerial significance of Jesus breathing upon them and saying, *Receive the Holy Spirit*, neither does he come down upon one side or the other in the debate about whether the authority of Jesus in verse 23 is given to the whole Church corporately or to a particular order or ministry within it, as is argued by Gregory Dix (1946, p. 104) and Gabriel Hebert (1946, pp. 531-534).

Matthew records the Lord in conversation with the Twelve (without Judas) before his Ascension in 28:18-20. Whether or not this section is a later interpolation into a basically Jewish text which blends Mark's account with material from the mystery Q, as B.H. Streeter (1924, pp. 273-292)) and his successors would have us think, the Lutheran theologian E. Schweizer (1982, p. 15) is inclined to date the first Gospel between 70 and 80. W.D. Davies and D.C Allison (1988, p. 128) state that the majority of scholars favour a date in the final quarter of the first century. Certainly Irenaeus, Bishop of Lyons was already familiar with it as early as the second half of the next century. Matthew reports Jesus as commissioning the Apostles with these words:

> *All authority has been given to me in heaven and on earth. Go therefore and make disciples of all nations, baptising them in the name of the Father, and of the Son and of the Holy Spirit, and teaching them to obey everything that I have commanded you.*

In Matthew's account, therefore, the Apostles are called to first to evangelise, then to baptise converts in the name of the Trinity and finally to teach them the entirety of the Lord's message and its demands upon their lives.

Luke, according to Schnelle (1998, p. 243), probably writing in the final decade of the first century, but maybe some time earlier, records in Acts 1:21 how in the days following the Ascension, Peter stood up in the assembly of around 120 Christian believers and declared that somebody should be added to the Apostolic band of Eleven to replace Judas, who had, in the very significant words of verse 20, vacated his position of *episkopos*. In this passage Peter lays down clearly both the purpose and the qualifications of the original Apostolate. The person to be chosen as Judas's replacement must be:

> *"One of the men who have accompanied us throughout the time that the Lord Jesus went in and out among us, beginning from the baptism of John until the day that he was taken up from us—one of these must become*

a witness with us to his resurrection." So they proposed Joseph . . . and Matthias. Then they prayed and said, "Lord, you know everyone's heart, show us which one of these two you have chosen to take the place in this ministry and apostleship from which Judas turned aside to go to his own place." And they cast lots for them, and the lot fell on Matthias; and he was added to the eleven apostles.

Some clear conclusions may be drawn from this passage. As John Stott asserts (1990, pp. 57-58), in the eyes of the earliest Christians the Apostles had to be those who had physically accompanied Jesus throughout the three years of his public ministry, right up to the moment of his Ascension; and all of them had to be eye witnesses of his Resurrection. These two qualifications could clearly not be reproduced in a literal sense among those who were later to succeed them. Yet, in some sense, as Peter's reference to Judas demonstrates, the Apostles considered that the task to which they had been appointed by Christ himself was very much in the nature of *episkope* or oversight. Thus we are immediately forced to face up to tricky issues concerning the relationship of the Twelve to those Christian leaders who came immediately after them and to whom they inevitably passed on that selfsame *episkope*.

Bishop J.B. Lightfoot (1901, pp. 23-34) makes the telling point that the functions of the Apostles and their successors differed widely. The Apostle, like the prophet or the evangelist, held no *local* office. He was essentially, as his name implies, a missionary moving about from place to place, founding and confirming new brotherhoods of Christians.

Lightfoot goes on to identify two major events that may have propelled the fledgling Church into making its ministerial arrangements more settled and locally focussed. He sees the martyrdom of Peter, Paul and James as crucial in removing the key figures from the Apostolic leadership, while the Roman overthrow of Jerusalem in 70 removed the visible focus of the Church—these events coming together to create *a crying need for some organisation which should cement together the diverse elements of Christian society and preserve it from disintegration.*

He backs up his case by quoting Eusebius. This 4th century historian records the surviving Apostles and personal disciples of the Lord, together with those of his relations still alive, meeting to consult together and unanimously appointing Symeon, son of Clopas to the leadership of the Jerusalem Church in succession to James, the Lord's brother, who had been summarily executed as part of Herod Agrippa's outburst of persecution. (Acts 12:1-2) .

Not long after this point the New Testament evidence becomes tantalisingly fragmentary. Most of the Apostles never reappear in Luke's fast-moving narrative of the growing Church in the years and decades after Pentecost and we can glean only unrelated scraps of their subsequent ministry from passing references in later documents.

Whatever scholars may say about the relationship between the Apostolate instituted by Jesus himself and those who took over the leadership of the churches immediately afterwards, there is no way of avoiding the unique status the Lord accorded to the original Twelve. Soon after he told them how hard it was for rich people to enter the Kingdom of God, Peter responded by reminding him that they had left behind all their earthly possessions to follow him. What was in it for them? The Lord's reply was, *Truly I tell you . . . when the Son of Man is seated on the throne of his glory, you who have followed me will also sit on twelve thrones, judging the twelve tribes of Israel (Matthew 19:27-28).*

This amazing promise is fulfilled in Revelation 4:4, where around the great throne of God are twenty four other thrones, on which are seated 24 crowned *presbuteroi*, twelve of them the patriarchs and prophets of the Old Testament and twelve of them those the author calls in Revelation 21:14 the *twelve apostles of the Lamb*, whose names are also inscribed upon the twelve foundations of the city wall of the New Jerusalem. The Apostles are clearly in a league of their own in the honours of Heaven!

Paul—the thirteenth apostle?

However, there is one major event that must be judged to have had a huge bearing upon the crucial issue of the precise nature of the Apostolate. It is the arrival of the ardent Pharisee Saul, later to be renamed Paul, upon the scene. He is reported by Luke (Acts 9:1-19) and in his own words (1 Corinthians.15:8) to have had a direct encounter with the risen Jesus when the searing light from heaven shone down upon him as he was on the road to Damascus to ferret out and arrest the members of its Christian community. After some time it appears that he was introduced to the fellowship of the Apostles in Jerusalem by Barnabas. Acts 9:28 refers to Paul going *in and out among them,* which implies that he had ample time to hear from them the entire Apostolic message before they sent him off to his home city of Tarsus. When he reappeared in Antioch, the prophets and teachers there fasted and prayed, laid hands upon Paul and Barnabas and then sent them away to preach the Gospel.

Although by his own admission on many occasions, just one of many evangelists and leaders in the diverse development of the infant church, Paul seems to have become, certainly in his own eyes, as Stott (1990, p. 165) interprets Romans 11:13, a sort of *thirteenth* Apostle. In nine of the thirteen epistles that bear his name, Paul makes his introductory greeting to his readers by calling himself an Apostle. He goes on to reinforce this impression in Galatians 1:17, where he refers to the Jerusalem leadership as *those who were Apostles before me.*

This Galatian passage, when set alongside the record of Acts 9:19-30, throws up problems about exactly when Paul first came into physical contact with the first Apostles in Jerusalem and precisely what was the nature of his relationship with them. He claims in Galatians 1:17-23 that after his conversion on the Damascus road he did not confer with any human being:

> *... nor did I go up to Jerusalem ... but went away at once into Arabia ...*
> *Then after three years I did go up to Jerusalem to visit Cephas and stayed*

with him for fifteen days; but I did not see any other Apostle except James the Lord's brother . . . Then I went into the regions of Syria and Cilicia, and I was still unknown by sight to the churches of Judea that are in Christ; they only heard it said, "The one who formerly was persecuting us is now proclaiming the faith he once tried to destroy."

The commentator Bishop Alfred Blunt (1925, p. 65) considers that in these verses Paul is merely going out of his way to show that he has no anarchic feelings towards the Jerusalem leaders, even though he finds himself driven to assert the independence of manoeuvre to which he feels himself entitled as an Apostle himself. Blunt reads Paul's intentions this way:

. . . he recites all the occasions on which he might possibly have come within the scope of their authority, and vehemently asserts that no such transaction in fact took place. Any details which did not bear on this question would only confuse the direct purpose of his narrative. The author of Acts, on the other hand, is interested in the process by which the Church grew and opened its door to the Gentiles; his concern is therefore with public developments, not with private negotiations.

Thus, whatever the exact sequence of events after his conversion, it is obvious that Paul seems in a certain sense to bridge the gap between Christ's chosen Twelve and a second generation of leaders who, although they might not have physically lived and worked with Jesus and witnessed the great events of Easter and afterwards, nonetheless shared with the original Twelve the Apostolic mission and authority given them by Jesus, and which Peter, in his address to the nascent Church (Acts 1:20) so clearly thought of as the very essence of *episkope.*

There may be some oblique confirmation of this second wave of Apostles in 2 Corinthians chapters 11 and 12, where Paul warns his readers that other men have visited the Corinthian Church and claimed the status of Apostles while preaching a different Gospel. He suggests that the validity of their Apostolic call will be vindicated only if they have experienced beatings, sufferings, deprivation, shipwreck and other tribulations in the same way as he has done. In 12:12 he reminds them that in his ministry at Corinth *the signs of a true apostle were performed among you with utmost patience, signs and wonders and mighty works.*

evidence for oversight in Acts and the Pastoral Epistles

The earliest evidence to be found for an embryonic ministerial structure appears not long after Stephen was martyred and Peter made his momentous visit to the Roman centurion Cornelius at Caesaria in response to the vision of the heavenly sheet he had received while falling into an exhausted sleep on the rooftop in Joppa. In Acts 11:29-30 Luke records that the Christians in Antioch sent their famine relief contributions to the *presbuteroi* of the Church in Jerusalem by means of Barnabas and Paul. This makes it clear that the first Christian community was headed not just by James, but also by a team of *presbuteroi* working alongside him.

The fruits of Apostolic evangelistic endeavour appeared with extraordinary rapidity. Peter's sermon to the Jews and proselytes on the Day of Pentecost produced about 3,000 new Christians (Acts 2:5-41) and as the crowd contained people of every conceivable nationality in the known world, from Rome right round the Mediterranean coasts to Libya, we can assume that local groups of believers must have emerged in some of these places soon after. A short time later the martyrdom of Stephen led to an outburst of persecution which drove Christians out of Jerusalem and scattered them across the countryside of Judaea and Samaria and then farther away into Phoenicia, Cyprus and Antioch (Acts 11:19). It must soon have become obvious that all these widely scattered little groups of new believers would require the provision of proper teaching, pastoral care and oversight.

Not long after, when the necessity arose for key policy decisions to be taken by the Jerusalem Church because of the influx of gentile converts, Barnabas and Paul came to Jerusalem to seek the views of the Apostles, *presbuteroi* and the rest of the church. The decision to relax Jewish ceremonial demands upon the gentile Christians was explained by James and agreed to by his team of *presbuteroi*, with the people giving their consent (Acts 15:1-29) and the explanatory letter containing their decision was sent to the churches in Antioch, Syria and Cilicia in the name of the Apostles, *presbuteroi* and brethren of Jerusalem by the hand of Paul, Barnabas, Barsabbas and Silas.

Paul went on to preach the Gospel in company with Barnabas on his first missionary journey via Cyprus to Pisidia and Pamphylia and then with Silas on his second journey to Asia as far west as the main cities of Greece. These campaigns produced many new churches. Later in Acts 20:28 Paul sends for the *episkopoi* from Ephesus on his way back to Jerusalem after having spent nearly three years of urban evangelism in their city during his third missionary journey. He makes no mention of how they had been chosen for their task, or who had admitted them to it, but he says to them:

> *I did not shrink from declaring to you the whole purpose of God. Keep watch over yourselves and over all the flock, of which the Holy Spirit has made you* episkopoi, *to shepherd the church of God that he obtained with the blood of his own Son.*

From this particular passage it is clear that the Christian leadership of Ephesus, the capital city of the Roman province of Asia, was multiple in nature like that of Jerusalem and had been soundly and intensively taught what Luke calls *the Apostles' doctrine* (Acts 2:42) by Paul himself.

The same pattern emerges when Paul writes to the Philippians in one of his undisputed epistles, which Schnelle thinks was probably composed about 60. Here he greets *all the saints in Christ Jesus,* together with the *episkopoi and diakonoi,* clearly demonstrating that in this strategic city on the main east-west road of the Roman Empire, the church was led by the joint ministry of a group of elders, together with a team of diaconal helpers (Philippians 1:1).

The Pastoral Epistles seem to display a similar pattern of ministry. The writer of the letter to Titus, reckoned by Dix (1946, p. 263) to have been composed not much later than 90, tells him (1:5-7):

> *I left you behind in Crete for this reason, that you should put in order*
> *what remained to be done, and should appoint* presbuteroi *in every town,*
> *as I directed you: someone who is blameless, married only once, whose*
> *children are believers, not accused of debauchery and not rebellious. For*
> *an* episkopos, *as God's steward, must be blameless . . .*

Schnelle (1998, pp. 328-332) follows Martin Dibelius and many other German scholars in considering this and the other Pastorals to be pseudepigraphical, largely on account of their exceptional linguistic features, but the quoted passage and the emotionally touching nature of the closing personal instructions in 3:12-14 demonstrate that the Epistle to Titus could perfectly well have been written by Paul himself sometime before his martyrdom under Nero around 67.

Although missing from Marcion's Canon (c.140), Titus and the other Pastorals, like the rest of Paul's epistles, each have their Marcionite Prologue, itemised by A. Souter (1913, p. 207). Bruce Metzger (1987, pp. 194-201) adds the important evidence that the Pastorals were also included in the late 2nd century Muratorian Fragment. They were also extensively quoted by the early Fathers from Polycarp onwards and there are possible traces in both the epistles of Clement of Rome and Ignatius of Antioch.

It is therefore abundantly clear that in the Pastorals, as well as in Acts, the two original nouns used for the local leaders of the new Christian communities are both *episkopoi* and *presbuteroi,* generally used interchangeably, but perhaps representing two different descriptive strands of the same ministerial character and function. In many English translations both Greek words are somewhat unhelpfully rendered as *elder*.

It seems that these elders were *presbuteroi*, in the sense that they were seniors in the local Christian community, whether by age, by experience or both, but *episkopoi* in their function as overseers or guardians of that community. Throughout the first century we seem to see this pattern of ministry referred to again and again, with both the seniority and the functional aspects of local leadership being combined into this single comprehensive leadership role.

As we saw earlier in Jerusalem, Ephesus and Crete, these leaders never seem to operate alone. The writer of the Epistle of James (5:14) calls on the sick to summon the *presbuteroi* of the church for prayer and anointing with oil. In Acts 14 Paul and Barnabas strengthen the disciples of Lystra, Iconium and Antioch and appoint *presbuteroi* for them in each church. Seniors, guardians—and yet again referred to in the plural, as if, in this earliest phase of the Church's existence, elder-guardianship was invariably exercised within a team setting.

Peter's first Epistle to the Jewish Christian converts dispersed around Asia Minor, reckoned by Bo Reicke (1964, p. 71) and C.E.B. Cranfield (1964, p. 17) to date from before Peter's Death in Rome in 65, reminds them how they have been rescued by Jesus from going astray like lost sheep, but adds that *you have now returned to the shepherd and* episkopos *of your souls* (2:25). It is Jesus, the Good Shepherd, who is here portrayed as the guardian, who keeps the wayward sheep penned safely and happily within the fold, around which are many wolves waiting for their chance to pounce, the very same danger alluded to by Paul in his farewell to the Ephesian leaders in Acts 20:28-30. If Jesus guards and protects, then the lesser guardians who operate under the Master's direct orders must be equally careful to guard and protect the flock.

From the earliest days of the Church, this joint ministry of eldership and guardianship seems to have been bestowed with prayer and the laying on of hands, although curiously, almost the only direct New Testament evidence for this procedure was when Stephen and six other men were ordained *diakonoi* (Acts 6:5-6) to look after the material welfare of the first Christian community in Jerusalem. Beyond that single instance, the only other hint comes when Paul encourages Timothy (2 Timothy 1:6) to stir up the gift that has been given him through the laying on of the Apostle's hands and those of the council of *presbuteroi* (1 Tim. 4:14).

The qualifications for oversight

When it comes to the qualifications necessary for entry to this elder—guardian ministry, we seem to be on much firmer ground. In his first letter to Timothy Paul elaborates at some length about them (3:1-7):

> *The saying is sure: whoever aspires to the office of* episkopos *desires a noble task. Now an* episkopos *must be above reproach, married only once, temperate, sensible, respectable, hospitable, an apt teacher, not a drunkard, not violent but gentle, not quarrelsome, and not a lover of money. He must manage his own household well, keeping his children submissive and respectful in every way—for if someone does not know how to manage his own household, how can he take care of God's church? He must not be a recent convert, or he may be puffed up with conceit and fall into the condemnation of the devil. Moreover, he must be well thought of by outsiders, so that he may not fall into disgrace and the snare of the devil.*

Later in the same letter (5:17), the writer says that those *presbuteroi* who rule well should be accorded double honour, especially those who engage in preaching and teaching, and he urges Timothy not to lay hands upon anyone in haste, a thought clearly related to the very questions about the nature and character of the eldership he has just been discussing.

In his letter to Titus, whom he left behind in Crete to organise the church and appoint *presbuteroi* in every town, Paul returns again (1:6-9) to the qualifications needed for this ministry. He insists that an elder-guardian should be:

> *Someone who is blameless, married only once, whose children are believers, not accused of debauchery and not rebellious. For an* episkopos, *as God's steward, must be blameless; he must not be arrogant or quick-tempered or addicted to wine or violent or greedy for gain; but he must be hospitable, a lover of goodness, prudent, upright, devout and self-controlled. He must have a firm grasp of the word that is trustworthy in accordance with the teaching, so that he may be able both to preach with sound doctrine and to refute those who contradict it.*

Peter, writing in his first letter specifically as a *presbuteros* himself from Rome to the Jewish Christians of Asia Minor, also has something to say about the qualifications and conduct of the ordained ministry (5:1-4):

> *I exhort the* presbuteroi *among you to tend the flock of God that is in your charge, exercising the* episkope, *not under compulsion but willingly, as God would have you do it—not for sordid gain but eagerly. Do not lord it over those in your charge, but be examples to the flock. And when the chief shepherd appears, you will win the crown of glory that never fades away.*

the Proto Orthodox case against the Pastorals and 1 Peter

It is however, only fair to point out that trends in modern scholarship have been very clearly against accepting the Pastoral Epistles or 1 Peter as of genuinely Pauline or Petrine authorship. Many scholars have based their doubts upon the vocabulary differences between the Pastorals and Paul's undisputed epistles, yet these might be accounted for quite simply by the fact that the two writers are addressing distinct audiences in order to present contrasting aspects of teaching in a variety of contexts and environments.

However that may be, one of the principal reasons for the scepticism of W. Bauer (1971, pp. 77-94) and many other scholars before and since is the very fact that in their detailed and focussed coverage of church order, these four epistles seem to them to be reflecting a later, professional and more hierarchical concept of the episcopate and the presbyterate. They offer the beguiling suggestion that this later thinking developed in the second century out of the writings of Ignatius and is therefore not really consonant with what they consider would have been the simpler and probably more *ad hoc* arrangements made for the rule of the churches in the early days of their spontaneous and somewhat chaotic growth.

Not surprisingly therefore, Burkett (2002, p. xiv) considers these documents a product of Gentile Proto-Orthodoxy, which he suggests originated in a desire to oppose divergent teaching by marginalizing the older Judaic and Gnostic views and imposing upon the Church an ordered Christology and a more hierarchical system of government.

If Burkett, Schnelle and many other modern scholars are to be believed, then these four epistles should be considered pseudonymous, written by later followers of Paul and Peter, anxious to take advantage of the cachet of their Apostolic standing and authority. Burkett (2002, p. 427) goes so far as to say that along with 1 Clement and the letters of Ignatius these epistles could form a body of writings that might date from as late as 150 and thereby reflect the development of a later pattern of professional clergy, as first century leadership began its steady transformation into third century hierarchy.

The principal difficulty with this view of the Pastorals and 1 Peter is that if they really are as late as Burkett and others claim with such confidence, then they might indeed be considered part of a corpus that should include 1 Clement.

However, when it comes to including the letters of Ignatius within this group as well, we are probably taking a step too far. Whatever the ultimate truth about the authorship of the Pastorals and 1 Peter, throughout these letters we see only a twofold ministry of deacons and elders on clear display: *presbuteros* and *episkopos* are without doubt interchangeable titles for the same office. Nowhere is there the slightest hint at Ignatius's excursion into a threefold ministry, with its freestanding episcopate. Not surprisingly therefore, despite the arguments marshalled by the many proponents of Proto-Orthodoxy, the Scottish scholar Howard Marshall (1999, p. 57) is still prepared to say that *on the whole the Pastoral Epistles reflect an undeveloped ecclesiology.*

eldership in the Jewish setting

The American scholar Joseph Thayer (1896, p. 243) finds that in the Old Testament, although it probably owes its origin to a meaning akin to the head of a family, the Hebrew word *zaquen* is used frequently to describe the elders of Israel, the elders of the people and the elders of the congregation. One of the earliest references comes in Numbers 11:18-30, where God tells Moses to gather together the seventy elders of the people to receive some of his spirit so that they can share the burden of leadership with him. All of these references apparently derive from the noun for a man of advanced age, who not only in Jewish society, but elsewhere throughout the ancient world, would invariably be accorded respect and authority and maybe also the formal role of a judge. Along with the priests, such men were entrusted with the written law and charged to read it to the people.

The Hebrew texts of the Old Testament were translated into Greek in Alexandria during the third century BC at the behest of King Ptolemy Philadelphus (Bamm, 1959, p. 143). In this Greek Septuagint translation the key word *zaquen* is often rendered *presbuteros*, as it is in Genesis 18:11, where Abraham and Sarah are described as being advanced in age and therefore beyond the age of conception, or in Sirach 6:34, where children are advised to seek out the company of senior citizens in their community.

This same word later reappears in the Gospels to denote members of the Sanhedrin of Judaea. *Presbuteroi* are also used in this way, along with the chief priests (*archiereis*) and scribes (*grammateis*), to describe the composition of the Council before which Jesus was brought after his arrest (Mark 14:53). *Presbuteros* is also employed to describe a member of the ruling body of a local Jewish synagogue, as for example in Luke 7:3, where the centurion from Capernaum sends *presbuteroi* to Jesus to ask him to heal a highly regarded slave.

However, and perhaps equally significantly, Thayer shows (1896, p. 535) how the Greek Septuagint version of the Old Testament also uses the word *episkopos* four times, in Judges 9:28, Nehemiah 11:9,14 and 22, 2 Kings 11:15 and 1 Macc 1:51.

The first of these Old Testament references concerns Zebul, ruler of Shechem, who is named as an *officer* of Abimelech, who was one of the grandsons of the national hero Gideon. In this instance the meaning of the word *episkopos* must approximate most closely to someone who is an *ally* or *confederate* of another ruler.

Nehemiah 11 lists the members of the Israelite tribes who volunteered to live in Jerusalem after its walls and temple had been rebuilt by those who returned from the Babylonian captivity. There Joel is described as the *overseer* of the Benjaminite warriors, Zabdiel *overseer* of the Levite warriors and Uzzi, *overseer* of the Levite singers and others who worked in the temple.

The use of *episkopos* in its military sense in the case of Joel and Zabdiel reveals itself again in the reference from 2 Kings when the priest Jehoida commands the *captains* who were set over the army to capture Athaliah for murdering the king's sons, whereas Nehemiah's Uzzi is clearly the *director of music* for the temple worship that had once again become the religious focus of Israelite life.

The 1 Maccabees reference furnishes the single example of the Jewish use of *episkopos* from the two centuries before the birth of Christ. It comes when Antiochus Epiphanes writes to all the countries of his Greek empire instructing them to give up their own particular customs in order to facilitate the creation of one people. He appoints *inspectors* right across his dominions to ensure that they will comply with his edict.

All this implies that the word *episkopos* would have been in established Greek usage long before the coming of Christ and that within its overall compass as a term of leadership, invariably involving responsibility for others, there were also distinct military, supervisory, inspectorial, musical and diplomatic nuances to its meaning.

However, *episkopos* already existed as a classical Greek word quite independently of its use by translators of the old Hebrew scriptures. Alongside its employment as a noun for every variety of responsible leadership, such as that of the foreman, curator, guardian or superintendent, it may have had another quite specific meaning as the title given to the official whose duty it was to remove blockages in the public water supply of the cities, so that all the connected houses were properly and reliably supplied with nature's most vital commodity.

There is thus a huge linguistic portmanteau to the word *episkopos* by the time the New Testament writers come to employ it later in the first century as one of the two nouns they find most appropriate to identify the sort of leadership that they wanted to see develop within the Christian Church.

the original purpose of the elder-guardians

Taken together then, the Biblical references to *presbuteroi-episkopoi* should hold the key to understanding what was the status and purpose of the elder-guardians in these earliest Christian communities scattered around the eastern Mediterranean coasts of a largely unsympathetic Roman Empire. Perhaps it is no surprise that in the pen of Peter, the metaphor of the Good Shepherd comes conveniently to hand as an easily recognised didactic focus (1 Peter 5:1-5). Like their master Jesus Christ himself, the *episkopoi* are to take care of their flock of sheep, who look to them for protection, reassurance and sustenance, both while they are within the Christian community and when they venture outside into the wider world, where they have to face many dangers which could easily overwhelm them. This pastoral care and oversight is meant to be exercised in a tender and considerate fashion, with never so much as a hint of an overbearing or domineering manner.

As well as being *episkopoi*, the elder-guardians are also *presbuteroi* in the sense that they hold a senior position within the local Christian community, not necessarily because of their age, but because of their doctrinal wisdom, maturity and integrity and also because they are able to teach and communicate the faith. Their seniority comes also by virtue of their developed Christian character and the sum of their graces, which enhance their standing not only among the believers, but also out in the hostile world, where their impeccable conduct earns them sufficient respect to be effective ambassadors for both their Christian faith and for the Christian communities which they have the privilege to lead.

Yet they are also *episkopoi* because they have a guardian role. They protect the body of Christian belief that has been passed on to them by their Apostolic predecessors, *the faith which was once for all entrusted to the saints* (Jude, 3), but they also guard the flock of God, keeping them safe within the Christian fold and rescuing them when they get into difficulties outside it. It may be at this point that the more ancient diplomatic sense of the word also impinges upon the function of *episkope*. In order to exercise their protective role adequately, the elders might have to talk with the pagan authorities on behalf of members of their *ekklesia* when in danger of persecution, but they might also have to exercise an ambassadorial function on behalf of the Christian community as a whole or indeed for the integrity of the very faith itself, as Paul hints when he talks (Acts 25 and 26) about the significance of appealing to Caesar, rather than letting the Jewish authorities decide his fate.

The *episkopoi* also possess a role akin to that of a conductor in an orchestra. They are to make sure that the gifts distributed by the Lord to every individual within the local Christian community (1 Corinthians 12:27-30) are properly developed for the good of all. Everyone's contribution is to be welcomed and held in perfect balance, so that teaching, prophecy, pastoring and administration all play their part in the building up of a mature and effective communal life and witness, which will not only make a sweet and harmonious sound to God himself, but will also play an attractive melody to capture the attention and ultimately the faith of the unbelieving world around.

The *episkopoi* must also be inspectors, making sure that there is an effective system of quality control to ensure that the Christian community is living at peace within itself, loyal to the Gospel it professes and beyond reproach by what is likely to be a critical, maybe even downright hostile Roman administration. There is also that intriguing Classical Greek allusion to keeping the routes of divine grace free of obstruction and in full flow, making sure that the whole Christian community and all its individual members remain constantly open to the prompting of the Holy Spirit and are able to gain regular nourishment from God through both his written Word and his holy sacraments.

Then last, but not least, comes the quasi-military function—*episkopoi* being in some sense the platoon commanders in what was seen by both Peter and Paul as an ever present struggle against *principalities and powers* (*Colossians 2:15*)—a struggle in which both were to give their lives as martyrs in Rome, the capital city of a political system and empire that was for these early Christians the ultimate personification of evil. John the Divine went so far as to describe it in his Apocalypse, written right at the end of the first century as *Babylon the great, mother of whores and of earth's abominations . . . drunk with the blood of the saints and the witnesses to Jesus.* (*Revelation 17:5-6*).

Christians suffered these draconian persecutions firstly under Nero and later under Domitian, but the messages to the seven churches recorded in Revelation chapters 2 and 3 demonstrate that these young communities faced not just physical violence, but also more subtle temptations to compromise their faith through daily contact with Roman-Hellenistic culture and society around them. It was in the shadow of these constant threats and distractions that the first *presbuteroi-episkopoi* exercised their team ministries. If any of their number happened to be singled out for imprisonment, torture or death by the emperor or his officials, others remained to plug the gap. Damaged it might be, but the local church could live on to fight another day.

CHAPTER TWO

The Early Church Develops
A Separate Episcopate

the immediate post Apostolic period

John seems to have been the last survivor of the Apostolic band. He is said by Irenaeus to have taught Polycarp of Smyrna (Needham, 2002, p. 98) and therefore to have lived into the reign of Trajan, who did not become emperor till 98. John had pondered deeply over the Christian tradition and passed it on by writing his Fourth Gospel, probably near the very end of the first century. Others, like Paul, had passed on that tradition firstly by word of mouth and later in writing to the Christian communities they had themselves founded. Countless others must have passed on the tradition by word of mouth alone. Once all the eye witnesses of Jesus's earthly life, death, resurrection and ascension had left the scene, the churches could no longer amplify or develop the Apostolic tradition by personal discussion and enquiry with those who had constructed it upon their intimate knowledge of Jesus Christ and their relationships and experiences with him. The patristic epoch had begun.

The first of the patristic documents to mention church order happens to be one of the earliest survivors, the *First Epistle of Clement*, which, according to Bart Ehrman (2003, pp. 167-168) seems to have been written by Clement, fourth Bishop of Rome to the strife-ridden Church in Corinth. He considers it to have been written around 95, at much the same time as John's Gospel was compiled. It was considered a part of the New Testament canon by many local churches for another two hundred years, partly because of its apparent antiquity and probably also because of the striking similarity of its teaching passages to those of Paul's Epistles. Although it was included within the fifth century *Codex Alexandrinus*, it had already been finally rejected in Bishop Athanasius of Alexandria's thirty ninth festal letter of 367 (Souter, 1913, p. 157), a decision supported by the Third Synod of Carthage twenty six years later.

Clement's letter was written because the Corinthian church had forcibly deposed its elders from office by the actions of a *vile and profane faction* (I:1) at the instigation of one or two persons. Clearly at this time the ministry of the church was still composed of interchangeable *episkopoi-presbuteroi* and *diakonoi*. Clement explains their origins (XLII: 4-5) like this:

> *As they (the Apostles) preached throughout the countryside and in the cities, they appointed the first-fruits of their ministries as bishops and deacons, of those who were about to believe, testing them by the Spirit. And this indeed was no recent development. For indeed, bishops and deacons had been mentioned in writings long before. For thus the Scripture says in one place, "I will appoint their bishops in righteousness and their deacons in faith"' (quoting the Septuagint version of Isaiah 60:17).*

Although there can be little doubt that Clement still considers *presbuteros* and *episkopos* to be one and the same ministry, he also makes passing mention of how they were appointed and already gives a clear hint at that essential sense of continuity in ministry which later came to be considered as the Apostolic Succession. He explains (XLIV: 1-3) that:

> *So too our apostles knew through our Lord Jesus Christ that strife would arise over the office of the bishop. For this reason, since they understood perfectly well in advance what would happen, they appointed those we have already mentioned; and afterwards they added a codicil (the text here appears to be corrupt) to the effect that if these should die, other approved men should succeed them in their ministry. Thus we do not think it right to remove from the ministry those who were appointed by them, or afterwards, by other reputable men, with the entire church giving its approval.*

The writer of the *Didache*, a compendium of apostolic teachings reckoned by L.W. Barnard (1966, p. 99) to have been produced in Syria between 100 and 120, but using earlier sources, deals with the welcome that should be accorded to itinerant prophets and teachers and then goes on to talk about local ministry. In the same vein as Clement he says (15:1):

> *So elect for yourselves bishops and deacons who are worthy of the Lord, gentle men who are not fond of money, who are true and approved. Therefore do not despise them, for they are the honourable men among you, together with the prophets and teachers.*

Thus in the *Didache* the ministry still appears to be twofold, elected by the local Christian community, committed to exemplary conduct and, echoing the letter to Titus, still very much concerned with sound teaching and prophetic insight, although it has to be said that for Simon Tugwell (1989, p. 1) the very primitiveness of these ministerial arrangements pushes the Didache's date back into the first century.

The same ministerial pattern is evidenced in a very short quote from the allegorical *Shepherd of Hermas*, according to Ehrman (2003, p. 251) written by a brother of the Bishop of Rome in the first half of the second century, included within the fourth century *Codex Sinaiticus* and, like the *Didache*, considered by Athanasius as worthy of reverence and study, although in his eyes, not properly canonical. The writer of the *Shepherd* tells the reader in II: 4 to read one of his books in a specified but unknown city with *the presbyters who lead the church.*

Not surprisingly therefore, J.T. Burtchaell (1992, p. xiii) concludes that the consensus of historians since the nineteenth century is that for the first two generations of Christian history, the Holy Spirit was given free rein, leaving the Church without more formal structures until divisions and heresy led to greater institutionalisation. This very much echoes Adolf von Harnack's theory of a *charismatic* ministry—the original Spirit-filled ministry of apostles, prophets and teachers, which was succeeded, as the Pentecostal inspiration died away, with the less exciting *official* ministry—those he somewhat disparagingly calls *the routine executive officers* of the local churches (1910, pp. 239-242).

the arrival of the solo bishop

Whether Burtchaell is right or not, things certainly start to change later in the second century. The Italian historian Marta Sordi (1983, pp. 182-186) suggests that the fledgling churches may have used the pattern of the pagan *collegia*, set up as associations or clubs for religious activities and mutual benefit, especially within the Roman army. Here members elected *magistri* as their local leaders, with district *seniores* above them, both sets of officials being chosen especially for their moral integrity.

Roger Beckwith's thesis (2003, pp. 28-41) seems more likely. He posits that because there were usually several teaching elders or *presbuteroi* within the synagogues of Judaism, by New Testament times it had become common practice to make one of them synagogue ruler, which would quite naturally lead to the development of a similar leadership pattern among the earliest Judaeo-Christian communities. In a not dissimilar vein, Kenneth Kirk (1946, p. viii) traces this development of a two-tier eldership to the early Church's growing discovery of Old Testament paradigms, where *the Apostles, reading their Greek Bible, found types of the ministry bedded within its pages.*

This very much echoes what Streeter had to say (1929, p. 77):

> *The nucleus of the body of converts in the churches founded by Paul consisted of Jews and proselytes; and since he regarded the Christian Church as being the authentic Israel, it would have been natural for him to view the newly founded local communities as synagogues—and to organise them accordingly.*

This tendency for the Early Church to search out and follow Jewish precedents wherever they could find them, sometimes even in an obsessive and slavish fashion, leads Bishop Tom Wright to observe unsurprisingly (1992, p. 453) that . . . *all early Christianity was Jewish Christianity.*

Beckwith, however, also suggests (2003, pp. 69-74) that the rise of a distinct episcopate may be intimately concerned with the special place that the eucharist came to have in local church discipline. By the end of the second century, two heresies, Docetism and Ebionism had already been widely propounded. The Docetists believed that Christ's humanity was more apparent than real, °whereas the Ebionites held tightly to Jewish tradition and considered Paul to be a traitor. The orthodox response was to bar their followers from the fellowship of the eucharist. It fell to the eldership to excommunicate them and make sure that they could not set up unauthorised competitor centres of communion elsewhere. Beckwith argues his point this way:

> *If this reconstruction is right, it means that . . . in the interests of order and unity, the presbyter-bishops decided that one of their number in each*

church should in future perform three functions which had previously been open to them all, namely: the direction of worship, the practice of ordination and the exercise of discipline. Where this was first decided, and whether all three prerogatives were transferred to the bishop at once, is impossible to say with certainty, but the effectiveness of the transfer in each case meant that it was rapidly imitated elsewhere (2003, p. 58).

A different and maybe slightly less plausible explanation of the rise of the solo bishop was advanced by A.M. Farrer (in Kirk, 1946, p. 8). He argues that the ministry of word and sacraments and the power to confer orders originally rested with the Apostles, and that they in turn ordained presbyters as an extension of their Apostolate. These then went on to ordain bishops as supervisors, and from that point onwards, it was these bishops and their duly ordained successors who held the chief responsibility for the ministry of word and sacraments and for conducting future ordinations. The monk Gregory Dix qualifies the cruder concepts of *apostolic succession* by saying that for him each new bishop is not so much a successor of the Apostles as an actual addition to the apostolic college, as were Paul and Matthias (in Kirk, 1946, p. 200).

The problem for Farrer's hypothesis is that there is precious little New Testament evidence for the central sacramental role of the Apostles. Apart from Paul's oblique reference to the Lord's actual words of institution at the Last Supper in 1 Corinthians 11:23-26, we do not read of any of the Apostles actually presiding at a eucharist, although in practice they must have done so all the time. Although Luke reports Peter baptising the centurion Cornelius, his family and his friends (Acts 10:47-48), Paul seems to make almost a virtue out of his constant round of preaching and teaching and his infrequent forays into sacramental acts. He tells the Corinthian church quite bluntly that he thanks God he baptised only Crispus and Gaius (1 Cor. 1:14-16), nonetheless going on to admit that he has also baptised the household of Stephanas and maybe others as well, although his memory is now hazy.

However, it is quite clear that the change from *presbuteroi-episkopoi* to a separate episcopate and presbyterate came about in due course, sooner in some places than in others. The earliest evidence for it occurs when Ignatius, Bishop of Antioch, writing to the Smyrnaeans (C:8) on his way to Rome around 110, urges their Church to avoid divisions at all costs:

> *Avoid divisions as the beginning of evils. All of you follow the bishop as Jesus Christ followed the Father, and follow the presbytery as the Apostles . . . Let no man perform anything pertaining to the church without the bishop. Let that be considered a valid eucharist over which the bishop presides, or one to whom he commits it. Wherever the bishop appears, there let the people be, just as, wherever Christ Jesus is, there is the Catholic Church. It is not permitted either to baptise or hold a love feast apart from the bishop. But whatever he may approve, that is well pleasing to God, that everything which you do may be sound and valid.*

Writing to the Ephesians (IV: 1-2) Ignatius talks of their leadership as . . . *your worthily reputed presbytery, worthy of God is attuned to the bishop like strings to a cithara.*

In Antioch therefore, and presumably in Ephesus also, there was clearly a separate episcopate at a relatively early date, with some sort of embryonic theology to undergird the practice. Ignatius sees himself as the focus and guarantee of the church's unity, but this is still at a purely local level and seen as a bastion against spurious leaders who might lead the people astray. The validity of Ignatius's stance in the difficult circumstances then prevailing in Antioch might well be seen as proved by the viciousness of Domitian's persecutions not very long before his own arrest and later martyrdom in Rome soon after 110.

Yet towards the end of the second century, Bishop Irenaeus of Lyons (*Adv. Haer, IV: xxvi*), likewise writing within the setting of schisms arising out of heresies, advises his readers to *obey only those presbyters who are in the Church, who have their succession from the apostles . . . who with their succession in the episcopate have received the sure gift of the truth . . .* Thus towards the close of the third quarter of the second century, it appears that *presbuteroi/episkopoi* are still the norm in at least one major city of Southern Gaul.

Cyprian defines the episcopate

In the middle of the 3rd century, at the very time that Decius and his successor Valerian were undertaking an intense, empire-wide persecution of the Christians, Cyprian, Bishop of Carthage in his treatise *On the Unity of the Church* makes a compelling case for the unity of the Godhead to be expressed in the unity of what had by now become the episcopate. In I:5 he says, *The episcopate is one, each part of which is held by each one for the whole.*

Although Cyprian considers that the Apostolic commission was originally given by Christ specifically to Peter (Matthew 16:18-19), he qualifies this by going on to say *. . . to all the Apostles after his resurrection, he gives an equal power and says, "As the Father has sent me, even so send I you: receive the Holy Ghost . . .", yet, that he might set forth unity, he arranged by his authority the origin of that unity, as beginning from one. Assuredly the rest of the Apostles were also the same as was Peter, endowed with a like partnership both of honour and power, but the beginning proceeds from unity. (Treatise I:4).*

Nick Needham (2002, p. 131) notes Cyprian's often-quoted sentence *Where the bishop is, there is the Church* and then goes on to surmise that in the eyes of this North African, the distinction between Apostles and bishops faded away almost entirely. The Apostles were themselves the first bishops and the bishops the new apostles, invested with absolute disciplinary authority over their congregations and clothed with the supernatural power to administer the life-giving sacraments.

In a letter to Antonianus written in 252 (letters LI:24), Cyprian talks of the unity of Christ's Church . . . *and also one episcopate diffused through a harmonious multitude of many bishops* . . . but this is tempered by a letter written to Cyprian in 256 by Bishop Firmilian of Caesaria in Cappadocia (letters LXXIV:7), who says . . . *all power and grace are established in the Church where the elders preside, who possess the power both of baptising, and of imposition of hands, and of ordaining* . . . thus there still seems to be a hint of a joint ministry of *episkopoi-presbuteroi* here.

Cyprian's teaching might sound like the birth of the monarchical episcopate, but it makes considerably more sense when one remembers the persecutions, heresies, schisms and cowardice which confronted this episcopal martyr on every side and the consequences of which he had constantly to address. In these desperate circumstances, it is no surprise he was so anxious to run a tight ship! Drawing upon the images of Christ's seamless coat (John 19:23-24) and Rahab's safe house (Joshua 2:19) as divine patterns for the Church, he says of the schismatics:

> *These are they, who of their own accord without any divine arrangement,*
> *set themselves to preside among the daring strangers assembled, who*
> *appoint themselves prelates without any law of ordination, who assume to*
> *themselves the name of bishop, although no one gives them the episcopate*
> *(on the Unity of the Church, Treatise I:9).*

For all this weight of evidence pointing to the development of a separate and superior episcopate over time, John Chrysostom, in his exposition of the opening sentences of Paul's letter to the Philippians in one of his homilies composed in the fourth century nonetheless asks a pertinent question:

> *Were there several bishops in one city? Certainly not, but he called*
> *the presbyters so. For then they still interchanged the titles . . . so then,*
> *as I said, both the presbyters were of old called bishops and deacons*
> *of Christ, and the bishops presbyters; and hence even now many*

bishops write, "to my fellow presbyters" and "to my fellow deacons."
(Philippians 1:1)

Even Jerome, Bishop of Alexandria, writing towards the end of the fourth century *(Epistle 146 to Angelus)* about the post-apostolic period, although he mirrors what Ignatius and Cyprian had to say about bishops, schisms and unity, nonetheless hints that in North Africa, at any rate, bishops possessed a solo function only in relation to passing on holy orders, his preamble being that *the apostle clearly teaches that presbyters are the same as bishops*:

> *When ... one presbyter was chosen to preside over the rest, this was done to remedy schism and to prevent each individual from rending the church of Christ by drawing it to himself. For even at Alexandria from the time of Mark the Evangelist until the episcopates of Heraclas and Dionysius (in the mid third century) the presbyters always named as bishop one of their own number chosen by themselves and set in a more exalted position, just as an army elects a general ... For what function, excepting ordination, belongs to a bishop that does not also belong to a presbyter?*

problems in the Eastern Empire

Once Constantine the Great died, the Roman Empire was been split between his sons, each becoming joint emperor. The Eastern Church, now based in Constantinople, seems to have experienced the greatest difficulties in stabilising the episcopate after the key doctrinal decisions reached at the Council of Nicaea. Probably this was because it was in the East that Arianism, the Origenists, Gnostic heresies and straightforward personality clashes had wreaked the most havoc. Basil, Archbishop of Caesaria in Cappadocia spent much time using his skills of patient diplomacy to bring together those who had broken the old unity of the Church by separating over comparatively trivial issues. In a letter to his young friend Bishop Amphilochius of Iconium in 374, Basil explains how the earlier Fathers would have analysed their current divisions, in all of which bishops had played a depressingly pivotal part:

> . . . by heresies they meant men who were altogether broken off and alienated in matters relating to the actual faith; by schisms men who had separated for some ecclesiastical reasons and questions capable of mutual solution; by unlawful congregational gatherings those held by disorderly presbyters or bishops or by uninstructed laymen (letter CLXXXVIII concerning the Canons).

For Basil, as an episcopal guardian of orthodoxy within his province, there could be no compromise on the matter of heretics. Each person of the Trinity was equal and co-eternal and in *de Spiritu Sancto,* written in 375, he gives a masterly exposition of the Holy Spirit's equal place of honour with both the Father and the Son.

Problems with Arianism continued at intervals during the reigns of Constantius, Julius and Valens until Theodosius the Great became Eastern emperor in 375. He issued an edict from his capital city of Constantinople in 380 announcing that he intended to lead all citizens in his domain to accept Nicaean Christianity, which led in its turn to orthodox Catholics gaining legal possession of all church buildings. This may have been widely welcomed, but in its train lay the inherent dangers of too close a tie between Church and State which were to cause the great preacher John Chrysostem such problems.

Egged on by Chrysostem's criticisms of the moral laxity of the imperial court and the convenient arrival of a hostile envoy from the Patriarch of Alexandria, the emperor Arcadius sent a squad of troops to arrest him and send him into exile. A great earthquake a few days later convinced the empress Eudoxia that Chrysostem's banishment had been a mistake. However, only a few months later, she had a silver statue of herself erected near his Church of the Holy Wisdom.

Because games and festivities around it were upsetting the services of worship there, Chrysostem expressed his strong disapproval. This time Arcadius's patience was exhausted and he suspended him from his episcopal duties. He was sent into a second exile from which he never returned. He thereby shared the same fate as did the great anti-Arian champion Athanasius of Alexandria, exiled five times during his 45 years as bishop.

choosing new bishops

Excellent evidence survives from the middle of the third century about how a bishop was appointed and ordained. Streeter (1929, pp. 111-12) quotes Pionius's Life of Polycarp, which describes these procedures in considerable detail, but somewhat in contradiction to Irenaeus, who accords this illustrious martyr a directly Apostolic appointment by John himself. Despite the doubts surrounding the texts, Pionius's narrative of such an occasion is none the less a compelling one:

> ... On the Sabbath, when prayer had been made a long time on bended knee, Polycarp, as was his custom, got up to read; and every eye was fixed upon him. Now the lesson was the Epistles of Paul to Timothy and Titus, in which he says what manner of man a bishop ought to be ... He was so well fitted for the office that the hearers said one to another that he lacked none of the qualities which Paul requires in one who has the care of a church. When then, after the reading, and the instruction of the bishops and the discourses of the presbyters, the deacons were sent to the laity to enquire whom they would have, they said with one accord, "Let Polycarp be our pastor and teacher." The whole priesthood then having assented, they appointed him ... Accordingly the deacons led him up for ordination by the hands of the bishops according to custom ... and being placed in his chair by them ... Then the company present urged him,

since this was the custom, to address them. For they said that this work
of teaching was the most important part of the communion.

Here we find obvious evidence for the importance the early Church attached to what Apostles like Paul had taught were the necessary qualities for church leadership, including the overriding importance of teaching among the episcopal functions. In this account of the choice of a bishop, the laity were first consulted and then the presbyters. Ambrose varies this by stating (*Epistle XV: 12*) that, *the people demanded, requested or acclaimed someone as bishop, and he was then elected, if they thought well, by the clergy.* More often the surviving evidence, like that recorded in Hippolytus's *Apostolic Traditions* of c.215, points to a decision of the whole local church acting together for this particular purpose at their Sunday worship, with the bishops of neighbouring churches also in attendance (Dix (1946, p. 196).

J.R. Willis (1966, p. 478) recounts how Cyprian, Bishop of Carthage, writing to the clergy and people in Spain around the middle of the 3rd century (*letter LXVII:5*) says:

... divine tradition and apostolic observance, which is also maintained among us, and almost throughout all the provinces (say) that for the proper celebration of ordinations, all the neighbouring bishops of the same province should assemble with that people ... and the bishop should be chosen in the presence of the people, who have most fully known the life of each one, and have looked into the doings of each one as respects his habitual conduct. And this also, we see, was done to you in the ordination of our colleague Sabinus; so that by the suffrage of the whole brotherhood, and by the sentence of the bishops who had assembled in their presence, and had written letters to you concerning him ... hands were imposed on him in the place of Basilides.

Although J.T. Lienhard (1984, pp. 43-44) mentions how the early 3rd century *Didascalia Apostolorum* advises that candidates for the episcopate should be *not less than fifty years of age, now removed from the manners of youth,* this was clearly a quirky opinion and not borne out by general practice. More significantly A.D. Lee (2000, p. 215) points out that in 343 the Council of Serdica decreed that new bishops should have previously served as reader, deacon and presbyter, thereby proving their ministerial worth over a long period of time. However, this gathering in what is now Sofia did not have the status of a full ecumenical council and it cannot be assumed that at this time all bishops were necessarily elected from among the presbyterate alone.

The choice of the provincial governor Ambrose by acclamation of the crowd as Bishop of Milan in 374 to follow the Arian Auxentius is well known enough, but more easily overlooked is Gregory of Nazianzus' record (Oration XVIII: 13) of how the layman Eusebius, who, like Ambrose, had not even completed his preparation for baptism, came in 362 to be elected bishop of a major city in Cappadocia:

> *The city of Caesaria was in uproar about the election of a bishop; for one had just departed and another must be found, amidst heated partisanship not easily to be soothed . . . owing to the fervour of its faith, and the rivalry was increased by the illustrious position of the see. Several bishops had arrived to consecrate the bishop; the populace was divided into several parties, each with its own candidate . . . but at last the people came to an agreement, and with the aid of a band of soldiers quartered there seized one of their leading citizens, a man of excellent life, but not yet sealed with the divine baptism, brought him against his will to the sanctuary, and setting him before the bishops, begged, with entreaties mingled with violence, that he might be consecrated and proclaimed . . .*

It seems clear from these instances at least that the choice of bishop could be largely determined by whom the people perceived to have sufficient standing to fulfil the vital task of leadership, both within the church and in the wider community. In the third century Origen (*Contra Celsum* VIII: 75) asserted that, *It is both necessary and right for them (bishops) to be leaders and to be concerned about all men, both those who are within the Church . . . and those who appear to be outside it.*

Occasionally a contested episcopal election could turn ugly, as it might have done in Milan in 374 when Ambrose was sent into the church by the government to quell the very disturbance that ended up in him being proclaimed bishop. The historian Socrates Scholasticus adds a more frightening dimension when he records (Book 2: XVI) how the Emperor Constantius sent Philip, the Praetorian Prefect to eject Paul from the see of Constantinople and substitute the Arian Macedonius as its bishop. In the angry scenes that followed, Philip's guard of soldiers hacked down 3,150 of the crowd.

Perhaps incidents such as this led the Council of Laodicea in the middle of the fourth century to decree in canon XIII that elections were not *to be committed to the multitude*. This helped to underline the decision made at the Council of Antioch in 341 that elections to fill an episcopal vacancy were to be conducted among all the bishops in a province and that a majority vote could suffice, although it would need ratification by the metropolitan of the province (canon XIX). Thus the East became the first to seriously diminish the role of the local presbyters and laity in choosing their bishop.

handling episcopal heresies and misconduct

J.W. Trigg (1983, p. 143) says that Origen considered bishops should combine irreproachable virtue with skill in argument and the ability to seek out hidden truth in the Bible. Augustine of Hippo, writing at the beginning of the fifth century in his *City of God (Book 19:3)*, summed up most early wisdom about the episcopate, when he wrote that being a bishop *is a task, not an honour . . . a bishop who loves to govern rather than do good is no bishop.* The true spirit of his own episcopate is encapsulated in his memorable words, *With you I am a Christian, for you I am a bishop (Sermon 349:1).*

Trigg (p. 28) also explains how bishops could be deposed by their fellow bishops after being found guilty of heresy or misconduct at a trial before their own congregation. Any who might still accept them as bishop suffered the same fate, ensuring that *the bishop was thus the congregation's link with the Church as a whole in a flexible but resilient structure* . This turned out to be little more than an ideal, since many deposed bishops simply carried on their ministry precisely as before and exported their loyal congregations with them to establish a rebel worship centre elsewhere.

In 325 the Council of Nicaea condemned the Arian heresy, which denied the divinity of Jesus. This caused considerable turmoil among the churches, which were already in disarray over Novatian's strict and inflexible discipline against those who had succumbed to pressure and denied Christ during the Decian persecutions at the end of the 3rd century. Both Socrates Scholasticus and Sozomen's histories of the 4th century Church are littered with references to the consecrations of Arian and Novatian bishops, especially in the East, most of them having small local followings but some enjoying considerably more backing and prestige.

Sozomen (Book VII: 2) may be slightly pessimistic when he records that towards the end of the fourth century all the churches of the East, with the exception of Jerusalem, were in the hands of the Arians. The Second Ecumenical Council held at Constantinople in 381 at the behest of the emperor Theodosius finally settled the doctrine of the Holy Trinity to the satisfaction of both the orthodox and the Origenists through devising the careful and studied words of the Nicene Creed. This decision was ultimately to unite the doctrine of both East and West in the century that followed.

According to the 4th century compiler of the *Apostolic Constitutions* (VIII: xlvii), bishops may also have been open to deposition for serving in the army or in public administration, but as this document is considered somewhat muddled and contradictory in both content and date, it is probably referring to the situation in the later second or third centuries, when the Christian community suffered spells of violent persecution at the hands of emperors like Marcus Aurelius, Decius and Diocletian (Needham, 2002, pp. 80-82 and 284). Their punishments would invariably have been handed down and administered through soldiers and public officials.

Nonetheless, as time went on and the political situation for Christians became less threatening, other secular occupations followed by local church leaders could give rise to equal headaches. The Fourth Ecumenical Council held at Chalcedon in 451 determined (canon III) that:

> ... no bishop, clergyman or monk shall hire possessions, or engage in business, or occupy himself in worldly managements, unless he shall be called by the law to the guardianship of minors, from which there is no escape ...

Clearly this decision was a response to two temptations to which the clergy were especially prone. Firstly, they could be side-tracked into neglecting their spiritual duties in order to wander abroad in search of financial gain. Secondly, they could be tempted into making money by managing other people's property, since their position as leaders of Christian congregations made them appear uniquely fit persons to hold such offices of trust (Allen in Francis and Francis, 1997, p. 56).

the earliest consecration liturgy

Only one account survives of the actual liturgy used for the consecration of a new bishop. It is recorded by Hippolytus, who was a presbyter of the church in Rome, but fell out with Bishop Callistus and set himself up as a rival bishop. He was later reconciled with the Roman congregation and died a martyr's death in 236. Although Hippolytus was writing early in the 3rd century, it is generally reckoned that he was talking about the settled tradition of the Roman church, which therefore probably takes us back into the 2nd century.

Hippolytus describes the ceremony this way:

> *The bishops shall lay hands on him and the presbytery shall stand by in silence. And all shall keep silence, praying in their heart for the descent of the Spirit. After this, one of the bishops present, at the request of all, shall pray thus, laying his hand on him (who is made bishop) saying:*

> *"O God and Father of our Lord Jesus Christ, Father of mercies and God of all comfort, who dwells on high yet has respect to the lowly; who knows all things before they come to pass; who gave ordinances of your Church through the Word of your grace; who foreordained from the beginning the race of the righteous from Abraham, instituting rulers and priests and not leaving your holiness without ministers; who from the foundation of the world has been pleased to be glorified in those whom you have chosen:*

> *Now pour forth that power which comes from you, from the princely Spirit which you gave to your beloved servant Jesus Christ, which he bestowed on your holy Apostles who established in every place the Church which hallows you, to the glory and endless praise of your Name:*

> *Grant the Spirit, O Father, who knows the hearts of all, upon this your servant whom you have chosen for the episcopate, to shepherd your holy flock, to serve as your high priest, blamelessly ministering by night and day, ceaselessly to propitiate your face, and to offer to you the gifts of your holy Church; and by the high priestly Spirit to have authority to forgive sins according to your command, to ordain according to your bidding, to loose every bond according to the authority you gave to the*

Apostles; to please you in meekness and a pure heart, offering to you the
savour of sweetness through your servant Jesus Christ, to whom be glory
and praise, to the Father and the Holy Spirit, in the holy Church, now
and for ever."

When he has been made bishop, let everyone give the kiss of peace . . .
To him then let the deacons bring the oblation . . . (Dix in Kirk, 1946,
pp. 196-97).

The new bishop then goes on to preside at the Eucharist.

In the second part of this consecration prayer Hippolytus defines what he considers to be the nature of the bishop's office, what comprises his *episkope*. It centres upon two particular relationships. In the first place, the bishop stands for God in relation to the church, incarnating the Lord's own office of the Good Shepherd to his holy flock; secondly, he is the representative of the people to God as they together plead the supreme sacrifice of Jesus, the Great High Priest in the Eucharist. Hebrews 4:14-16 makes it plain that Christ alone has entered the heavens as our victorious Saviour over sin and death, but here on earth his people plead the merits of that sacrifice before the Father every time they celebrate the Eucharist, the bishop himself fulfilling a function akin to the high priestly role as he leads their worship upwards. Hippolytus joins his contemporaries Tertullian and Cyprian in this view of the bishop's functions within his own church, but his presentation of them within the exceptionally complete form of the consecration prayer itself, is a unique and coherent statement of great value.

the Church and changes in imperial organisation

The Christian churches these bishops governed were for the most part based in the cities of a far-flung empire whose capital was the city of Rome itself, where their two most prominent early leaders had met their martyrdom. Within a century of their deaths the empire grew to its farthest extent, with the Antonine Wall, the Rhine and the Danube its boundaries in the north and the Euphrates its limit to the east. Even with an excellent road network and an established pattern of sea routes, such a mammoth territory was not easy to govern and with the increasing risk of invasion from outside, especially from the end of the third century onwards, changes in its cumbersome organisation were inevitable. These took place under Diocletian, who began by strengthening the entire frontier system and then set about a wholesale reorganisation of provincial government.

The archaeologist Peter Salway (1993, pp. 204-205) explains how the existing provinces were grouped together into *dioceses*, headed by a *vicarius* and his staff, civilian administrators who were responsible to the regional praetorian prefect and ultimately to the emperor in Rome.

Only a few years after Diocletian came Constantine the Great. His conversion seems to have been a complex affair, but it was clearly influenced by the failure of Diocletian's persecution of the Christians and the evidently greater power of the Christian God, particularly as it was so practically demonstrated, when, under a Christian banner, Constantine defeated Maxentius at the Milvian Bridge. However lukewarm his devotion to his new faith may have been, the very fact that he had joined the Church could not help turning Christianity into the official religion of the Empire, as was inevitable in a regime where the Emperor was deified by virtue of his very position.

With this change came important secular consequences for the Church and increasing civic responsibilities and status for its bishops. A.D. Lee (2000, p. 219) records how the emperor placed them alongside the regular judiciary by allowing them to be chosen as an alternative by litigants in any case, even if the other party objected and by making their rulings unalterable and imperishable. Dix (1946, p. 278) points out that by the end of the fourth century the imperial constitutions gave bishops the office of *defensores* of their see cities, thereby practically replacing the old elected magistrates as the only truly elected officials able to defend local liberty against the oppression of central bureaucracy. Ramsey MacMullen (1984, p. 49) also relates how, by a now lost decree, Constantine exempted church lands from taxation, ordered provincial officials to make materials and provide labour for church construction, set up a system of gifts of food to the church and excused clerics from onerous civic obligations.

MacMullen summarizes the fruits of establishment for the bishops under Constantine and his successors like this (1984, pp. 113-114):

> Bishops now dined with Constantine himself; they used Constantius's palace as their headquarters. They were seen riding along provincial highways in state conveyances, bent on their high affairs, as guests of the government. All the world could behold what fantastic changes had come about in the repute and position of ecclesiastical officials. What they said now had an authority acknowledged by the emperors themselves.

W.H.C. Frend (1991, p. 238) shows how these secular rewards expanded even further:

> The bishop of a large see was now a great officer of state, paid 720 solidi a year like a provincial governor and expected, as Gregory of Nazianze complained during his short tenure of the see of Constantinople (380/1) "to rival the consuls, the generals, the governors, the most illustrious commanders", to eat well and to dress splendidly.

While this extravagant lifestyle may have become *de rigeur* for bishops in the Eastern Empire, things changed dramatically in the West when Rome fell to Alaric in 410. In the aftermath of its sack by the Visigoths, a serious power vacuum emerged at the heart of the old empire. After occupation by a succession of soldier kings, the centre of political influence shifted northwards in the direction from which the invading hordes had come, yet the centre of the Western Church remained in Rome, the home of what had by then become the senior see of the Christian Church.

CHAPTER THREE

The British Episcopate till the End of the Middle Ages

the Church in Late Roman Britain

The precise nature and extent of Christianity in the final century of the Roman occupation of Britain still remains something of a mystery. In a major survey of this field, the archaeologist David Petts (2003, pp. 96-99) can point only to the wide distribution of what are presumed to be lead baptismal tanks as archaeological evidence of its geographical distribution. The so-called *church* discovered within the deserted Roman city of Silchester in Hampshire has been identified almost entirely on the grounds of its cruciform plan. The only totally undisputed Christian attributions are in fact the house chapel at Lullingstone in Kent with its praying figures (mid to late fourth century) and the numerous chi-rho monograms found on mostly fourth century portable objects, some of which are likely to have been items of communion plate (Thiede 1992, pp. 100-101). The male figure which features in a panel of the late fourth century mosaic floor in the villa at Hinton St. Mary, Dorset, is superimposed upon a large chi-rho monogram, but this may or may not make it a representation of Jesus Christ or one of his Apostles.

We are on firmer ground when it comes to British attendance records for one of the early church councils at Arles in 314. Perhaps because of growing military threats both from inside and outside the empire, Rome divided the two existing provinces of Britannia Inferior and Superior into four smaller units early in the fourth century and this may explain why the Church was represented at Arles by Bishop Restitutus of London, Bishop Eborius of York, Bishop Adelphius of Lincoln and a presbyter and deacon, the latter two maybe representing either a vacant see or a bishop who was unable to attend through sickness or some other obstacle (Petts, 2003, p. 38).

Sheppard Frere (1967, p. 333) points out that the British Church was poverty stricken enough to accept Constantius's offer of free transport by the imperial posting service for some of its bishops attending the Council of Ariminum in 359. It had nonetheless spawned its first known martyr many years before in 208/9, when a Roman soldier, Alban, was condemned to death at Verulamium by Geta Caesar while he was in Britain governing the civil province (Salway, p. 515-16).

Towards the end of the fourth century, however, the British Church achieved notoriety on account of a heresy propagated by one of its presbyters Pelagius, which postulated that as man is captain of his own soul, he is capable of exercising his own free will to achieve his own salvation. In 429 Germanus, Bishop of Auxerre arrived from Gaul with Bishop Lupus of Troyes to arrest the progress of the heresy and to counter the influence of a certain Agricola, son of a bishop, who had become its leading spirit. Germanus routed the Pelagians at a great assembly in Verulamium and soon afterwards seems to have won a major military victory over the Picts and Saxons, probably in North Wales (Salway, 1993, pp. 320-322).

The golden age of Celtic Christianity

Nonetheless, the proud days of the Roman Empire were almost over. Successive waves of invaders from across the North Sea during the fifth and sixth centuries drove the Romano-British westwards and northwards into the mountain fastnesses of Wales and Northumbria, and with them the Christian faith that many of them had espoused. It seems that the Christian faith had already gained a foothold in Ireland, since in 431 Pope Celestine sent Palladius to be its bishop and to engage in further evangelism. Palladius seems to have been succeeded by the Romanised Briton Patrick, who set up his see at Armagh. From then on, historians find the situation confusing and increasingly murky.

All that we can say for certain, with D.H. Farmer (1983, pp. 13-14), is that these Celtic Christian communities of the west and north were based, not so much upon bishops and settled dioceses, but rather upon small monastic communities, some of them mixed because of the family-orientated nature of Celtic society. The abbot's authority would hold sway, even if a bishop were a member of his community, as happened when a resident bishop in Iona who was reluctant to ordain a man to the priesthood, did so after Columba had assumed responsibility for it.

As Margaret Deanesly points out (1961, pp. 38-39), the Celtic lands could not develop a territorial episcopate because they lacked the Roman *civitates* upon which to base them. The great Celtic characters, like David, Ninian and Patrick may have held episcopal rank, but according to Ian Bradley (2003, pp. 14-20) their reputations grew, not from settled local ministries, but from long evangelistic treks by land and sea, setting up new Christian communities as they went, with links from Britanny constantly augmenting and refreshing their work. Germanus came from this part of Gaul in the 5th century and maybe he is commemorated through his Welsh name Garmon in the dedication of many churches in North and Mid Wales, although recently some have considered that this may refer to some other Garmon.

Like their Apostolic forbears, the Celtic bishops were once again teachers and preachers, bringing the faith to places where the good news of Christ was not yet known. Nonetheless, despite its attractive character and notable successes, the Celtic Church was operating on the remotest island fringes of the Christian world, in very difficult mountainous terrain far away from the hub of the Western Church in post imperial Rome. Not surprisingly, it grew apart from it in its organisation, spirituality and habits.

Perhaps Aidan exemplifies the attractions of the Celtic bishop. He was the first Bishop of Lindisfarne, but also a monk, living under monastic vows and responsible to his abbot. Henry Mayr-Harting (1972, p. 95) wonders whether Aidan would have thought of himself as Bishop of Lindisfarne at all: he was at heart a wandering missionary bishop and would more likely have thought of himself as bishop to the Northumbrians.

In his *Ecclesiastical History* (quoted by Mayr-Harting, 1972, p. 95) Bede describes Aidan in these touching words:

> *He neither sought nor cared for worldly possessions but he rejoiced to hand over at once, to any poor man he met, the gifts which he had received from kings or rich men ... He used to travel everywhere, in town and country, not on horseback, but on foot, unless compelled by urgent necessity to do otherwise, in order that, as he walked along, whenever he saw people whether rich or poor, he might at once approach them, and if they were unbelievers, invite them to accept the mystery of faith; or if they were believers, that he might strengthen them in the faith, urging them by word and deed to practise almsgiving and good works.*

the Saxon Church

While the Celtic Church was making its mark in the West and North of Britain, Pope Gregory had dispatched Augustine to evangelise the pagan

Saxons. Upon his arrival in Thanet in 597 he converted King Ethelbert of Kent and later went on to establish his own see at Canterbury and consecrate Mellitus bishop for London and Justus for Rochester to serve those southern and eastern kingdoms of England whose monarchs had embraced the new faith. So successful was the mission that some 10,000 Englishmen were baptised on Christmas Day that year. Augustine had been sent from Pope Gregory's own monastery on the Coelian Hill in Rome, where despite the final collapse of the Roman Empire at the start of the fifth century, the old habits and customs of imperial rule and administration lived on in the structures, personnel and expectations of its Catholic Church.

In the nature of the case, the ministry of Augustine's bishops was primarily itinerant, pastoral and didactic, and as their spheres of operation moved northward and westward, they could not help coming into contact with churches and men who had been moulded by the colourful characters and rugged individualism of Celtic Christianity.

The Synod of Whitby was summoned by King Oswiu of Northumbria in 664 to bring together the old Celtic churches of the North and West with the new churches of England founded by Augustine. Although talks were ostensibly about harmonising the date of Easter, in reality Whitby was about beginning the slow process of reintegrating Celtic Christianity into the mainstream of the Catholic Church (Farmer, 1983, p. 29).

However, not everyone could accept its conclusions: Colman, Bishop of Lindisfarne decided to withdraw to Ireland with forty of his monks. Although Wilfrid was a Northumbrian who had been trained as a boy by Irish monks at Lindisfarne, he had later gone to study in Rome. He had been much impressed during a stay in Lyons by the majestic cathedrals and courtly establishments of the Frankish bishops. Not surprisingly, it was he who led the pro-Roman contingent at Whitby.

The Celtic Christians, no doubt because of the close ties between their own languages and Breton, had maintained regular contact with the Armorican

Peninsula. The Saxon Church, however, had active links with the more strategically important central areas of Gaul and from there came conflicting ideas, both about the episcopate and the nature of a diocese. Frankish bishops were known for their splendour, political prowess and influence, while their dioceses were based upon the Roman cities, with all their history, buildings, fortifications and places of learning. In England most of the Roman cities were at best deserted ruins and people were scattered thinly across the countryside. It is therefore no surprise that the Gallic episcopal model came to dominate the thinking of the Saxon Church in the centuries that followed.

Political prestige for an Anglo Saxon bishop, says Mayr-Harting (1972, p. 135), lay in identifying with an entire tribe or kingdom, which helps to explain why the bishops summoned by Archbishop Theodore to the Synod of Hertford in 673 wished to retain the principle of one bishop for each kingdom, although there was an ever-present temptation towards creating bigger dioceses which could guarantee them bigger revenues. Hertford also completed the Romanisation of the Church which had begun at Whitby. The itinerant bishop and priest and the cosy informality of the Celtic Church were finally rejected. From now on no bishop could invade the territory of another; no cleric could leave his bishop without permission or enter the diocese of another without letters of commendation and no one could exercise a priestly ministry without the permission of the bishop within whose diocese he intended to work.

It was Theodore too who, according to D.J.V. Fisher (1973, p. 91) embarked upon a programme which began by the assertion of his own authority, leading in turn to a spirit of unity, proper organisation and finally to reform. The number of sees was increased, bishops met in synod and there was an increased supply of trained priests. Bishoprics could, however, only be founded as kings made grants of lands and privileges that were thought to be adequate for the proper endowment of a bishop and his household.

The gradual interweaving of the great Celtic and Roman traditions produced some outstanding bishops like Cuthbert, Wilfrid and Cedd. Cuthbert's elevation to the see of Hexham by Archbishop Theodore of Canterbury in 684 epitomised the fusion of the best qualities in both streams of Christianity, a fusion which was to create within only a century of Augustine's arrival a fully articulated, conventional diocesan system under one archbishop and later a second based at York.

Church life generally centred upon the minster, which was often the mother church of a large territory more akin in size to a diocese than to a parish. These royal or episcopal foundations would be served, says Deanesly (1961, pp. 191-210), by Benedictine monks, monks in the Celtic tradition or by a group of priests and men in minor orders living together. Some bishops, like those of Sherborne and Hexham, worked their dioceses from these minsters.

By the middle of the C10, episcopal power and the influence of the minsters was regularly challenged as wealthier theigns began to build churches in villages on their estates and to appoint the priests whom they wanted to serve in them. King Edgar of Mercia passed a law early in his reign which established the ecclesiastical tithe as a major source of church income, with the important proviso that a theign with a church possessing its own churchyard, could pay his own priest a third of the tithe instead of sending the entire amount to the minster from whom the lesser church had been severed. Edgar's Archbishop of Canterbury, Dunstan, formerly the Abbot of Glastonbury, was responsible for a major overhaul of monastic life, which resulted in bishops being drawn almost entirely from the ranks of monks. All this helps to explain the origins of the parochial system as we know it today.

The growing economic and political links between monarch and bishops had become plain by the end of the Saxon period. In 1032 Canute gave the see of Winchester to Aelfwine, the first time a man had been elevated in reward for service to the royal household, while in 1033 Dudue was given Wells, probably because his wide knowledge of European affairs was vital to the king (Fisher, 1973, p. 335).

As there were no independent church courts in the Saxon kingdoms, it was the duty of the local court to interpret and enforce the ecclesiastical law as well as the secular. This fact explains the presence of the bishop in the shire courts, where he very probably assumed a leading place, perhaps as presiding officer, when such cases came to trial (Adams and Schuyler, p. 21)

the Norman Conquest

William the Conqueror's policy for the English Church after he won the Battle of Hastings in 1066 was clear enough. It was to be brought into the mainstream of continental church life, but at the same time to remain firmly under the leadership of the king himself. What few Saxon bishops remained in post were deposed if they looked likely to be troublesome, while Norman bishops who had been appointed by Edward the Confessor were quickly joined by other Normans, including William's loyal servant Lanfranc, who came from Caen to replace Stigand as Archbishop of Canterbury. Over the next century new churches and cathedrals were constructed from Cornwall to the Orkney Islands in the muscular Romanesque style of France, many, like Durham, Rochester, Peterborough and Kirkwall, on the grandest of scales, with enormous drum columns and arcades (Cormack, 1984, pp. 26-35).

The historian John Gillingham summarises the Norman achievement succinctly, when he states (1984, pp. 154-155):

> *During the course of the twelfth century, the English Church established the diocesan and parochial organisation under which it was to live for centuries. The last new dioceses to be created were Ely (1108) and Carlisle (1133) . . . as before, new parishes were created almost at will—the will of the local lord; but thereafter it became much harder. The territorial organisation of the Church became, as it were, frozen in its twelfth century state.*

According to Michael Keulemans (2004, pp. 19-20) and others the archaeological and architectural evidence from pilgrimage sites like Pennant Melangell and elsewhere in Wales and Northern England, shows that even after almost a century of Norman rule, the English kings were careful to keep alive the heroic Celtic tradition in order not to upset potentially difficult subjects in the remoter parts of their realm. At the same time, according to Nerys Jones and Morfydd Owen (2003, p. 66), the new foreign bishops defined and demarcated afresh the Welsh dioceses, exploiting the traditions of their sees and collecting the relics of their saints, so that they could strengthen their control over the local church.

In 1170 Archbishop Thomas a Becket was slashed to death in Canterbury Cathedral by four knights who had come over from the royal court in France in response to Henry II's famously rhetorical question *Who will rid me of this turbulent priest?* On the face of it, Becket's murder was a victory for a king who wanted to smash anarchy and make the common law apply to all within his realm, clergy as well as lay people, but this may be to sell the martyr-archbishop short. Henry's relief was short-lived and the Church hit back swiftly. So it was that until the Reformation, Church courts continued to function and clergy could appeal to Rome against a royal verdict. While the power of the state could do little to interfere with the spiritual, the prelates of the Church—rich, powerful and educated—grew ever more indispensable to the effective government of the English kings.

Plantagenet England was run to a quite extraordinary extent by administrator-prelates like Hubert Walter, justiciar, papal legate and Archbishop of Canterbury from 1193, and Stephen Langton, Archbishop of Canterbury and virtually the architect of *Magna Carta*, which King John was forced to sign at Runnymede in 1215. These were the sort of churchmen whom Simon Schama (2000, p. 144) concludes were *politically shrewd, intellectually subtle and administratively tireless.*

the king consolidates his powers over the Church

Throughout the later Middle Ages, royal power grew as papal influence diminished. The Papacy was to be severely weakened both before and after its 68 year exile to Avignon, but in England the growing demands of royal finances featured prominently in causing this change. Gillingham observes (1984, p. 157) that although from 1200 onwards, the Papacy had a continuous series of tax collectors in England bearing the title of *nuncios*, all of them Italians, by 1300 it was the king who received the lion's share of tax proceeds, no doubt to help finance costly military campaigns in the Holy Land, Wales, Scotland and Flanders (Powicke, 1962, p. 798).

Alongside this change, the Crown's influence in the making of episcopal appointments was extended by Richard II's Statute of Provisors in 1351. The papal right to *provide* men for English benefices and more senior appointments had become increasingly unpopular, but especially after the Pope had moved to Avignon and come under French influence at the very time when England was fighting the Hundred Years War against France. Elections and presentations to benefices and other church offices by the king and others with ancient rights were to continue to be free. If the Pope infringed the royal prerogative by appointing aliens and cardinals to such dignities, those who accepted office would be banished from the kingdom and their property forfeited to the king.

Two years later Richard brought forward the Statute of Praemunire, which was drawn up in the light of the Pope moving bishops and other high-ranking ecclesiastics around the country or even abroad, often without the king's consent or even their own, causing serious financial losses to the Crown. Praemunire declared that any who went to Rome to appeal against the decisions of the king or his courts would lose his protection and forfeit their property to him. For the first time the Crown articulated a doctrine which was to become central 150 years later—... *the crown of England ... has been so free at all times that it has been in no earthly subjection, but immediately subject to God and none other (Bettenson 1943, pp. 243-253).*

Niall Barr notes similarly increased powers for the Crown in the Church life of mediaeval Scotland, although he draws passing attention to the Papal approval demonstrated by the bestowal of the Rose and Sceptre upon James IV in 1494 (2001, p. 23).

There seems to be no evidence that either Provisors or Praemunire were ever used against the Pope, but they were reserve powers which hinted at the growing displeasure which later mediaeval monarchs felt at foreign interference in English affairs, not least by aliens who were appointed to English church posts by Rome and then asset-stripped them before returning home with the proceeds.

filling an episcopal vacancy

When a vacancy occurred, there would often be a spirited three-cornered contest between the local cathedral chapter, the monarchy and the papacy, to be settled by a series of compromises between the wishes of all three. The king would do his best to select a man whom he thought would be helpful to him and then forward his name to the Pope for ratification. If the Pope did not approve, the see remained empty until some settlement had been reached. When the candidate had been finally agreed, the cathedral chapter, who were in theory the electors, were ordered by the king's *conge d'elire* to choose the man proposed, either by persuasion or threat. Once elected by the chapter, he paid homage to the king and only then was he duly consecrated and enthroned.

If the king's intentions were baulked by Rome, there were always other ways for him to achieve his ends. As the king held the temporalities of a vacant see, he could make it difficult for the Pope to appoint his own nominee, but a much easier way for the king after the passage of Praemunire was to translate an existing bishop to a more important diocese. J.D. Dickinson (1979, pp. 253-254) observes that:

> the possibilities for Crown manipulation of episcopal appointments were augmented by the ease with which it was possible to translate a bishop ... It was a weapon which could be and now was used by the king to advance a favoured bishop from one see to another which was, in the worldly sense, more desirable, or occasionally to downgrade a bishop no longer in favour by moving him to a lesser sphere of influence.

bishops as officers of state

Not surprisingly, as the Middle Ages wore on, many new bishops proceeded straight back to court to continue their political careers and visited their dioceses only on very rare occasions, leaving most of the routine work to their chancellors, to Irish bishops beyond the Pale or to bishops *in partibus,* who were often in local or mendicant orders and only too glad of the opportunity to augment their meagre incomes by serving their richer brethren. E.F. Jacob (1961, p. 275) records that John Chourles from the Irish see of Dromore was out of his diocese between 1419 and 1426 to undertake episcopal duties in Canterbury, London and Rochester.

High-flyers would be marked out by the king to become Chancellors or Treasurers or hold some other high office of state, for as T.M. Parker (1946, p. 378) points out, *the Crown tended to look upon bishops as counsellors to whose services it had a prescriptive right.* One of many such high fliers was Henry Beaufort, half-brother of Henry IV. He was appointed Bishop of Lincoln in 1398, where the income from wool grown on his extensive manorial estates became an important prop to royal finances hard-pressed by the French Wars. He became Lord Chancellor of England in 1403 at the age of only 29 and was translated to Winchester the following year. His loans to the Crown probably came to the incredible sum of more than £200,000 (Jacob, 1961, p. 442). He was an aristocrat to his fingertips and enjoyed a long although sometimes difficult career in national government.

Dickinson points out that there were undoubted practical advantages for the mediaeval kings in using bishops to undertake secular responsibilities. Not only were they sometimes appointed judges of assize because of their assumed impartiality and rectitude, but they frequently had the charge of royal castles or royal treasure for similar reasons. He also remarks on an important development:

> ...from the late 13ᵗʰ century onwards all the diocesan bishops were liable to be summoned to the new thing they called Parliament, thereby being liable to involvement in tedious travel ... the king obtaining the service of men who were like to have greater integrity and much less concern for family interest than the lay barons (1979, p. 29).

With mediaeval bishops having so many irresistible distractions from what must have seemed their more mundane and humdrum pastoral and ecclesiastical duties, G.R. Elton's assessment comes as no surprise (1991, p. 115):

> ... the way to the bench had lain through the king's service: good grace made the leaders and guardians of the Church active or retired ministers of the crown rather than prelates obeying their spiritual head.

big dioceses with big responsibilities

Deanesly (1950, p. 199) notes only seventeen dioceses in early mediaeval England, two of them of immense size, Lincoln stretching from the Humber right down to the Thames and York reaching from the Cumberland coast right down to Nottingham (see fig.1).

Fig. 1

ENGLISH AND WELSH BISHOPRICS AROUND 1300
cathedrals marked by crosses
(adapted from Deanesly, 1950, p. 199)

In such large dioceses many new bishops found themselves instant and often wealthy landowners. In the middle of the 15th century, land holdings brought the Bishop of Winchester the colossal annual income of £3,900 (Dickinson, 1979, p. 30). Episcopal manors stretched right across the dioceses, Lincoln alone possessing nine. These houses served a useful purpose for bishops as they travelled round with their entourage listening to disputes and administering the law. Because they had the power to deprive clergy of their benefices and to flog the laity, the bishop and his advisers were viewed as a formidable body, whose displeasure even the most powerful of magnates had cause to fear. Dickinson, (1979, p. 169) records how Bishop Swinfield of Hereford had 36 horses so that he and his extensive household could move 81 times in 296 days! No wonder Bishop J.R.H. Moorman (1973, p. 102) comments that *as pastor and landowner, judge and magistrate, civil servant and member of parliament a bishop's time was fully occupied.*

Sometimes, however, the piety of the bishops was more than merely superficial and produced its glossier fruits within their own dioceses. Thomas Beckington, a 15th century occupant of Bath and Wells, not only built fish breeding tanks in his palace, but established an excellent school with a resident schoolmaster and gave the little town its water supply *along with troughs, pipes and other necessary engines above and below ground.* (Dickinson, 1979, p. 254)

Two bishops may be reckoned to encapsulate the principal but contrasting dimensions of the mediaeval episcopate, Robert Grosseteste of Lincoln the spiritual in the 13th century and William of Wykeham of Winchester the political in the next.

Robert Grosseteste of Lincoln

Robert Grosseteste came to Lincoln in 1235 as bishop of a diocese containing 1600 parishes in eight archdeaconries with around a fifth of the entire population of England (Southern, 1992, p. 235). He had studied in Paris and taught in Oxford, where he first adopted the voluntary poverty of the Franciscans. He was no mean theologian, being conversant with Hebrew and having translated the *Testament of the Twelve Patriarchs* from Greek into Latin, as well as being considered a great authority on God and the created order. He also wrote extensively on astronomy and farming.

He lived a simple and frugal life himself, but commended food, sleep and a good humour to others, telling a melancholy friar that he should drink a cup of the best wine as a penance (Moorman, 1946, p. 184). He was passionately concerned to raise the low standards of the parochial clergy and, in line with his Franciscan sympathies, to release a powerful force through the land that would bring before people's minds a stirring vision of what God had called the Church to be.

Following the wishes of the Fourth Lateran Council, summoned by Pope Innocent III in 1215 to provide a body of disciplined, educated and dedicated clergy to instruct their parishioners, Grosseteste set to work with characteristic energy. In his first year at Lincoln he deposed eleven heads of religious communities and promulgated a set of constitutions as a guide to his parish priests, brief, practical and, in his own words, *with strict attention to immediate problems (Powicke 1964, pp. 452-456)*. Clergy were to be expected to know their basics; the Ten Commandments, the Seven Deadly Sins, the Seven Sacraments, the Creeds and how they should conduct themselves. Homilies were to be preached in English, the sale of sacraments was denounced, offices were to be said at times that would allow the laity to attend, daily prayer and Bible reading were encouraged and clergy were discouraged from having the distraction of a secular job—in Grosseteste's eyes everything must be subordinated to the supreme task of gaining the salvation of human souls.

Grosseteste embarked upon a two-year visitation of the diocese with his officials in 1246. This involved precise investigations, during the course of which people would be required to make sworn testimonies, a procedure which was prohibited by the king, but which the bishop considered necessary to avoid the subversion of the pastoral office and the eternal damnation of souls.

Grosseteste's honest single-mindedness was shown at national level too. At a meeting of King Henry III's Great Council at Merton in 1236, only one year into his episcopate, he brought himself into collision with the barons by defending the Church's right to override civil practice by declaring children born to a couple before wedlock to be legitimate if their parents subsequently married.

Explaining his sometimes controversial conduct as a diocesan bishop to Pope Innocent IV and his cardinals at Lyons in 1250, just three years before the end of his life, Grosseteste says:

> *When I became bishop I believed it to be necessary to be a shepherd of the souls committed to me, whose blood would be required of me at the Last Judgement unless I used all diligence in visiting them as Scripture requires. So I began to perambulate my bishopric archdeaconry by archdeaconry, and rural deanery by rural deanery, requiring the clergy of each deanery to bring their people with their children together at a fixed place and time in order to have their children confirmed, to hear the Word of God and to make their confessions. When the clergy and people were assembled, I myself frequently preached to the clergy, a friar, preacher or minor preached to the people, and four friars heard confessions and imposed penances. Then, having confirmed the children on two days, I and my clerks gave our attention to enquiring into things which needed correction or reform ...*
>
> (Southern, 1992, p. 258)

William Wykeham of Winchester

William of Wykeham came from comparatively humble Hampshire stock and after being educated in Winchester through the munificence of an unknown patron, became secretary to the Constable of Winchester Castle. He then entered the royal service as an underling in the office of the Constable of Windsor Castle, becoming Clerk of Works there at the wage of two shillings per day. S.C. Carpenter (1954, p. 181-183) says that he showed a remarkable talent for the economical management of buildings and estates, being involved in the design and construction of Edward III's Round Table house for the new Knights of the Garter and the completion of the royal apartments at Windsor in 1359.

He had already taken his first tonsure after the Black Death and in 1357 was appointed Rector of Pulham, a Norfolk parish in the gift of the king. As recognition for his architectural achievements at Windsor and the other royal castles, Edward showered ecclesiastical benefices upon him—a deanery, eleven prebends and two rectories—all between 1357 and 1361, even though he was still a layman. He was ordained to minor orders in 1361 and to the priesthood a year later, when he received five more prebends, two archdeaconries and another rectory.

In 1363 the King appointed him Lord Privy Seal, which meant that he was in effect the monarch's private secretary and probably one of the most influential men in the land. Months after being appointed to Canterbury from Winchester, Bishop William Edington, who had ordained Wykeham an acolyte, died. The king promptly nominated Wykeham for the Winchester vacancy, but the Pope dithered and in the meantime Wykeham was given the Great Seal as Chancellor and then the see of Winchester into the bargain. Thus at the age of 43 he came to occupy the highest administrative post in the land and also its richest see. Following the French sacking of the Cinque port of Winchelsea and the kidnap of its women and girls in 1359, the king gave him the additional appointment of Chief Keeper of Dover Castle and three other strategic Kentish fortresses. He went to Calais in 1360 to witness Edward sign the Treaty of Bretigny with King John of France and also represented the king in his tortuous dealings with the Scots.

He resigned from the Chancellorship in 1372, ostensibly because of a Commons petition against churchmen holding offices of state without being answerable to the courts, but more likely on account of the poor outcome of the French Wars and several dubious accusations of financial abuses brought against him by John of Gaunt and other jealous members of the court (Saul 1997, pp. 295-96). The following year he started a programme of works to restore the fabric of his twelve episcopal palaces and castles and began a visitation of every church and monastery in his large diocese, while also reforming abuses at St. Cross Hospital in Winchester and at Selborne Priory. He nonetheless remained active as a trusted advisor to the increasingly senile king, lending him large sums of money on several occasions.

He was recalled to the Chancellorship by Richard II on his accession in 1389, with the proper defence of the realm his priority, but he served for only a couple of years before retiring to his palace at North Waltham, where he died in 1404 after using some of his own considerable fortune to rebuild the nave of his own cathedral.

According to Carpenter (1954, p. 192) *he made a good bishop and did much to organise both Church and State during the difficult years after the Black Death and the second pestilence of 1361.* However, he is most remembered for founding Winchester College to provide an education for *seventy poor and needy scholars, clerks, living college-wise therein and studying . . . in grammaticals, or the art, faculty or science of grammar.* Pupils spent four to five years in the school. Winchester College was intended as a nursery for his other great foundation of New College, Oxford, where the seventy students received three years of tuition from the older fellows. All of this immense largesse was ultimately directed towards what Wykeham called *the cure of the common disease of the clerical army, which we have seen grievously wounded by lack of clerks, due to plagues, wars and other miseries.*

Looking ahead towards the transformation of many of the mediaeval cathedral and charitable foundations like Winchester into the major and minor public schools of the Victorian era, G.H. Moberly astutely observes that

Wykeham *directly moulded the education of the upper middle classes of the nation (1887, pp. 267-268).*

Perhaps it is an interesting exercise to speculate as to why so many bishops fell into one or other of these two major preoccupations, politics and education. With degrees in ecclesiastical or civil law they were ideally placed to be spotted as capable and knowledgeable administrators by the monarch or the Church and in the course of their experience they probably became skilled in managing people and astute in handling property and money. Once again, those with a penchant for education will have earned degrees in the arts and maybe later in law or medicine and had ample opportunities to make their mark on promising choristers in the cathedral and song schools that were invariably linked to the big cathedrals and on the boys in the grammar schools that nestled in the shadow of some of the collegiate and larger parish churches.

Thus Euan Cameron (1991, p. 34) neatly summarises the background of the 15th century bishop like this:

> *In the English case, a typical bishop in the late 15th century was of modest social origins, trained in canon law at a university, and experienced as an administrator or functionary in the household of another prince of the Church or of the king himself . . .*

Right at the end of the Middle Ages, Henry VII's 24 year reign produced 46 new bishops. Of these only three were from noble families, far fewer than before and reflecting the tighter controls that the founder of the ever-suspicious Tudor dynasty was imposing upon the nobility. Of the total, a stunning 32 had given previous governmental or diplomatic service, while six were Italians and 24 had studied law, ten theology and one medicine in the higher university faculties (Thomson, 1992, pp. 46-47). It is worth noticing that by this time bishops and abbots constituted a good half of the members of the House of Lords (Maitland, 1955, p. 507)

Yet, in summing up the mixed legacy of the Middle Ages Parker declares (1946, p. 378):

> *The chief count against the mediaeval bishop is not that he abused a system good in itself, but rather that he was a living representative of a system vitiated by its secular contacts since the establishment of Christianity in the later Roman Empire. That, no doubt, was not his fault; he was a victim of the past and could not have extricated himself from the system even had he wished.*

CHAPTER FOUR

✳

The Reformation and the Creation of the Classic Anglican Bishop

The causes of the Reformation

There had been rumblings of religious discontent in Catholic England long before the Reformation cataclysm struck. In the fourteenth century John Wycliffe, the first translator of the Scriptures into English, had been instrumental in founding the Lollards. Although this movement paralleled some of the wandering preaching tradition made popular in Italy by the Franciscans, it was organised, not through normal Church structures, but through the personal initiative of a Leicestershire rector. Hence it was rapidly perceived as a threat and cruelly suppressed.

The immediate cause of England's rupture with Rome was not the ungodly exercise of episcopacy, but Henry VIII's need to have his marriage with Catherine of Aragon set aside, so that he could pursue his sexual intentions with the country girl Anne Boleyn. The Pope had refused to grant him an annulment, even though Henry claimed that God was angry with him and granted him no son and heir because he had married his brother Arthur's widow, so the king

---

turned to his Archbishop of Canterbury instead. Thomas Cranmer obliged, as he was to do again later when Henry grew tired first of Anne Boleyn and then Anne of Cleves.

To wreak easy vengeance upon an unpopular aspect of the old Roman order, but also to fill his coffers for the defence of his beleaguered realm and to reward those whom F.H. Crossley (1935, p. 104) called *the jackals who dogged the heels of a spendthrift monarch*, Henry closed all the religious houses of England. Hundreds of monasteries, friaries and nunneries were left as empty shells to be sold off, torn down by speculative builders, left to rot in remote countryside, ransacked for building stone or converted into country houses for wealthy gentlemen. The Dissolution of the Monasteries may have been intended primarily as a huge money spinner for the hard-pressed royal finances, but it undoubtedly had the effect of nudging the progress of reform up a gear.

The English Reformation, although very different in its origins, nature and outcome from the European, could not help being profoundly affected by events on the Continent, not least because of the constant comings and goings of theologians from Germany, Switzerland, the Netherlands and France to the University of Cambridge, which had become the hub for most of the new thinking (Neill, 1977, p. 47).

Doctrinal and liturgical change came slowly and with relatively little iconoclasm. The Psalter was translated into English from the Latin Vulgate by Miles Coverdale in 1535 and the Great Bible in English ordered to be placed in every parish church in 1536, but then, apart from the Dissolution of the Monasteries, little of major significance happened until Edward VI came to the throne and Cranmer's first Book of Common Prayer appeared in 1549, to be followed a year later by the Ordinal, which includes the form for *ordaining or consecrating an archbishop or bishop*.

We find the earliest indications of Cranmer's thinking on the question of episcopacy in the Questions and Answers he is reputed by John Strype

(1694) to have written for commissioners appointed to draw up a declaration of Christian doctrine in 1540 (quoted in Duffield, 1964, p. 28). In answer to the perennial question of which came first, bishop or priest, Cranmer says, *The bishops and priests were at one time, and were not two things, but both one office in the beginning of Christ's religion,* later on affirming that:

> *A bishop may make a priest by the Scripture, and so may princes and governors also, and that by the authority of God committed unto them, and the people also by their election; for as we read that bishops have done it, so Christian emperors and princes usually have done it, and the people, before Christian princes were, commonly did elect their bishops and priests.*

Charles Neil and J.M. Willoughby (1912, pp. 497-505 and 529-533) explore how Cranmer's 1550 Ordinal discontinued some old customs of the Sarum Pontifical like the unction of the head and hands and the delivery of the ring and mitre to the bishop elect, but retained the giving of the pastoral staff, the wearing of the cope and the laying of the Bible upon the head of the candidate.

This Ordinal was revised in 1552, along with the rest of the Prayer Book, in order to complete the Evangelical overhaul of liturgy and to remove the last vestiges of what were considered to be those unhelpful mediaeval externals which had survived hitherto. As in the other new ordination services, Cranmer introduced a public question and answer session before the laying on of hands which demonstrated with extraordinary clarity what the Church was entitled to expect from a newly consecrated bishop, in terms of his functions as well as his beliefs and conduct. After asking the candidate if he felt genuinely called by God and the Church to the work of episcopal ministry, the second, third and fourth of the other six questions were almost exclusively concerned with its teaching function:

...Are you determined out of the ... holy Scriptures to instruct the people committed to your charge ... ? (Q2)

Will you then faithfully exercise yourself in the same holy Scriptures, and call upon God by prayer for the true understanding of the same; so that you may be able by them to teach and exhort with wholesome doctrine and to withstand and convince the gainsayers? (Q3)

Be you ready, with all faithful diligence, to banish and drive away all erroneous and strange doctrine contrary to God's Word; and both privately and openly to call upon and encourage others to do the same? (Q4)

In a passing hint at the bishop's need to act as a focus of unity for his diocese, but more obviously his obligation to administer ecclesiastical discipline, question 6 called upon the candidate to promote *quietness, peace and love among all men* and to correct and punish *such as be unquiet, disobedient and criminous* within his diocese. A seventh question concerning a bishop's duty to perform ordinations was not in the 1552 revision, but added in 1662.

In the 1552 rite, after delivering the Bible to the newly consecrated bishop, the Archbishop said:

Give heed unto reading, exhortation and doctrine. Think upon the things contained in this Book ... Take heed unto thyself, and to doctrine and be diligent in doing them: for by so doing thou shalt save both thyself and those that hear thee. Be to the flock of Christ a shepherd, not a wolf; feed them, devour them not. Hold up the weak, heal the sick, bind up the broken, bring again the outcasts, seek the lost. Be so merciful that ye be not too remiss; so minister discipline that you forget not mercy ...

Taken together then, most of the 1552 consecration service is concerned in one way or another with the episcopal teaching function. Clearly, for the Reformers, as for the Fathers of the early Church, Christian teaching, focussed clearly upon the Holy Scriptures, along with pastoral care and an exemplary lifestyle were considered of paramount importance to the nature and exercise of the episcopate. Little else seemed important enough to warrant more than a fleeting mention.

Significantly, when Bishop Hugh Latimer was preaching before the young King Edward VI in 1549, he revealed some of the true intention behind the reform of the episcopate begun in the 1550 Ordinal. It was time to put an end to the days of Morton, Wolsey and Gardiner and turn bishops into full-time churchmen, who could care for God's Church and people without the distractions of major responsibilities of state. *I mean not that I would have prelates lords presidents, nor that lords bishops should be lords presidents . . . The office of a presidentship is a civil one and it cannot be that one man shall discharge both well (Corrie, 1845, p. 176).*

England's short and nostalgic return to the Catholic fold under Mary I saw the Prayer Book's major contributor and editor Thomas Cranmer and his episcopal colleagues Latimer and Nicholas Ridley burnt at the stake in Oxford, but no sooner had Elizabeth I ascended the throne in 1558 than she set in train a return to most of what had been so summarily cut short in 1553. In spite of those more colourful and retrospective ceremonies (Johnson 1974, p. 89), which might have gone on in the privacy of her own domestic chapel at Whitehall, Diarmid MacCulloch comments (1999, p. 12):

> *Edwardian government decisions moulded the church settlement restored in 1559, equally in liturgy, theological confession and church polity. Elizabeth put Edwardian structures to rather different uses to those originally intended, but even so, the Church of England is the Church of Edward VI more than it likes to admit. Thomas Cranmer, that editorial*

genius, bequeathed Elizabeth the Book of Common Prayer, which
(perhaps against her personal inclinations) she restored in its more radical
version of 1552, virtually unaltered.

Only one bishop—Anthony Kitchin of Llandaff—took the oath of allegiance to the new queen. The rest were either deprived or went into exile, which made it difficult to muster the requisite number of bishops to consecrate Matthew Parker as Archbishop of Canterbury. Moorman (1973, p. 203) records that in the finish the ceremony took place in Lambeth Palace Chapel in 1559 at the hands of William Barlow, formerly of Bath and Wells, Miles Coverdale, formerly of Exeter, John Scory of Chichester and John Hodgkin, Suffragan Bishop of Bedford, two of whom had been consecrated according to the Roman rite back in Henry VIII's reign.

the pressures upon the Elizabethan bishops

After the ecclesiastical upheavals of the Reformation era and the final removal of the Spanish threat through the destruction of the Armada by Sir Francis Drake in 1588, both Church and State settled down into a quieter mode. The task to which Elizabeth had devoted herself, the consolidation of the English Church, was one forced upon her not by any strong convictions of her own, but mainly by the pressure of political difficulties, such as the Papal Bull of 1570 which attempted to depose her from her throne, the St. Bartholemew's Eve Massacre of the French Huguenots in 1572 and the secret Jesuit mission to England in 1580. On top of these external threats she had to face the schemes of the French Guises to bring about an armed uprising in Scotland and the possibly dire domestic consequences of the assassination of the Prince of Orange in 1584, while all the time being acutely aware of repeated attempts being made upon her own life.

Scory of Hereford may have provided a favourite illustration of venality and maladministration, Richard Curteis of Chichester may have been a dishonest drunkard, but by the later years of John Whitgift's Elizabethan archiepisco-pate, it seems that the Reformation bishops had acquired a range of attractive attributes. As P.M. Dawley (1955, pp. 105-106) argues so cogently:

> *Elizabeth's average bishop was a conscientious prelate, beset with problems that defied easy solution. Surrounded by changing social and political patterns that he scarcely understood, he was uncertain of the extent of his episcopal authority and the precise nature of his administrative functions in a national Church that had not yet reached its maturity. The Elizabethan bishops were pioneers, bringing the traditional Catholic episcopate into an ecclesiastical settlement at once broadened by the religious reformation and constricted by the association with the Crown. Past experience contributed little to the solution of their problems. Like all pioneers, they were forced to decisions and actions out of which, at least in part, the future would be shaped. Theirs was the immediate responsibility of steering the Elizabethan Church through the narrow straits between the Scylla of Rome and the Charybdis of Puritanism. It was an uncharted course between the rock of Peter and the ever-widening whirlpool that spread out from Geneva. They not only had to find the channel, but mark its path in their writings . . . the buoys, so to speak, along to the safer waters of Hooker's Laws of Ecclesiastical Polity.*

However, despite the undoubted qualities of these studied and conscien-tiously moderate men, the Elizabethan bishops appeared quite different to those contemporaries who lived outside their immediate world. R.L. Ottley (1894, pp. 25-42) comments that to most of the English people, and especially to the growing Puritan party:

> *Bishops appeared to be little more than government officers, enforcing by legal powers a conformity which was odious to multitudes of earnest*

men, and which seemed opposed by its very nature to the essential spirit
of religion.... The Church of England held as yet somewhat loosely and
with hesitation to the via media. She seemed to be the natural refuge for the
lukewarm, the indolent and the temporising spirits among the clergy. The
cautious and tentative attitude forced upon her by the circumstances of the
time was one that repressed ardour while it invited attack ... Elizabeth
had subdued them (the bishops) and ordered them about like servants.
Under James they were raised to a position of dignity; they were the equal
of statesmen and courtiers; they were trusted advisers to the Crown.

The Elizabethan Church faced constant challenges from two sides, the newly confident and assertive Roman Church of the Counter-Reformation and the uncoordinated criticisms of full-blown Protestantism both in Continental Europe and at home. Bishop John Jewel of Salisbury's *Apologia pro Ecclesia Anglicana* of 1562 set out its case capably against the Roman Church. He takes his stand on the Scriptures and the primitive Church of the first six centuries and affirms that by this date, the clear outlines of Christian doctrine had been drawn and that any further developments will be found firmly within those outlines and not beyond them. He does not devote much specific attention to the episcopate, but asserts:

We believe that there is one church of God, and that the same is not
shut up ... into some one corner or kingdom, but that it is catholic and
universal and dispersed throughout the whole world ... Furthermore that
there be divers degrees of ministry in the church: whereof some be deacons,
some priests, some bishops: to whom is committed the office to instruct
the people, and the whole charge and setting forth of religion.

He declares those people wrong who ask *that we allow every man to be a priest, to be a teacher, and to be an interpreter of the scriptures (Works, part III, pp. 59-60).*

In 1594 the Kent parish priest Richard Hooker addressed the challenge the Church faced from the extreme Protestant side. Since he had been only a small child when Elizabeth came to the throne, he had experienced none of the bitter religious struggles that had characterised the middle decades of the 16th century. For a short time he was Master of the Temple, the London hub of the legal profession, but then he held a number of quiet country cures which gave him the opportunity to acquire his huge breadth of knowledge of Scripture, the Fathers, the Schoolmen, Church history and indeed almost everything that had ever been written of profit in the Christian world. All this varied material he used to mature his thinking into the creation of a harmonious exposition of a truly distinct Anglicanism, demonstrating both how it was truly Catholic and validly Reformed, but also to show precisely where it was forced to differ from the strident *sola scriptura* of Genevan Protestantism and its band of henchmen in England.

On the thorny question of bishops, Hooker takes matters right back to the beginning, stating unequivocally that *the Apostles did no less perform the offices of their episcopal authority by governing, than of their apostolical by teaching (Book VII, iv.1)*. Later he asserts just as confidently, quoting Cyprian of Carthage, that *it was the general received persuasion of the ancient Christian world that the outward being of a church consisteth in the having of a bishop (Book VII, v.3)*. For Hooker one of the chief functions reserved to a bishop alone is to ordain others to the sacred ministry, *for that no man is able to shew either deacon or presbyter ordained by presbyters only, and his ordination accounted lawful in any ancient part of the Church . . . (Book VII, vi, 5)*.

Hooker makes use of perhaps the most compelling reason for having bishops. He infers that they were universally appointed in the early centuries because *it plainly appeared that without them the Church could not have continued long . . . Episcopal authority was even in a manner sanctified unto the Church of Christ by that little bitter experience which it first had of the pestilent evil of schisms. (Book VII, xiii, 3)*.

The Anabaptist threat had already made itself evident in the early years of the Virgin Queen's reign, especially in London and other big cities, but by the time of James I's coronation the Puritans were becoming noisy as well as numerous. The problem had become sufficiently alarming for him to call the Hampton Court Conference in 1604 in an attempt to ward off their criticisms of the episcopal system and the Anglican liturgy and wheedle them into a more co-operative frame of mind. In the event James's fuse was short and he largely ignored their demands, offering them merely a new translation of the Bible. Instead he began to bolster his bench with new men like Lancelot Andrewes, who could be relied upon to develop the steadier and more conciliatory Anglicanism so beloved by Elizabeth and so brilliantly portrayed by Jewel and Hooker.

It was indeed the publication of Hooker's seminal *Laws of Ecclesiastical Polity* that ultimately came to encapsulate the spirit and character of the 17th and 18th century Church of England. *Ecclesia Anglicana* did indeed hold to the primacy of Scripture and its inherently supreme authority in the ongoing life of the Church, which the Reformation had rediscovered, but it also accorded high regard to the writings of the early Fathers and their significance in the formation of Christian tradition, while at the same time giving full rein to the use of human reason in interpreting both the Scriptures and Christian tradition in the light of changes in society and circumstance. This distinctively Anglican position, which would eventually come to be set out in the Lambeth Quadrilateral of 1888 (Carpenter, 1959, pp. 425-426), was the one which largely guided the memorable episcopates of men like Lancelot Andrewes in the 17th century and Thomas Wilson in the next.

Lancelot Andrewes

James I appointed Lancelot Andrewes from the Deanery of Westminster to be Bishop of Chichester and Lord High Almoner in 1606. Three years later he was translated to Ely and nine years after that to Winchester and the

Deanery of the Chapel Royal, both of which posts he held until his death in 1626. Andrewes was an accomplished scholar, having been previously Master of Pembroke Hall, Cambridge. He had a superb knowledge of the Latin authors and the early Fathers and had taken part in translating the Pentateuch and the historical books for the Authorised version of the Bible published in 1611. His intellectual capacities strongly appealed to the King, who liked nothing better than to express his own love for learning and indulge his interest in discussing theological matters with his church leaders.

However, Andrewes had an appeal far beyond the claustrophobic confines of James's Court. He was one of the first to articulate what was to become the prevailing philosophy of Anglicanism. By the time he first entered the field of controversy with his *Responsio* in 1610, it had become essential for the Church of England to have a solid foundation upon which to base its claim to true catholicity in response to the searching challenges presented by Cardinal Bellarmine and other Roman apologists, alongside its need to assert clear Evangelical credentials against a clutch of Protestant critics on the Continent.

Andrewes unashamedly rests the Anglican title to catholicity upon the simple fact that its faith is that of the primitive Church. It believes neither less nor more than the Fathers to whom it makes its appeal. In the primitive Church public prayer in an unfamiliar language, the denial of the cup to the laity, image worship, invocation of saints, masses celebrated by priests alone, seven sacraments, the primacy of the Roman see—all these would have been unknown. The English Church therefore deliberately rejects them. As Andrewes puts it so graphically and memorably in one of his sermons recorded by Ottley (1894, p. 163), it believes in:

> One canon reduced to writing by God himself, two testaments, three creeds, four general councils, five centuries, and the series of Fathers in that period—the three centuries, that is, before Constantine, and two after, determine the boundary of our faith.

Although he wrote briefly upon the subject of bishops, the aims of Andrewes's episcopate must be judged largely from the articles he submitted to churchwardens before his primary visitation of the Winchester diocese. His sheer practicality shines out: he is concerned for the cleanliness, order and decency of churches and their furniture; for the proper and regular administration of the sacraments; for the genuine care of the sick and poor, and above all for the moral condition of the people in the parishes. Andrewes is particularly concerned about the lifestyles of the clergy and he has no compunction about asking his leading laity bluntly whether their minister resorted to taverns and ale houses or occupied himself in *base or servile labour, riot, dice, cards, tables or any other unlawful games.* They were also asked whether he was *contentious, a hunter, hawker, swearer, dancer, usurer, suspected of incontinence, or hath given any evil example of life* (Ottley, 1894, p. 110).

Andrewes's demands of the laity were no less severe. The churchwardens are directed to fine those who have absented themselves from church without good cause and during service times they are to *walk out of the church and see who are abroad in any alehouse, or elsewhere absent or evil employed,* and report any offenders to the ordinary. The minister is to keep a record of those who have been excommunicated, and once every six months *to denounce them which have not received their absolution on some Sunday in service time, that others may be admonished to refrain from their company* (Ottley, 1894, p. 111).

Andrewes took great care in the use of his episcopal patronage. Ottley says (p. 112):

> *He would send for a likely man, and with thoughtful kindness defray the travelling and other incidental expenses of one he had decided to promote. He was noted for his special abhorrence of simony: he refused to admit men to livings whom he suspected to be simoniacally preferred, and on this account he was content to suffer on several occasions by suits of law.*

Although Andrewes was a great episcopalian, he was no narrow minded bigot and he resolutely refused to unchurch otherwise orthodox Christian bodies who had jettisoned the office of bishop. Bishop Stephen Neill (1977, p. 136) quotes him saying:

> Even if our order be admitted to be of divine authority, it does not follow that without it there can be no salvation, or that without it a Church cannot stand. Only a blind man could fail to see Churches standing without it. Only a man of iron could deny that salvation is to be found within them.

Archbishop John Williams of York, like Andrewes, had first been appointed Dean of Westminster in 1620 by James I before becoming one of the king's closest advisers as Lord Keeper of the Great Seal. The extraordinary range of Caroline episcopal interests and the humility with which they were exercised, no less than the continuing priority of the teaching function, comes out exquisitely in the words Williams (1979, p. 14) records him saying not long before his death in 1650:

> I have passed through many places of honour and trust, both in Church and State, more than any of my order in England these seventy years before. But were I but assured that by my preaching I had converted but one soul unto God, I should take therein more spiritual joy and comfort than in all the honours and offices which have been bestowed upon me.

bishops go underground in the English Civil War

This comparatively peaceful period for the English Church came to an end with the increasing hostility of the House of Commons to Charles I and his use of the Royal prerogative and to Archbishop William Laud, who supported the king with the efficiency and loyalty equal to Henry VIII's statesman-bishops. Laud's tragedy was that although he stood in the noble Anglican tradition of Hooker and Andrewes, he possessed neither the breadth of their understanding nor their eirenic temper. The casual way in which people dumped their hats and coats upon the holy table and let their dogs roam around the chancel makes perfect sense of his introduction of communion rails in 1636, but the imposition of the 1637 Prayer Book upon the fiercely independent Scots was asking for trouble.

The sentences which Charles I's Court of Star Chamber handed out, under Laud's influence, to those who had the temerity to publicly oppose episcopacy were draconian in the extreme. The most notorious offenders, the lawyer William Prynne, Puritan rector Henry Burton and physician John Bastwick were each fined £5,000, had their ears cut off, were forced to endure the stocks and sentenced to perpetual imprisonment (Neill, 1977, pp. 145-46). But perhaps Laud's greatest mistake, and the one that was ultimately to take him to the executioner's axe on Tower Hill, was to turn the clock back by bringing churchmen into occupying some of the great offices of state, not least in Scotland. This was to arouse the anger of the entire nobility and most of the new merchant classes as well.

Civil War broke out in 1642. The Church found itself suddenly propelled by state edict from episcopacy into a Presbyterian form of government (Neill, 1977, p. 156). Many clergy simply drifted along with the new arrangements, hoping that better times lay ahead.

Bishop Matthew Wren of Ely was incarcerated in the Tower of London, but most bishops seem to have gone underground and did nothing to ensure their succession, which could have been disastrous were it not for the fact that the new regime unravelled rapidly after Head of State Oliver Cromwell's death in 1658. The surviving Laudian bishops were waiting in the wings for Charles II's return from the Continent and in only a couple of years the Act of Uniformity had guaranteed the return of episcopacy along with the Book of Common Prayer and its Ordinal.

The Cavalier Parliament imposed the Clarendon Code (against the wishes of Lord Chancellor Clarendon) which banned dissenting ministers from officiating within five miles of any town, thereby attempting to sever the links between the new sects and the artisan and merchant classes who had supported them during the Civil War. In Simon Schama's words (2001, p. 258) ... *a whole culture of teaching, preaching, praying and singing ... was made to go away.* Alongside this legal move against dissent came the expulsion of the not inconsiderable rag-bag of those Presbyterian and Independent clergy who could not bring themselves to conform, including not just eminent Puritan divines like Richard Sibbes and John Owen, but also the saintly Richard Baxter of Kidderminster, whom the king tried to tempt into remaining in the Church of England by offering him the bishopric of Hereford.

the bishops succumb to new political pressures

Despite the optimistic start to Charles's reign, problems soon arose, not just because the king had married a Portuguese Catholic, but also because his Declaration of Indulgence in 1672 seemed to be kinder to Roman Catholics than to Nonconformist Protestants. Lord Danby's incoming administration that year replaced the Declaration with the Test Act, which required all holders of public office to deny Catholic doctrine and conform in every way with the Anglican settlement. This was, of course, entirely at variance with Charles's own ecclesiastical sympathies, as well as his friendship with Louis XIV of France and his prosecution of the war with Protestant Holland. When James II decided to flaunt his Roman Catholicism in even more overtly dangerous ways, it was a step too far for the Anglican gentry and the Nonconformist business classes alike. The Prince of Orange was invited to cross the North Sea and take the place of the fugitive king.

Changes in the English constitution after William III's arrival in Torbay from Holland in 1688 saw the final burial of the Stuart obsession with the royal prerogative in both Church and state. With its increased ability to raise taxes with which to fight wars, there was not surprisingly a vast increase in the powers of Parliament. And with these powers came the rise of two political parties, the Whigs and the Tories, who would contest the right to use these powers. Gordon Rupp (1986, p. 73) notes the effects of these changes upon the bishops:

> Inevitably ... the leaders of the Church were sucked into all these pressures, since for almost a thousand years bishops had acted as counsellors of state. But now they were commanded to attend parliamentary sessions less and less widely spaced in time, and to devote many months each year to residence in London ... They were expected to give the services of vote and voice in favour of the political party to which they owed their elevation.

Thomas Wilson of Sodor and Man

The dominant impression of the Church of England in the early 18th century has long been considered that of a moribund institution lulled into a protracted, cosy sleep, awakened only by the coming of the Wesleys and Whitefield and their Evangelical Revival. The century did indeed begin with the Deists, who reduced Christianity to the mere worship of the God of nature, aloof in his heavenly realm and encouraging a vague moral goodness among his creatures, but this was brilliantly answered in 1736 by Bishop Joseph Butler's *Analogy of Religion, Natural and Revealed, to the Constitution and Cause of Nature*. In fact this period produced some other fine bishops like Gilbert Burnet of Salisbury, who for 26 years genuinely cared for his clergy and was a true father-in-God to his people.

The Church historian Moorman considers that perhaps the finest of all was Thomas Wilson, a Cheshire man and graduate of Trinity College Dublin, who was appointed under protest to Sodor and Man in 1697 by William III on the nomination of the Earl of Derby, Lord of Man. Sodor and Man was the poorest and most isolated of all the English sees. Though the endowment was but slender, Wilson refused to supplement it by accepting the offer of the living of Baddesworth in Yorkshire. Having set his face against pluralities of parishes and non-residence of incumbents, devices often used unscrupulously by other bishops and senior clergy to augment their incomes, he managed instead to give away nearly half his income in charity. Since the Crown did not take over the lordship of the island till 1765, Wilson was not bound by English Acts of Parliament and could rule his diocese strictly according to ecclesiastical law.

At the annual synod of his clergy held in 1704, he promulgated Ten Constitutions which dealt with the duties of the clergy, education and church discipline. He set about enforcing his discipline with the full rigours of public penance. He proceeded against his own housekeeper Catherine Crumbleholme for her fornication with a fellow manservant and sentenced her to fourteen days' imprisonment and a display of her misdemeanours listed on a placard round her neck at the four market crosses of the island. In 1721 he sentenced Mrs. Horne, the wife of the island Governor to do penance for slander, while the following year he suspended his own archdeacon for heresy. The Governor was forced to hear appeals from both parties and not surprisingly decided against the bishop, fining him and his two vicars-general £90 each, putting them into Castle Rushen prison when they refused to pay.

During the 57 years of his episcopate he hardly ever left the island, refusing the chance to desert his lonely outpost for the more lucrative and attractive see of Exeter. Instead he devoted himself to the care of his clergy, the preparation of his ordinands, the promotion of education and the teaching and nurture of his people. He learnt the Manx language, ran a college for students in his own house and taught there daily, translating Christian literature for the humbler folk and working as a physician among the sick.

His devotional book *Sacra Privata* was acclaimed throughout the land and Queen Caroline said as she saw him approach, *Here is a bishop who does not come for a translation,* while crowds in the streets of London thronged him for a blessing (Linnell, 1964, p. 5). He was buried in Kirk Michael churchyard in a coffin made from an elm tree he had himself planted. A tiny island out in the Irish Sea might indeed have been a manageable proposition for a noteworthy episcopate, but it must have been hard for Wilson never to succumb to the lures of fame, wealth and an altogether easier life on the mainland (Moorman 1973, pp. 280-281).

a sad picture of episcopal decline

By and large, however, the episcopal situation in the 18th century was far bleaker nationally, if at least understandable. With such great distances, dangerous roads, slow means of travel and treacherous English weather, with all the best will in the world, a bishop could hardly be expected to see much of his clergy, or even to know who they were. Moreover, the difference in class between the exalted prelate and the humble parochial minister was so great that they were bound to have little in common and would inevitably feel uneasy in each other's company.

Moorman (1973, p. 296) gives an account of how the death, or even the expected death, of a prelate sent a sheaf of letters to the Prime Minister from earnest clergy begging to be considered for preferment. Dr. Thomas Newton wrote to the Duke of Newcastle in 1761:

> . . . the Archbishop of York lies a dying, and, as all here think, cannot possibly live beyond tomorrow morning . . . Upon this occasion of two vacancies, I beg, I hope, I trust your Grace's kindness and goodness will be shown to one who has long solicited your favour.

Newton's appeal must have had the desired effect, for in the reshuffle after the Archbishop of York's death, he was appointed Bishop of Bristol!

Yet the eighteenth century was also a momentous one, setting in train many of the influences that fashioned the modern world, such as the rise of science and technology and the phenomenon of urbanisation. Moorman comments disparagingly of the Church of England (1973, pp. 296-97):

> The attitude of the Church ... to the vast changes which were taking place all over the world was largely one of indifference. The immense social changes which began with the coming of the Industrial Revolution, the political questions caused by the French Revolution and the international problems created by the expansion of the Empire all contributed to the making of a new age ... Convocation being virtually dead, there was no meeting place where policies could be thought out and action prepared. Most of the bishops were prevented, by temperament and by their position, from exercising any real leadership. For the most part they were trying to build up family fortunes by the most flagrant place-hunting and nepotism ... sensitive to their privilege and their prestige among the upper classes.

Into this somnolent atmosphere came the wake-up call of the Evangelical Revival, spearheaded by John and Charles Wesley and George Whitefield, all of them determined Church of England clergymen, but equally determined that their special ministry of converting the masses to Christ and spurring them on to holiness of life could be accomplished only by an itinerant ministry, in which the parochial and diocesan organisation of the Church was *not so much denied as disregarded* (Neill, 1977, p. 188).

It was the Bishop of London's refusal to ordain one of Wesley's preachers for his newly established churches in America that finally convinced Wesley he should himself set apart Richard Whatcoat and Thomas Vasey as presbyters and institute Anglican priest Thomas Coke as Superintendent Minister in Bristol in the autumn of 1784 for his growing work across the Atlantic (Davies, 1963, p. 128).

Despite the coming of the Evangelical Revival, little changed among the bench of bishops, even when it came to dealing with what might appear relatively straightforward social issues to the Christian conscience. Beilby Porteous, the Bishop of London may have preached against slavery to the Society for the Proclamation of the Gospel in 1783, yet incredibly, the very next year that same society decided to forbid Christian instruction to slaves! In 1804 William Wilberforce finally managed to get his bill to abolish slavery through the House of Commons at the second attempt, but sensing a danger to their valuable estates and tithes, the Lords adjourned the matter, with only two peers and one bishop speaking in its favour (Howse, 1971, p. 59).

When it came to calls for the Church to be true to its own supreme vocation as the guardian and proclaimer of the Gospel, the bishops behaved with no more than their customary indifference. Charles Grant and Henry Venn joined Wilberforce on an errand to see the Archbishop of Canterbury with a set of rules and a prospectus for the establishment of the Church Missionary Society, which they hoped would be able to tackle the urgent task of evangelism in the colonies of India and Africa. In spite of repeated approaches, it took the Primate of All England more than a year to make a formal reply and then it was merely to state that he *could not with propriety at once express his full concurrence and approbation (Howse, 1971, p. 77).*

Meanwhile in 1780 the Gloucester journalist Robert Raikes had opened his first Sunday School in Sooty Alley opposite the city jail for educating poor children through teaching them to read the Bible. In only seven years the total number of Sunday scholars in England had reached a quarter of a million. Bishop Samuel Horsley scathingly declared that there was *much ground for suspicion that sedition and atheism were the real objects of some of these institutions rather than religion (Howse, p. 96).* Matching this shameful response was the fact that in the years 1815 and 1816, the Bishops of Lincoln, Chester, Carlisle and Ely all singled out the newly established British and Foreign Bible Society for criticism in pastoral charges they delivered to their clergy .

Despite this constant sniping at any signs of *enthusiasm* among either priests or lay people, most influential Evangelicals, like John Newton of Olney, John Berridge of Everton and William Grimshaw of Haworth shut their ears to episcopal warnings and did their share of preaching outside their own parish boundaries. They steadfastly remained within the Church of England and put their greatest efforts into making a success of their own parishes and churches. There was sufficient critical mass in the quality of their pastoral work and the number of their parishes to enable some of the next generation to catch the notice of the Crown and reach the episcopal bench during the first half of the next century.

CHAPTER FIVE

English Episcopal Appointments in an Increasingly Comprehensive Victorian Church

Palmerston and the Evangelical ascendancy

During the 64 years of Victoria's long reign, the considerations taken into account in the making of episcopal appointments and the patterns of consultation before they were announced, become more formalised and easier to track, especially from the 1850's onwards.

The primacy of the old Latitudinarian position, which was still the hallmark of the bulk of Church of England clergy when George III came to the throne in 1760, had been somewhat weakened by time Victoria was crowned in 1837. It was an assortment of old fashioned High Church, Evangelical and Tractarian-leaning bishops who tried to block the Oxford Regius Professor of Divinity Renn Hampden's appointment to the see of Hereford in 1847 on account of his perceived doctrinal unorthodoxy on questions of Christology and the Trinity. Nigel Scotland (1995, p. 112) says that it was because Bishop John Bird Sumner

---

of Chester was one of the few on the bench who had not joined the signatories against Hampden, that Lord John Russell translated him to Canterbury to replace Archbishop William Howley in 1848. Sumner was considered a moderate *Claphamite* Evangelical of great pastoral zeal and considerable academic accomplishment, whose appointment delighted both Victoria and the Prince Consort. One of his first episcopal acts was generous to a fault. Even before the day of his enthronement, he went ahead with the consecration of Renn Hampden, despite being less than sympathetic to the professor's doctrinal leanings.

Prince Albert's own feelings about bishops were clear from a letter he wrote to his former chaplain, Samuel Wilberforce after he had been appointed Bishop of Oxford in 1845 (Carpenter, 1959, p. 260):

> *A Bishop ought to abstain completely from mixing himself up with the politics of the day and beyond giving a general support to the Queen's Government, and occasionally voting for it, should take no part in the discussion of State affairs (for instance, Corn Laws, Game Laws, Trade or Financial questions, etc.); but he should come forward whenever the interests of humanity are at stake, and give boldly and manfully his advice to the House and Country (I mean questions like Negro Emancipation, education of the people, improvement of the health of towns, measures for the recreation of the poor, against cruelty to animals, for regulating factory labour, etc).*

The Tory Prime Minister Lord Palmerston came to power in 1855. He came from the social background of the Anglo-Irish landlord class, which Ridley (1970, p. 500) found a very significant factor in the colour of his ecclesiastical appointments. As Palmerston possessed no religious enthusiasm, except for an innate anti-Papalism, and was somewhat irregular in his church attendance, it seems that he relied heavily upon the advice of his son-in-law, the doughty and respected Evangelical social reformer Lord Shaftesbury in making his ecclesiastical appointments.

Shaftesbury was consulted about all the five archbishops and twenty bishops whom Palmerston either appointed or translated in England, Wales and Ireland during his eight years as Premier. As John Pollock says, *Rather than dry dons, superannuated headmasters, or men with no claim but their lineage, Shaftesbury sought to make bishops of clergy who had worked hard in parishes, especially among the poor (1985, p. 116)*. This was exemplified by Palmerston's nomination of the unknown Montague Villiers to the see of Carlisle—a man who had been Vicar of St. George's Holborn and led a team of curates, Scripture readers and London City Missionaries in a ministry to the working class men of a parish which contained far more mean slums than it did leafy squares.

However, Palmerston was very conscious of the need to bring men of other churchmanships onto the bench and many of his choices were Broad church-men, whom he felt would help to mitigate religious conflict and promote a spirit of toleration. In 1860 the Queen wrote to Palmerston to express her concern that future appointments should include *university men of acknowledged standing and theological learning*, rather than merely what she called *respectable parish priests*, while her own Dean of Windsor, Gerard Wellesley argued for rotating the choice for bishoprics among the best men of each ecclesiastical party.

When a vacancy arose in London in 1856, Palmerston boldly disregarded the convention that a candidate should be promoted from a more junior see and instead chose Archibald Campbell Tait, the Dean of Carlisle. He was a Broad churchman, favoured by both Victoria and Albert and met the require-ment to be a good public speaker, who would be a valuable contributor in Lords' debates and also be a moderate spirit who could be relied upon not to take a narrow, dogmatic view, which might alienate popular opinion from the Church. Tait became Palmerston's sounding board to ensure that his appoint-ments were acceptable to groups other than the Evangelicals (Wolffe, 2005, pp. 923-926).

Jasper Ridley (1970, p. 500) records how in 1855 Palmerston explained the political purposes behind his episcopal appointments in a letter to Charles Wood, Secretary of State for India, a High Churchman who, like Gladstone and other High Church members of the cabinet, complained continually about the phenomenon of the *Shaftesbury Bishops*:

> *The population of England and Wales may be said to be divided into two thirds Church of England and one third Dissenters. The two thirds of churchmen are split into High and Low Church. The High Church are few in number and are found chiefly in the higher classes: the different degrees of Low Church, or at least of those who are against High Churchmen, are numerous among the higher classes, and one may say universal among the middle and lower classes of Churchmen. The dignitaries who are of the Low Church school are more forebearing towards their High Church brethren and are at peace with Dissenters. In this state of things it seemed to me that if one is to err on either side (and able and energetic men are not easily found among those who are neither one thing nor another) the safest course is to lean towards the Low Church, by which means a greater degree of religious harmony is obtained than by the other course.*

Despite this rather rough and ready analysis, Palmerston was too astute a politician to present anything other than a genuinely realistic picture of the lay scene. He was, after all, writing only just over twenty years after John Keble's famous 1833 Assize Sermon in Oxford, yet although Tractarian ideals had indeed sprouted rapidly among the university clergy, they had progressed a great deal less quickly in the ordinary parishes of the land.

Palmerston's analysis of the Evangelicals was no less accurate. They preached the same Gospel of personal salvation from sin through the propitiatory sacrifice of Jesus Christ as did most of their nonconformist compatriots, and shared many elements of their church life, especially the informal home prayer meeting.

Evangelical relationships were particularly strong with the Methodists, who, says L.F. Church (1949, p. 267), regularly administered the Lord's Supper *according to the form of the Established Church.* Most early Methodist chapel interiors were indeed little different from most parish churches newly constructed at that time, focusing upon a centrally placed or otherwise dominant pulpit and reading desk, with the holy table, communion rails and Ten Commandment boards insignificantly tucked away behind them at the east end.

Professor Nikolaus Pevsner's *Buildings of England* series show that there is little to choose internally between the liturgical arrangements in say, the parish church of St. John's, Chichester, built in 1815 (Sussex 1965, p. 170) and the parish church of Christ Church, Macclesfield, built in 1775 (Cheshire 1971, p. 268) or the roughly contemporary Wesley's Chapel in London, commenced in 1777 (London 4: North, 1998, pp. 606-607) and the Countess of Huntingdon's Chapel at Birdport, Worcester constructed in 1804 (Worcestershire 1968, p. 322).

the Tractarians make their mark

In finding Evangelical clergy more tolerant towards their Tractarian colleagues than *vice versa*, Palmerston again correctly gauged contemporary realities. In the later 1830s and 40s Anglo-Catholics were still considered a tiny and not particularly rebellious or noticeable oddity, based within the seclusion of the two ancient universities at Oxford and Cambridge and in a relatively small number of parishes that the more Tractarian Oxbridge colleges held within their patronage.

The earliest Tractarians were not liturgically adventurous. They were content to carry on using the Book of Common Prayer in time-honoured fashion. John Keble continued to take the north side position at the Holy Communion in his Hampshire village church at Hursley from the day of his induction in 1836 until his death thirty years later (Moorman, 1973, p. 351). Candles might have begun to appear on the holy table, but only in single pairs, while surplices and scarves were still standard wear for all clergy, High Churchmen included. Evangelicals did not yet perceive Tractarians as a serious threat and so relations remained civil, if not exactly cordial.

The art historian Kenneth Clark (1964, pp. 140-141) observes that after the foundation of the Cambridge Camden Society in 1839, the pious mediaeval artistic virtues of the Gothic Revival were praised relentlessly in the columns of its Tractarian-leaning magazine, *The Ecclesiologist,* leading to a burgeoning of new church building in the ancient Catholic style of arcaded naves and long chancels. The great new towns of the Industrial Revolution were growing apace from the 1850's to the 1880's and nearly all their new churches, even the most extreme Evangelical ones, like the Albert Memorial in the inner Manchester suburb of Collyhurst, were built under its all-conquering architectural influence. Despite their love affair with the Catholic Middle Ages, most Victorian Gothic architects were no less acceptable to Evangelicals than they were to the Tractarians, the style of their buildings being universally considered to be both picturesque and romantic.

Carpenter, (1959, p. 257) records that at about the same time as Gothic Revival church buildings came into fashion, the new Tractarian theological colleges in Chichester (1839) Wells (1840) and Cuddesdon (1854) started to pour out a steady stream of enthusiastic young ritualist clergy into the parishes, particularly into the poorer areas of Inner London and the teeming industrial cities and towns of the Midlands, Lancashire, Yorkshire and Tyneside.

Thus the people in the pews were now beginning to see and experience within their own parish churches and among their own clergymen the glossy fruits of High Church architecture and liturgical thinking. Despite their long national Protestant and Prayer Book tradition, many could not help liking what they encountered, and it was frequently their own energetic young curate or vicar who was responsible for making the changes and setting the pace that so perplexed them at first.

After a series of legal complaints and actions brought by extreme *no popery* Low Churchmen against younger, but hugely successful ultra-ritualist slum priests, like Robert Radclyffe Dolling of St. Agatha's Portsmouth, Charles Fuge Lowder of St. George's-in-the-East, Stepney and Alexander Heriot Machonochie of St. Alban's, Holborn, tender episcopal sensibilities like those of Bishop Harold Browne of Winchester found themselves severely assaulted. Low Church and even moderate bishops had their forebearance and tolerance tested to the very limits by the blatant exhibitionism, brinkmanship and sheer imagination of these pioneering spirits. Dolling's biographer, C.E. Osborne (1903, p. 116) rightly called his subject an *ecclesiastical Cecil Rhodes*. Not surprisingly the bishops were forced into the realisation that there had to be some adjustment within the Establishment to accommodate this oppressed, courageous, but increasingly well-respected body of clergy, who were willing to take on some of the most squalid and impoverished city parishes in the land and embrace their poor with a ministry of tireless love and care.

the Latitudinarians get a new lease of life

By the middle of the 19th century the steady trickle of new thinking in both theology and the study of the natural world had become a flood. Under the influence of German literary criticism, Benjamin Jowett, Professor of Greek at Oxford had boldly declared that scholars should interpret the Scriptures just like any other book and treat them in the same careful and impartial way that they might do in order to ascertain the meaning of the works of Sophocles or Plato (Cooper and Atterbury, 2001, p. 140). This trailblazing view was brilliantly developed by Jowett and six other academics in their controversial book *Essays and Reviews* of 1860.

At roughly the same time, ground breaking work by the geologist Charles Lyell on the fossil record in the cliffs of Dover, Lyme Regis and Whitby seemed to prove that the world could not have been created in just six days, while Charles Darwin's cruise on the *Beagle* and his twenty years' research on the evolution of species in natural selection suggested that creation might in fact be a continuous process. This prompted Adam Sidgwick, Professor of Geology at Cambridge to say that since sin appeared to be a mere organic misfortune, Darwin's thesis, if true, made religion nothing less than a lie (Cooper and Atterbury, 2001, p. 141).

When the dust had finally settled, Latitudinarian Churchmen discovered that the two sides of the argument could be comfortably reconciled by a broad shift in theological thinking, which allowed that science and religion could co-exist perfectly happily if the one were allowed total freedom within its own domain of the natural world, while the other were allowed to rule within the unseen world of the spirit. As Dean Stanley said at Lyell's funeral in Westminster Abbey (Cooper and Atterbury, 2001, p. 141):

> *The tranquil triumph of Geology, once thought so dangerous, now so quietly accepted by the Church, no less than by the world, is one more proof of the groundlessness of theological panics in the face of the advances of scientific discovery.*

Gone was the sedate and undemanding tolerance that had descended upon the Church in the years between the Restoration and the heady days of the Evangelical Revival towards the middle of the next century. By the 1870s there were three different and equally militant *parties* at work in the Church: the old Broad Church majority, increasingly willing to accommodate the new Biblical criticism and the principles of Darwinian science; the Evangelicals, now past their zenith and in slow numerical decline, especially among younger clergy; and the Anglo-Catholics, newly established and quirky, but growing rapidly in numbers, determination and influence.

Disraeli's personal dislikes and his appointments

Despite coming from a Jewish agnostic home and being educated in Unitarian establishments, Benjamin Disraeli was received into the Church of England at the age of twelve and worshipped regularly in his home parish church at Hughenden. Having left school at fifteen, he had nothing in common with the upper bourgeoisie, who were the most influential section of mid-Victorian society, especially within the Church. The moral and intellectual worries that obsessed so many of his contemporaries were of no interest to him and this invariably affected his policy towards episcopal appointments when he led the Conservatives to power in 1868. He detested Broad Churchmen because they tended to be Liberal in their politics and he was equally hostile to Anglo-Catholics because their extreme ritualism had alarmed public opinion. About these Tractarians he wrote sarcastically, *I don't know who is for them except some university dons, some youthful priests and some women: a great many perhaps of the latter. But they have not votes yet (Blake, 1966, p. 506).*

Although his first premiership lasted only nine months, he found himself involved in filling five episcopal vacancies. The last was Canterbury, where Archbishop Longley had died on the eve of the election. The Queen got in first by suggesting the name of Bishop Tait of London, a Broad Churchman and a notable supporter of the liberal *Essays and Reviews,* the very sort of candidate Disraeli would have gladly avoided. The Prime Minister responded with the name of Dr. Charles Ellicott, Bishop of Gloucester. Dean Wellesley of Windsor suggested to Victoria that she *could fairly begin by positively declining the Bishop of Gloucester. He is an amicable, insignificant man, talking constantly and irreverently.*

Disraeli was forced to look elsewhere, but there were difficulties of one sort or another with all his alternative names. In the end he had no choice but to give way and acqiesce in Tait's appointment. The Queen had managed to outmanoeuvre him.

Just after the start of Disraeli's second premiership in 1875, Dean Wellesley commented with some justification that *he regards the Church as a great State-engine of the Conservatives (Blake, 1966, p. 687).* Exactly this criticism was later levelled during Lord Salisbury's premiership and it resurfaced several times during the Conservative administrations of the first half of the 20th century.

One of Disraeli's more brilliant appointments must have been that of J.B. Lightfoot to Durham in 1879. This Hulsean Professor of Divinity left the senior common rooms of Cambridge for a large diocese of coal mines and steelworks, where he preached in every parish church, built new churches wherever needed, promoted mission work at home and abroad and encouraged every attempt at social amelioration. The dense crowds of miners who stood in silence as his funeral procession passed through Tudhoe and Spennymoor showed how deeply the episcopate of this shy scholar had affected the people of his diocese. A workman who was present in St. Hilda's Hartlepool when Lightfoot ordained seven deacons in 1884 later said of the occasion, *Man alive, I can hear him still with his "Take thou authority," in a voice that might have come out of a coal pit (Carpenter, 1933, pp. 288-89).*

Gladstone's attempts to achieve balance in episcopal appointments

It is in the setting of all these new considerations and challenges that Bishop George Bell (1935) opens up a revealing window into episcopal appointments in the early years of Gladstone's Premiership. The precipitating incident occurred when Bishop Jackson of London died early in January, 1885, leaving the next most prestigious diocese after Canterbury and York to be filled alongside another one at Lincoln. The principal actors in this drama amounted to five: Queen Victoria herself, Sir Henry Ponsonby (the Queen's Private Secretary),

the Prime Minister, Archbishop Edward Benson of Canterbury and Randall
Davidson, the Dean of Windsor.

On January 8th the Dean of Windsor suggests to Ponsonby three possible
candidates for the London vacancy—Bishops Lightfoot of Durham, Temple
of Exeter and Goodwin of Carlisle, adding by way of commentary that:

> I do not think that any man among the present bishops stands out as
> markedly suitable above all others... What is wanted is not merely a man
> of great power and ability, and liberality of view on church questions, but a
> man who adds to these qualities the weight and recognised position among
> English clergy which will enable him to hold his own.... He must also
> have marked business powers, for the Bishop of London is the principal
> manager of the enormous business of the Ecclesiastical Commission, in
> addition to all his other duties (pp. 168/9).

Reviewing the claims of Bishops Temple and Lightfoot, the Dean says of
the first that *his theological opinions have turned out to be quite safe after all,* and
then he goes on to draw attention to the qualities of the second:

> He combines with his scholarship and culture a wide liberality of thought
> and action in religious matters, of which I am sure the Queen must
> approve ... He would be quite invaluable as an adviser and helper for
> the Archbishop, and his speeches in the House of Lords and elsewhere
> would be of immense weight and would all be on the side of a wholesome
> and liberal theology, like that of Archbishop Tait. (p. 168)

On the 23rd January the Prime Minister submits to the Queen the names
of Temple of Exeter and failing him, Lightfoot of Durham, for the See of
London and a Mr. Bickersteth for the consequent vacancy at Exeter, enclos-
ing a memorandum to explain how he has decided upon these three and why

Professor King of Oxford is nominated for the vacancy at Lincoln created by the retirement of Bishop Wordsworth.

With regard to the order in which he has submitted the London recommendations, Gladstone demonstrates the importance he attaches to the intellectual strength of the Bench as a whole:

> *Inasmuch as the names of the Bishops of Durham and Exeter were those which had already suggested themselves to Your Majesty, Mr. Gladstone will only trouble Your Majesty by stating that that he has been prompted to submit first the name of Bishop Temple:*
>
> a. *by the great eminence of the See which Bishop Lightfoot already holds, and by the desire to avoid a double translation;*
> b. *by the likelihood that the offer, if made, might be declined;*
> c. *by a sense of the value of Bishop Lightfoot's studies to the Church, and by the high probability that acceptance of the See of London would put an end to them (p. 173).*

Turning to his attempts to secure some sort of balance in the *party* character of his suggestions to the Queen by nominating the Evangelical Mr. Bickersteth for Exeter, Gladstone observes that:

> *Your Majesty was undoubtedly most accurate in the appreciation of Bishop Boyd Carpenter (recently appointed to Ripon), as more nearly related to what is termed the Broad School than to that called Evangelical.... Searching among the clergy who bear the last named designation, Mr. Gladstone, after taking pains to inform himself, believes that the claim of Mr. Bickersteth, who has recently received a conspicuous mark of Your Majesty's favour (he had recently been appointed Dean of Gloucester), is upon the whole the best. (p. 173)*

This concern to preserve some sort of balance between the three *party* groupings into which the Church was now becoming divided is demonstrated again in that part of the memorandum dealing with Professor King's nomination for the Lincoln vacancy:

> *Dr. King would be reputed a divine of the High Church. At the time when he received his important professorship from Your Majesty, he had by a wise and loving spirit attracted confidence and attachment from many, bishops and others, within a wider circle than that of any special party. (p. 174)*

The Dean of Windsor similarly extols Dr. King's virtues in his letter to the Queen's Private Secretary on January 25th:

> *His own views are decidedly High Church, but he has never thrown himself actively into public controversies on these subjects, and he is so bright and cheery that he has done much to counteract the rather severe and gloomy views . . . which have characterised some of the other teachers who share his Church opinions . . . . He openly and emphatically avows decidedly High Church opinions, and must be distinctly classed as belonging to that school. But I imagine that Her Majesty will feel it to be necessary or desirable that there should be among the bishops some representative of a body so largely represented among the parochial clergy, and supposing Her Majesty to approve of the two other recommendations which have now been made, the High Church party would only have had one representative among the five bishops last appointed. (p. 175)*

The private opinions of Gladstone are known to have been sympathetic towards the Tractarian position and help to explain the rather harder test of acceptability within the wider Church set a moderate Low Churchman like Bickersteth, as against a much more definite Anglo-Catholic like King. Asked by Sir Henry Ponsonby to comment upon the Prime Minister's nominee for Exeter, the Dean of Windsor patronisingly compliments Bickersteth for his distinguished university career and for being *the author of much religious and other poetry of a high order, and a vigorous and earnest parish clergyman,* assuring the Queen's Private Secretary that:

> *He is a most liberal-minded Evangelical, of no party bias whatever, a man acceptable to all who know him as a refined Christian gentleman . . . . Narrow partisan Evangelicals regard him as too lax and wide in his sympathies to please them—and for that reason he is the better suited—as I believe Her Majesty will think—to be placed in a position of authority and influence. (p. 175)*

changes in the relative influence of the appointments players

As far as the mechanics of these appointments were concerned, it is quite clear that the Queen herself retained the final right to choose between the two names the Prime Minister submitted to her. She vetoed his first name a good many times. In 1906, five years after Victoria's death, Randall Davidson, himself now Archbishop of Canterbury, writes in a memorandum that, *She did not like to wait until a recommendation should arrive from the Prime Minister before forming opinions of her own about the vacant position and the sort of person who was to fill it.* (p. 164). In fact, her involvement came right at the outset of the process through the communications that passed backwards and forwards between herself, her Private Secretary and her Dean of Windsor. These two royal servants were both domiciled within the great castle upon its private mound and Victoria herself was in residence there as often as her business and circumstances required her to be close to her capital city.

The Archbishop of Canterbury was indeed part of the consultation process, but clearly in a less primary role than he had enjoyed in earlier centuries, thanks to the continuing involvement of the monarch and her entourage and the ever-increasing constitutional reach and significance of the Prime Minister. It was, after all, the Dean of Windsor who had apprised the Primate of the two runners for the London vacancy and in his reply of January 15th, 1885 Archbishop Benson elaborates at some length about the disadvantage of having to cope with Bishop Lightfoot's uncommunicativeness. He calls the choice between the two candidates *a nice balance,* but tips the scales a little towards Bishop Temple, adding significantly that, *It was a great pity that the question came to me in so narrow a form, and with such injunctions to secrecy.* (p. 170). This is clearly a hint at the fact that he would have appreciated a much greater role in considering possible candidates and assembling the shortlist, rather than being given not much more than a secret last-minute veto before the names of the finalists went to the Queen.

There was an interesting postscript to this incident in the Dean of Windsor's letter to Sir Henry Ponsonby two days before the Queen approved the appointments on January 27th. He says:

> *I rather wonder that Mr. Gladstone should have wished to send Mr. Bickersteth to Exeter and Canon King to Lincoln. The former is much more of a High Church diocese than the latter—notwithstanding the characteristics of their present bishops. (p. 176)*

This indicates that the needs of the diocese may indeed have been given some consideration in the selection process of a new bishop, but that, in these two cases at least, the official response was to give the diocese something quite different than its character might indicate—using an inverted argument in the attempt to prevent the development of churchmanship ghettoes, a technique which was to be deployed more frequently in the century ahead.

Lord Salisbury—trying to maintain the balance

Tory Robert Cecil first became Prime Minister in 1885 and in the course of his three administrations was responsible for the distribution of no less than 38 diocesan mitres. Like so many other Oxford men, he tended towards High Church, although not ultra-Tractarian views, but he had a lifelong fear of civil war in the Church, which he instinctively felt would irreparably harm the fabric of both nation and empire. Like Gladstone, he assessed that it was necessary to preserve a careful balance in episcopal appointments between the three main parties, and indeed, between the bishops and the deans of their cathedrals, bearing in mind that he considered the majority of the clergy supported the High Church faction and the majority of the laity the Low Church wing—a tussle in which he wryly observed that *the exasperation on both sides is equal (Roberts, 1999, p. 676).*

The delicate nature of negotiations between Victoria and her Tractarian Premier were revealed in 1888, when he wanted to appoint Canon Henry Liddon of Cuddesdon College to the see of Oxford. Although Liddon had not been a contributor to the formidable Catholic compendium of essays entitled *Lux Mundi,* Salisbury thought him *the most brilliant member of the clergy of the Established Church,* an ideal choice to preside over the diocese which he thought of as *the intellectual centre of the Church.*

The Queen's response to her Private Secretary Sir Henry Ponsonby was typically brusque. *The Bishop of Oxford he must never be. He might ruin and taint all the young men as Pusey and others did before him.* Randall Davidson, Victoria's longstanding domestic chaplain and Dean of Windsor agreed, but this opinion was not conveyed to Lord Salisbury, who instead acceded to the Queen's official refusal of Liddon on medical grounds. As it happened, Liddon was eventually offered the see of St. Albans in 1890 but refused it, dying only five months afterwards (Roberts, 1999, p. 678).

Lord Salisbury kept the biggest surprise up his sleeve for his final episcopal appointment in 1901, just after Edward VII had ascended the throne. In an impish, almost end-of-term mood, and with a more malleable monarch, he broke the habit of a lifetime and nominated Charles Gore, Canon of Westminster and Superior of the Community of the Resurrection at Mirfield for the diocese of Worcester. Gore had been editor of *Lux Mundi,* the great Catholic collection of essays on the theology of the Incarnation which had appeared in 1889. At that time there could not have been a more provocative appointment than Gore's, but much later in the 20th century, other Prime Ministers like Harold Macmillan and Margaret Thatcher were still perfectly capable of springing similar surprises.

CHAPTER SIX

***

The Changing Nature of
the English Episcopate
1905 to 2005

how to measure change

The *Crockford Clerical Directory* has always been reckoned the best single source of personal information about the English, Welsh and Scottish Anglican clergy. As it has done almost every year since 1858, it still provides fulsome information about their secular and theological education and itemises in exhaustive detail their appointments since ordination. From this rich mine of data it has been possible to extract nearly all the salient features of the three British mainland episcopal benches over the past century, examining them for any possible trends and then graphing them to see if these trends are actually confirmed by the statistics.

However useful they might be, *Crockford* directories list only a man's university education and qualifications and his subsequent ecclesiastical career. It was therefore also decided to consult retrospective editions of *Who was Who* to fill out other details of social significance such as family and marriage links, schools attended, hobbies and interests and club memberships.

Earlier editions of *Crockford* went into considerable detail about clergy academic careers, itemising not merely the subjects of first degrees, but also the class achieved. This bank of amplified material provided about bishops until the 1980s is therefore of great value in assessing their particular qualities and strengths. However, because more recent editions provide merely names of universities attended and titles of degrees earned, the comparative value of more recent information in assessing academic weight is unfortunately much reduced.

Taking a detailed snapshot of *Crockford* episcopal data every twenty years over the past century captures the flavour of the entire bench at six defined moments in time. To take statistical glances at only ten year intervals would have made the exercise unnecessarily detailed, cumbersome and diffuse, whereas to widen the gap to a whole quarter century would perhaps have skipped across the years too superficially and resulted in the omission of many episcopates of real significance, with inevitable damage to the value of the findings.

the situation at the start of the twentieth century

The Victorian age had just passed with the death of the Queen Empress one year into the new century and with Edward VII's accession, the slow march of political events unfolded that would culminate in the cataclysm of the Great War. 1905 also marked the start of a profound change in political thinking. It was only one year before Campbell-Bannerman's landslide Liberal victory in the General Election and only three years before Lloyd George was to bring his Pensions Bill before the Commons, a move which fired the starting pistol of a steady progress of social amelioration that forty years later would result in the Beveridge Report and the coming of the modern Welfare State (Hattersley, 2004, p. 152).

According to the *Official Yearbook* for 1905, at this time the Church of England had 31 diocesans and 29 suffragans in office to care for a a communicant roll of almost 2.2 million, a surprisingly meagre 7% of the population, all the worse if it is remembered that this figure also included no less than 152,000 resident in the four Welsh dioceses. However, it should also be noted that since Matins was at that time still the main Sunday morning service in a majority of parishes, communicant numbers cannot be considered anything like the bellwether of church attendance that they were to become in the wake of the new Parish Communion culture initiated by Ernie Southcott in Leeds and Alan Ecclestone in Sheffield during the 1950s (Welsby,1984, pp. 34-35). In terms of attendances at Matins, the actual strength of church membership in Edwardian times will have been very much higher. Andrew Marr (2009, p. 17) dismisses these worshippers somewhat cynically as people making *that little curtsey to the Church of England needed in a country whose spiritual life was dominated by frilly bishops, vicars and the Book of Common Prayer.*

In 1905 two Scotsmen were leading the Church of England, Randall Davidson at Canterbury and W.D. Maclagan at York. Both were special among the bench, Davidson having married a daughter of Archibald Campbell Tait, a previous Archbishop of Canterbury and Maclagan having served as a subaltern in the Indian Army as a young man, making him the only bishop at that time to have served in the armed forces of the Crown. The saintly Anglo Catholic Edward King was still at Lincoln, Boyd Carpenter, one of the leading exponents of Victorian broad churchmanship was still at Ripon and Charles Gore, one of the pioneers of a newer and more liberal Catholicism, had just arrived in the newly established see of Birmingham.

Not all 32 bishops divulged details about their education before university, but of the 26 who did, no less than twenty one (81%) had attended public schools, eleven (42%) of them the three most prestigious institutions of Eton, Harrow and Winchester. Only three (12%) had attended grammar schools and two had been educated at home, both of them notable Evangelicals, Handley Moule of Durham and F.J. Chavasse of Liverpool.

The entire bench had attended one or other of the two ancient universities, with Oxford in first place at twenty (63%). A surprising sixteen (50%) had spent more than ten years in parish ministry, while fourteen (44%) had taught in the universities, nine (25%) in the theological colleges and one in school.

No less than twenty of the bench (65%) reported themselves as members of the Athenaeum, a Pall Mall gentlemen's club populated, like its ancient Greek counterpart, predominantly by scholars and literati. Few gave any indication of their hobbies or pursuits, but G.W. Kennion of Bath and Wells indulged himself in hunting and fishing, Maclagan of York walked and rode, G.F. Browne of Bristol belonged to the Alpine Club and Moule of Durham was captivated by the telescope.

More significantly, ten of them (31%) had links with the titled aristocracy by birth or marriage and five (16%) were either related to bishops or had married into episcopal families. A similar pointer to the importance of social prestige was the fact that ten (31%) had served as Chaplains to either Queen Victoria or King Edward VII.

Only four (13%) had been suffragans, both A.W. Winnington-Ingram of London and Browne of Bristol at Stepney, Sir Edward Hoskyns of Southwell at Burnley and H.W. Yeatman-Biggs of Worcester at Southwark. Two others, Kennion of Bath and Wells and J.R. Harmer of Rochester had seen previous episcopal service overseas. By a curious quirk both had been Bishops of Adelaide! Earlier in their careers four (13%) had served as archdeacons and the same number as deans of cathedrals.

Only three (9%) of these diocesans had become bishops under 40 years of age, one being Winnington-Ingram, consecrated a suffragan at 39 and the two Australian bishops previously mentioned, consecrated at 37 and 38 respectively. Six (19%) had been appointed between the ages of 40 and 44, fourteen (44%) between 45 and 54 and nine (28%) at 55 and over. Four of these nine began their episcopal careers between the ages of 60 and 62, a surprising figure at a time when Butler and Butler (1994, p. 325) estimate that male life expectancy was only 46. Indeed Browne, appointed a suffragan to London at the already late age of 62, found himself translated to even greater responsibilities at Bristol only two years later.

in the middle of the roaring Twenties

By 1925 the Great War and the Treaty of Versailles were well past and Britain had begun its slide into the Great Depression, with the spectre of mass unemployment and widespread poverty (Schama, 2002, p. 463-470). Many of the old certainties had disappeared with the huge losses in the trenches of France and Belgium and the Government's abject failure to provide the country with a brighter future, despite the hugely optimistic promises made to the men who returned from the battlefields. The General Strike was only a year away and in just four years Ramsey Macdonald would head Britain's first Labour government.

Ecclesiastically it was only two years away from the first revision of the Book of Common Prayer since 1662, which was to be twice thrown out by the House of Commons after strenuous campaigning by both its protagonists and its opponents, in which some members of the episcopal bench played a very active and public part.

1925 saw Randall Davidson still at Canterbury, but Cosmo Gordon Lang in charge at York, leaving both the primatial sees still held by Scotsmen. Winnington-Ingram remained at London, but many new faces had appeared, including the wildly liberal E.W. Barnes at Birmingham, the controversial Hensley Henson at Durham and the highly regarded William Temple at Manchester. Seven new dioceses had been created since 1905, the largest by population being Chelmsford, aptly nicknaming itself *London over the border*.

Once again not all bishops divulged their pre-university education, but among the 32 that did, there had been an increase in the number from public schools to twenty eight (88%). Those from the three top schools had declined to eight (25%), but there was a wide representation from the lesser institutions, Marlborough and Charterhouse both producing three and Westminster, Christ's Hospital and Haileybury two each. As in 1905, there were only three (9%) from grammar schools and only one, Henson of Durham, claiming to have been educated at home.

Almost the entire bench of 38 had attended Oxford or Cambridge Universities, the only exception being C.L. Thornton-Duesbury of Sodor and Man, who hailed from Trinity College, Dublin. Oxford continued to maintain its dominance with twenty one (55%) of the total episcopate. Twenty (53%) had served more than ten years in parish ministry, Lang of York and Cyril Garbett of Southwark having been Vicars of the large, strategic parish of Portsea and F.T. Woods of Winchester and F.S.G. Warman of Chelmsford, Vicars of the populous, influential northern parish of Bradford. Twelve (32%) had taught in universities, six (16%) in theological colleges and three (8%) had been headmasters of public schools, two of them at Rugby. W.H. Frere of Truro was the first bishop since the Reformation to be appointed direct from leading a religious house, in his case the Community of the Resurrection at Mirfield.

Those posting up membership of the Athenaeum had dropped significantly to fourteen (37%), but there was one member of the Royal Yacht Squadron. There was a slightly wider representation of episcopal hobbies and interests than in 1905. Six played golf (15%), four were fishermen (13%) and there was a solitary gardener (A.A. David of Liverpool) and a lone cabinet maker (G. Nickson of Bristol).

Aristocratic links had slimmed down considerably to only eight (21%), although Robert Cecil of Exeter was a son of the Marquess of Salisbury and therefore a baron in his own right. Meanwhile Sir Edward Hoskyns was still at Southwell. Those born into episcopal families or married into them rose slightly to six (15%), among these being Archbishop Davidson and Temple of Manchester, while no less than six (15%) had served as honorary chaplains to King Edward VII or his son George V. Barnes of Birmingham had previously held the prestigious post of Master of the Temple, London's leading Inn of Court and the hub of the English legal profession.

There was a slight increase in the proportion of those who had already held senior church appointments. Eight (21%) had started their episcopate as suffragans, Stepney being used most frequently as a stepping stone, with Jarrow, Ipswich, Burnley, Hull and Lewes each making an appearance, indicating that the benefits of experience in both urban and rural situations were beginning to be recognised. Three bishops had been appointed from overseas, J.R. Harmer to Rochester from Adelaide, M.B. Furse to St. Albans from Pretoria and St.G. Donaldson to Salisbury from Brisbane and the Primacy of Queensland. Interestingly Donaldson's father had been the first Premier of New South Wales. In addition, eleven (29%) had held senior posts as archdeacons or cathedral deans.

A belated recognition of the increasing gap between the Church and the working classes is hinted at in the fact that there were now three bishops who had served as chaplains to the forces, one of them in the Boer War and the other two in the Great War. Equally significantly, Winnington-Ingram of London had served as Warden of Oxford House, Bethnal Green and Donaldson of Salisbury as Warden of Eton College Mission, Hackney Wick, both of them serious efforts on the part of the public schools and the ancient universities to offer help in notable areas of social deprivation within the industrial and dockside areas of London's East End and South Bank. Meanwhile Temple of Manchester was serving as President of the Workers' Educational Association, which pursued similar aims of communal amelioration, but upon a truly nationwide canvas.

In terms of age of appointment to the bench, there had been little change since 1905. Four (11%) were consecrated in their late thirties, including the two from Adelaide and Pretoria, while seven (18%) had been appointed between the ages of 40 and 44. Seventeen (47%) became bishops between 45 and 54 and nine (25%) at 55 and over. Three of this latter age group attained mitres only in their early sixties, including the noted Anglo Catholic liturgist W.H. Frere at Truro and the heavyweight all-rounder A.C. Headlam at Gloucester.

the situation at the end of the Second World War

By 1945 the nation was understandably exhausted after six years of conflict with Nazi Germany. Nevertheless social change was accelerating. The Butler Act of 1944 had introduced compulsory secondary school education for all, while that same year the Beveridge Report had heralded the establishment of the world's first free National Health Service. The cessation of hostilities in 1945 led to the setting up of the United Nations in the hope of promoting a more peaceful and secure future for all the nations of the world (Hattersley, 1997, pp. 14-15). Bishop G.K.A. Bell of Chichester had played no small part in this momentous initiative.

After the long period of armed struggle abroad and the bombing of major cities at home, the Church of England might well have suffered a greater loss of standing among the people had it not been for the wise and humble leadership of William Temple. Temple, the son of a previous Primate of All England and a former chaplain to another, had been Archbishop of Canterbury for just two years. Iremonger (1948, pp. 512-520) shows how he enjoyed a wide reputation within both Church and State throughout the war years, being both a respected theologian and a committed social reformer, but this huge, genial and loveable figure had just been struck down by a pulmonary embolism, leaving Canterbury vacant. Cyril Garbett of York was the first primate from a grammar school and yet another former incumbent of the showpiece Portsmouth parish of St. Mary Portsea. Significantly both Temple and Garbett had been translated from urban dioceses, the former from Manchester and the latter from Southwark.

Geoffrey Fisher was at London, A.T.P. Williams at Durham and Mervyn Haigh at Winchester. Fisher had been Headmaster of Repton School, Williams Dean of

Christ Church Oxford and Haigh a Chaplain to the Archbishop of Canterbury and Secretary of the 1920 Lambeth Conference. In terms of churchmanship, these five senior members of the bench shared a middle of the road standpoint, with perhaps most of them leaning towards the Catholic in ceremonial.

Of the 40 willing to divulge details of their education, a total of 32 (80%) had attended public schools, Eton and Winchester together contributing five (12%), Marlborough six (15%) and Bradfield three. Grammar schools were becoming more evident: they had educated eight (20%), including the formidable theologian K.E. Kirk of Oxford and the only serious scientist on the bench, the notoriously modernist E.W. Barnes of Birmingham.

Oxbridge continued to claim the vast majority of the 43 man bench (95%), with Oxford still the clear leader at 27 (63%). Only B.F. Simpson of Southwark was a provincial graduate (Durham), while W.W. Cash of Worcester, the only bishop not to have attended any university, had been a lay missionary in Egypt after leaving school and later Secretary of the Church Missionary Society and a considerable expert on Islam. Twenty (47%) had spent more than ten years in parish ministry, while sixteen (37%) had taught in university, nine (21%) in theological colleges and seven (16%) in schools.

Eleven (26%) of the total had previously served as suffragan bishops, mostly in the Canterbury Province, with Croydon appearing twice. Three had been consecrated for the colonies, J.W.C. Wand of Bath and Wells as Archbishop of Brisbane, Philip Loyd of St. Albans as Assistant Bishop of Bombay and N.B. Hudson of Newcastle as Bishop of Labuan and Sarawak. Eight others (19%) had previously served as archdeacons or cathedral deans.

Only some 12 of the bench (28%) now claimed membership of the Athenaeum, but two belonged to the Royal Commonwealth Society and a further two to the United Services Club. Only 13 bishops reported hobbies, golf and gardening claiming four each and tennis and walking two each. Contact sports were notably absent, but C.M. Chavasse of Rochester had competed in the 400 metres event at the 1908 Olympics. Interestingly, his twin brother Noel had the rare distinction of winning a double Victoria Cross while a doctor on the Western Front in the 1914/1918 War.

Of the 40 who gave their birth date, a major 24 (60%) had been appointed to the bench between the ages of 45 and 54, 9 (22%) when over 55, including two over 60 and five (13%) between 40 and 44. Only two had been consecrated under the age of 40, the socially well-connected P.M. Herbert of Norwich and Hudson of Newcastle, who had been a colonial bishop and then returned home to head the Society for the Propagation of the Gospel.

As if to emphasise the continuing importance of social connections, it is worth mentioning that 10 (23%) of the total had served as Chaplains to King George V or his son George VI. H.A. Skelton of Lincoln had been Chaplain to the Earl of Rosebery, Barnes of Birmingham had been Master of the Temple and Temple of Canterbury Rector of the fashionable London church of St. James, Piccadilly.

At the same time, as if to underscore their accessibility to the man in the street and the respect he might therefore accord them, a large 22 (51%) had served as chaplains or members of the armed forces during the Great War, no less than 10 winning the Distinguished Service Order or the Military Cross for gallantry. Many of the others had been either mentioned in despatches or awarded the French Croix de Guerre.

In a similar vein, two bishops, F.R. Barry of Southwell and Haigh of Winchester, had been Principals of the Knutsford Test School, which was opened in an old Cheshire prison after the Great War to give working class ex-servicemen with minimal academic qualifications or none the chance to study for ordination (Williamson, 1963, pp. 97-100).

half way through the Swinging Sixties

This was the decade that celebrated the final end of post war austerity and ushered in the economic prosperity that brought about the New Towns and the Beatles (Sandbrook, 2006, pp. 313-316), both of them symptomatic of a fundamental shift in society towards optimism, youth and novelty. Manufacturing industry was still in top gear, largely engaged in the long task of post-war reconstruction and trade with the developing Commonwealth countries. The foundations of the modern consumer society were being laid, with Conservative Prime Minister Harold Macmillan proudly announcing to the British people that they had *never had it so good*. It was also the decade when many former colonies followed Ghana's example of 1957 by declaring their independence from Britain.

Within the Church of England the slow march of canon law revision was absorbing the energies of the Church Assembly, but new theological thinking by Bishop John Robinson and Canon Douglas Rhymes on London's South Bank was gaining unprecedented publicity in the popular media at the same time as the Evangelical cause was experiencing an unexpected revival as a result of the boom in ordinands produced by Billy Graham's London crusades of the middle fifties.

Michael Ramsey occupied the seat of Augustine, bringing to the task his calm nerve and enormous theological brain, but only three years' experience in a parish. Donald Coggan was at York after a lifetime of distinguished teaching in the theological colleges, but his steady hand was also limited by parochial experience that amounted to just one three-year curacy.

Robert Stopford at London had been a teacher for most of his ministry, but proved to be an excellent diocesan administrator, while experienced parish priest Maurice Harland continued the break in what had by now become a longstanding tradition of academic theology at Durham, while S.F. Allison at Winchester possessed a happy combination of considerable parochial experience with theological college teaching. In churchmanship terms, Ramsey could be considered a moderate but orthodox Catholic, Coggan and Allison moderate Evangelicals and Stopford and Harland determined *middle of the road* men.

Of the 40 who provided detailed information about their education, 33 (82%) had attended a wide variety of public schools. Only two were alumni of Winchester or Eton, but Rugby featured with three and Westminster and Shrewsbury with two each. Seven (18%) had attended grammar schools, although four of these institutions might more properly be considered semi-independent.

The entire bench of 43 were university graduates. Oxbridge still claimed a vast 39 (91%), with Cambridge having the larger proportion at 22. Trinity College Dublin featured twice, with Manchester University and University College London scoring one each. A large 26 (60%) had more than ten years' parish experience, while sixteen (37%) had taught in theological colleges, eight (19%) in universities and three (7%) in schools.

Seventeen (40%) of the bench had been suffragan bishops, only four of them in the Northern province, with Willesden and Croydon each appearing twice. G.F. Allen of Derby had been previously Bishop in Egypt and J.L. Wilson of Birmingham Bishop of Singapore, although he spent most of World War II as a prisoner in the notorious Changi camp. Of those who had been appointed to the bench without a term as a suffragan bishop, twelve (28%) had been cathedral deans or provosts or archdeacons.

Only one bishop, Cyril Eastaugh of Peterborough now had aristocratic links, but 5 (12%) had been Chaplains to King George VI or Queen Elizabeth. L.M. Charles-Edwards of Worcester had been Vicar of London's fashionable St. Martin's-in-the-Fields, the parish church of Buckingham Palace.

The need for the Church to appeal to the intellectual world was hinted at by the fact that two bishops, Joe Fison of Salisbury and Mervyn Stockwood of Southwark, had come straight from the incumbency of Great St. Mary's, the University Church at Cambridge. Scott Fleming of Norwich had been Director of the Scott Polar Institute at Cambridge and W.D.L. Greer of Manchester on the staff of the Student Christian Mission. The growing significance of the ecumenical perspective is indicated by David Say of Rochester having been the Director of the British Council of Churches.

No bishop had been consecrated while under 40 and only 10 (23%) from within the 40 to 44 age bracket. Men appointed over the age of 55 had declined to only two (5%), whereas an even greater 31 (72%) had now been raised to the episcopate between the ages of 45 and 54.

Six bishops (14%) admitted to being members of the Athenaeum, but the spread of other club memberships was wide, ranging from the Automobile Association, through the various service and university clubs to the Alpine and the Middlesex Cricket Clubs. Interests and hobbies were widely represented, with walking the most popular at eight (18%), golf at seven (16%) and gardening at six (14%). Once again contact sports were barely mentioned, football and rugby scoring only once each, but television, the popular new indoor entertainment medium, managed to creep in at just two (5%).

the situation in the middle eighties

1985 came half way through a decade marked by an acceleration in the development of modern information technology, with a matching decline in the heavy manufacturing industries and the numbers of manual workers they employed. Margaret Thatcher had only just achieved her landslide Conservative victory at the polls, but comprehensive secondary education, introduced by Labour's Harold Wilson after the 1964 General Election, had long since become almost universal throughout Britain (Marr, 2007, pp. 245-251). Many new universities like Brunel and Liverpool John Moores had been created out of the old colleges of advanced technology as the government sought to improve the status of vocational degree level qualifications such as those in the fields of engineering and nursing.

Within the Church of England, Synodical Government had been in operation for fifteen years and on paper at least, there was now a well established system of consultation between bishops, clergy and laity, which was being put to the test in what became, at times, acrimonious discussions about whether women should be ordained to the priesthood and what should be the contents of the *Alternative Services Book*.

Both archbishops were English, Robert Runcie of Canterbury being a product, like so many of his predecessors, of the *Literae Humaniores* school at Oxford but John Habgood of York being a Natural Sciences graduate from Cambridge, who had gone on somewhat unusually to become a University Demonstrator in Pharmacology. Both shared a liberal Catholic stance, one having done his ministerial training at Westcott House, the other at Cuddesdon. Archbishop Runcie had also won a Military Cross in World War II while serving in the Scots Guards. Among the other senior bishops, a stalwart traditional Catholic, Graham Leonard, held London, while Colin James was at Winchester and David Jenkins at Durham, both of them ostensibly liberal Catholics, but the latter of a decidedly more provocative, avant-garde viewpoint.

Of the 38 who divulged information about their schooling, a still dominant 25 (66%) had attended public schools, Eton claiming four, Rugby three and Sherborne and Aldenham two each. A now significant twelve (32%) had attended grammar schools, although among this total were some institutions that were not entirely state funded and might strictly be counted as semi-independent. Only one bishop, R.K. Williamson of Bradford, had gone to a state comprehensive (in Belfast), and worked before ordination as a lowly layman in the London City Mission.

Oxbridge still dominated the bench with 33 (77%), split roughly 50:50, but there were now eight (19%) from other universities, three from London, two from Leeds and one each from Manchester, Nottingham and Trinity College Dublin, Williamson of Bradford being the only non-graduate. Seventeen (40%) had taught in theological colleges, fifteen (35%) in universities and two in schools.

Eleven (26%) had served as members of the armed forces or as chaplains, mostly during World War II and alongside Robert Runcie, Simon Phipps of Lincoln held the Military Cross. David Sheppard of Liverpool had spent a good proportion of his ministry as Warden of the Mayflower Family Settlement in London's East End, matched by Michael Whinney of Southwell's spell leading the Cambridge University Mission in Bermondsey. Only two had served as Chaplains to the Queen.

A considerable 17 (40%) reported having club memberships, but these were varied, five belonging to the Royal Commonwealth Society, four to the United Oxford and Cambridge University and four to an assortment of Service clubs. Only one now identified himself with the Athenaeum. A not insignificant 28 (65%) of the episcopate mentioned hobbies or pastimes, with walking proving to be one of the most popular at 13 (46%), two specifically mentioning hill walking. Music was entered by 14 (50%), with none of them willing to identify their particular tastes. Reading not surprisingly featured with seven (28%), travel and gardening came next with six each (21%) and theatre with four (14%). Significantly, sports never appeared more than once each for tennis, cricket and sailing—yet again, no mention of contact sports!

A large proportion, 31 (72%) were appointed to the bench between the ages of 45 and 54, with only five (12%) aged between 41 and 44 and five (12%) aged over 55. Of the two appointed at the age of 40 or under, Timothy Bavin of Portsmouth started his episcopal career as Bishop of Johannesburg while David Sheppard of Liverpool already possessed a high public profile as a former England cricket captain before becoming Mervyn Stockwood's suffragan at Woolwich.

A considerable twenty (47%) had previously served as suffragans, all but three of them in the Canterbury province, with Willesden, Bedford, Kingston and Tonbridge being represented twice each. Of the others, nine (21%) had been deans or archdeacons.

Only two bishops (5%), J.R.G. Eastaugh of Hereford and Simon Phipps of Lincoln, had aristocratic links, in both cases by marriage, but a handful had occupied posts of significance before their appointment to the bench. Of a surprising 13 (30%) who jumped straight to a diocesan bishopric without serving as suffragans, deans or archdeacons, David Jenkins of Durham and John Habgood of York had followed distinguished academic or theological college careers respectively, while Michael Baughen of Chester had established a considerable reputation for modern hymnody while Rector of London's fashionable Evangelical centre, All Souls, Langham Place. David Say of Rochester had spent eight years as curate of London's equally fashionable St. Martin's-in-the-Fields before becoming private chaplain to a notable Tory grandee, the Marquess of Salisbury. Austin Baker of Salisbury had been Rector of St. Margaret's Westminster and Speaker's Chaplain to the House of Commons, while Barrington-Ward of Coventry had headed the Church Missionary Society and Patrick Rodger of Oxford had occupied a senior post at the World Council of Churches.

the situation at the start of a new millennium

2005 marked not just the start of a new century and millennium, but also an era when profound changes seemed to be taking place in philosophical thought. Post modernism's increasing doubts about the inevitability of human progress were given an unexpected boost, not only by the terrorist destruction of the World Trade Centre and the bombings on the London Underground, but also by growing unease about the finite nature of fossil fuels, climatic change, and even the very future of the planet itself.

Within the Church of England the Decade of Evangelism had come and gone, as had two landmark reports analysing the Church's failures in the inner cities and the countryside, but despite these campaigns, communicant membership had fallen to below a million for the first time. Some encouraging shoots of growth had started to appear with the Alpha, Emmaus and Christianity Explored enquirers' courses, while various initiatives in local lay ministry and serious attempts on the part of the Church Army and others to employ *fresh expressions* of church were beginning to open up genuine engagement with the unchurched masses.

Archbishop Rowan Williams of Canterbury had just arrived from the primacy of the Welsh Church and John Sentamu was soon to fill the vacancy at York, the first a renowned heavyweight theologian of liberal Catholic stance without any parochial experience at all and the second a former South London Evangelical parish priest of considerable repute, who arrived in Britain as a refugee from Idi Amin's Uganda, where he had been a high court judge. Just as a century before, both archbishops were now from outside England, but these men were not home-grown products of the Church of England, but of other self-governing provinces of the growing Anglican Communion.

Richard Chartres, a rather more traditional Catholic with a good track record as a Westminster parish priest held the see of London, while Tom Wright, a moderate Evangelical theologian with no previous parochial experience was at Durham and Michael Scott-Joynt, another liberal Catholic and ministerial all-rounder, was at Winchester.

Oddly, in an era of increasing openness, only 29 of the 41 (67%) were willing to divulge their schooling and of these a considerable 18 (62%) had still attended minor public schools, with Eton, Harrow and Winchester no longer featuring at all. Eight (28%) had attended grammar schools, but only a tiny three (10%) comprehensive schools. Richard Harries of Oxford stood alone in having trained as an Army officer at Sandhurst.

The combined Oxbridge graduate total had now dropped to 22 (54%), plus another from Edinburgh, one of the four ancient Scottish universities. This group therefore still comprised 56% of the bench, with Cambridge alone contributing 13. The total from Victorian redbrick universities came to 12, plus one more from a modern university, which meant that this group now made up 32% of the bench, Leeds alone contributing three, all of them theology graduates. A not inconsiderable eleven (27%) had earned their doctorates rather than receiving them *honoris causa*. By contrast there were still only four non-graduates (10%) on the bench, one of whom, Hill of Bristol, had attended

Fig. 2

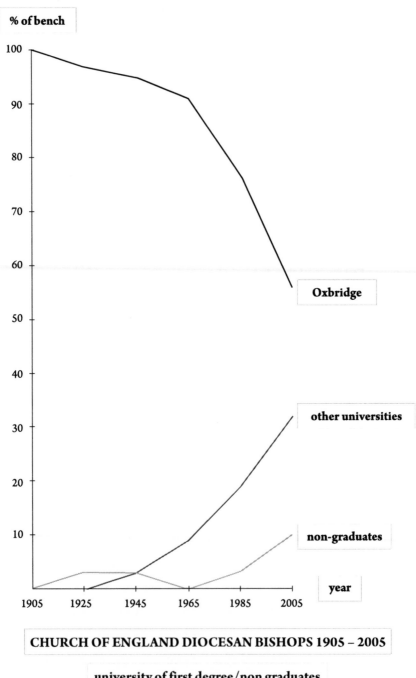

CHURCH OF ENGLAND DIOCESAN BISHOPS 1905 – 2005

university of first degree/non graduates

the pre-theological course at Brasted Place to qualify for theological college entry. Fig. 2 shows the changes in bishops' universities of first degree over the whole century.

Fifteen (37%) had worked in parishes for more than ten years, while 24 (58%) had taught in theological colleges, four (10%) in universities and just one in school. Fifteen (35%) had been diocesan or national bureaucrats. Only one, Anthony Russell of Ely, had previously been a Chaplain to the Queen.

In terms of theological training, the liberal Catholic colleges contributed 16 (40%), with Ripon/Cuddesdon the clear leader at 13. The open Evangelical colleges had eleven (27%) with Ridley Hall alone taking five. The more conservative Catholic institutions contributed five (13%), all but one from Mirfield, while the more conservative Evangelical colleges provided four (10%), half of them from Oak Hill. Only four (10%) came from institutions like Queen's College, Birmingham, that could still be reasonably considered *central* in churchmanship.

Theological colleges, however, do not necessarily prove to be good predictors of future churchmanship. Price of Bath and Wells might have gone to Oak Hill, but he spent five years heading the Catholic USPG, while the outspokenly liberal Tom Butler of Southwark might now feel himself quite out of place at Mirfield. Neither are the theological colleges themselves necessarily fixed in their churchmanship. While St. Stephen's House, Oxford and Oak Hill may have remained resolutely constant throughout their history, others, like St. John's College, Nottingham have lost their previously distinctive ethos and become more *central* in their outlook as a result of relocations and amalgamations. Trinity College, Bristol, Ridley Hall and Wycliffe Hall have functioned around a broadly Evangelical emphasis over the past half century, but veered in a more or less conservative direction according to who the current principal happened to be.

Fig. 3

CHURCH OF ENGLAND DIOCESAN BISHOPS 1905 – 2005

percentage with previous experience as suffragan bishop

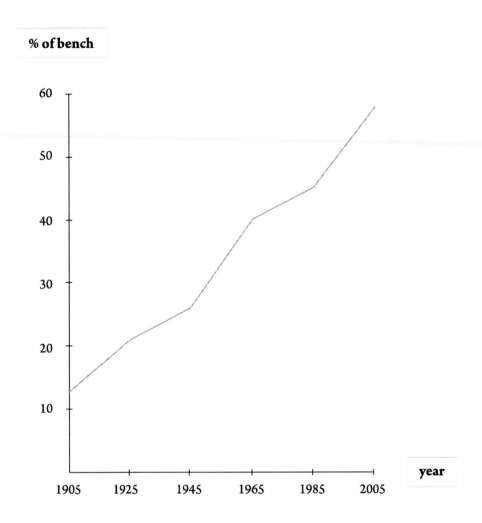

In 2005 a considerable 25 out of the 43 diocesans (58%) had previously served as suffragan bishops, but of those who had not, another nine (21%) had been cathedral deans or provosts, indicating that just under 80% had already held senior office within the Church. None had been elevated directly from a parish. The only other upward routes continued to be through academia or theological college teaching, as was the case with Williams of Canterbury and the just retired Hope of York respectively. Fig.3 summarises the percentage of new diocesans with previous service as suffragans over the whole century.

Club memberships were now mentioned by only six (14%), although three still belonged to the Athenaeum. One was a member of the Royal Commonwealth Society, one of the Royal Overseas League and another of the Royal Yacht Squadron. On the other hand no less than 33 (77%) were willing to admit having hobbies, which turned out to be surprisingly varied. For the first time music came top with 15 devotees (45%), while reading and walking were relegated to second place with twelve each (36%). Although Sentamu of York was interested in rugby, football and athletics, amazingly there were still no other mentions of contact sports. Jonathan Gledhill of Lichfield liked to sail and ski, while R. Lewis of St. Edmundsbury boasted an unusual combination of bricklaying, bees and kit cars.

A large majority (71%) had been appointed bishop in the 45 to 54 age bracket, with 17% at the age of 55 and over, 10% between the ages of 40 and 44 and only one (2%) while still under 40. This youthful exception was Michael Nazir Ali of Rochester, an acknowledged expert on Islam, who had originally been consecrated at the early age of 35 to an assistant bishopric in his homeland of Pakistan and had come to England to head the Church Mission Society. Significantly there was no longer a single bishop who had been appointed over the age of 60. Fig. 4 summarises the age breakdown of bishops on their appointment over the entire century.

Fig. 4

CHURCH OF ENGLAND DIOCESAN BISHOPS 1905 – 2005

age at first elevation to the episcopate

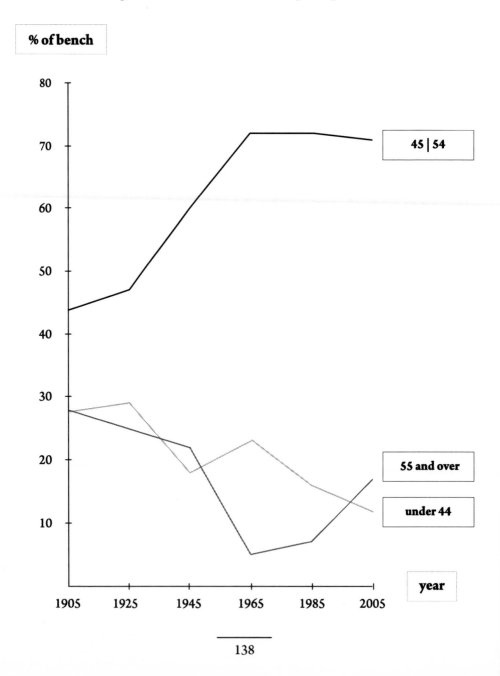

CHAPTER SEVEN

The Church in Wales: Disestablished in Name Rather than Reality?

how Disestablishment came about

Welsh Nonconformists had always been jealous of the position of members of the Church of England on their side of Offa's Dyke, who seemed to enjoy nearly all the material, historical and social benefits of being the Established Church, while ministering to what they considered to be a considerably smaller proportion of the population than did the chapels. J. Davies (1993, 45-47) observes that 80% of attendances recorded in the 1851 religious census were at the chapels, with only 20% at the parish churches. With the Nonconformists often having more than one service per Sunday, these percentages need to be treated with considerable caution, but they do indicate that there were reasonable grounds for complaint, especially after the boom in chapel attendances as a result of the 1859 and 1904 Welsh revivals. But in truth the Church of England had hardly served Welsh Anglicans any better than it had the English.

Philip Jenkins (1992, p. 107) found that under the Tudors and Stuarts Welsh bishops were native Welshmen and usually Welsh speakers too. The Bible and Prayer Book had indeed been early translated into Welsh (Ross, 2008, p. 143), but one of the great complaints of the Welsh Church from the Restoration onwards had been the remoteness of their episcopal oversight and the fact that their bishops were most likely to be Englishmen—and often monoglot Englishmen at that. Rupert Davies (1963, p. 29) mentions how the notorious George Hoadly was Bishop of Bangor for six years and during that time never managed to enter his diocese once, neither did he appear to have ordained anyone!

E.D. Evans (1993, pp. 27-28) points out that *the Welsh bench suffered through frequent translations of bishops to English sees, since Welsh ones were regarded merely as stepping stones to preferment.* Many indeed held a Welsh bishopric alongside a more influential and absorbing English office. Ordinands seeking laying on of hands from John Tyler of Llandaff were forced to seek him out in Hereford, where he happened also to be Dean. Many of the problems may be explained by the uneven incomes of the Welsh sees: in the early 19th century the Bishop of St. Asaph commanded the princely amount of well over £6,000 per year, but the two southern dioceses carried much tinier rewards, Llandaff offering a mere sixth of the richest. The holders of St. Davids and Llandaff therefore invariably held an English deanery to augment their incomes (Evans, 1989, p. 83).

With their having seats allotted to them in the House of Lords, the Bishops of Bangor, St. Asaph, St. Davids and Llandaff, like their English counterparts from sees away from the capital city, maintained courtly London establishments, the social whirl of which, according to Davies (1963, p. 28), invariably kept them out of their dioceses for perhaps as much as two thirds of the year. Eifion Evans (1985, p. 30) records how Daniel Rowland, a contemporary and colleague of the famous Welsh hymnwriter and poet William Williams, Pantycelyn, had to struggle on foot in the company of drovers all the way from West Wales to Duke Street Chapel in the fashionable London suburb of St. James's in order to be ordained to the humble country curacy of Llangeitho and Nantcwnlle by Bishop Nicholas Clagett of St. Davids.

Under pressure from the Welsh Church, anxious to avoid making itself a hostage to fortune, and no doubt influenced by Gladstone, who became a Member of Parliament in 1832 and lived just inside the Principality at Hawarden in Flintshire, Downing Street began to take more care over Welsh appointments towards the middle of the 19th century. Jenkins (1992, p. 292) points out that some of these Victorian bishops, like Connop Thirlwall of St. Davids (1840-75), Vowler Short of St. Asaph (1846-70) and Alfred Ollivant of Llandaff (1849-82), were leaders of great merit, who were responsible for huge school, church and parsonage building programmes within their dioceses and a big rise in communicant numbers. It is worth noting that, according to Roger Brown (2006, p. 2), bishops appointed to the four dioceses from 1840 onwards were once again able to speak the Welsh language to a greater or lesser degree.

Jenkins observes (1992, p. 292) that:

> *Unlike so many of their predecessors, they were usually resident and they took care to make or encourage appropriate appointments to livings. They were increasingly unwilling to tolerate the old compromise whereby a squire appointed an English incumbent, who then employed a Welsh-speaking curate to serve the parish. The new bishops travelled to every one of their dispersed parishes—a mobility made possible by the railways . . .*

However, Nonconformist pressure against the Church remained unrelenting. The first motion to disestablish the Church of England within the four Welsh dioceses was brought before the House of Commons in 1870 by the lawyer Watkin Williams, the text of the bill making clear his intention that the ancient endowments of the Church should be removed and applied instead to supporting a national and interdenominational system of education right across the Principality (Edwards, 1912, pp. 252-53). It failed.

The second attempt to disestablish the Church of England within Wales was made in 1895 by no lesser a personage than the Home Secretary, H.H. Asquith himself. He described it unflatteringly as an *alien* institution (Edwards, 1912, p. 255). Among the provisions in his bill was the removal of the four ancient cathedrals from the Church and their vesting in a body of commissioners. This cost the bill Gladstone's support and ensured its failure.

In 1909 Asquith, by now himself Prime Minister, was the mover of yet another Disestablishment bill, which this time limited the confiscation of endowments to simply the tithes and that part of the Church's assets acquired since 1662. It passed the Commons, but failed through the opposition of the natural Tory majority in the Lords. D.T.W. Price (1990, pp. 3-4) draws attention to a protest rally of some 15,000 Welsh churchpeople in Hyde Park, followed by a big meeting in the Albert Hall in 1912, but despite this impressive show of strength, the next bill passed the Commons with ease a couple of years later, the Parliament Act of 1911 having by then curtailed the Lords' powers of obstruction. The Welsh Nonconformists may at last have got what they wanted onto the statute book, but with the outbreak of the First World War, the attention of Lloyd George's Liberal government was rapidly diverted elsewhere to far more pressing affairs.

Disestablishment was eventually implemented in 1920 in the peace that followed the Armistice. The tithes and endowments were to be dispersed among the counties and county boroughs of Wales as the Welsh Church Funds, which provided that income earned from capital should be distributed in grants for charitable purposes, almost invariably to aid community and educational causes. However, Price (1990, p. 5) notes that only in 1942 and 1947 were three and a half million pounds finally transferred to the Government by the Church, just under one million alone being earmarked for the University of Wales.

During the locust years of mass unemployment and widespread poverty, which descended upon Wales in the 20s and 30s and might be expected to have preoccupied the Church's attentions (Evans, 2000, p. 43), the Anglicans of Wales were instead busy responding to the financial, legal and constitutional challenges of Disestablishment. In order that the new province should be placed upon sound financial footings, an immediate Million Pound appeal was launched and despite seriously adverse economic conditions, by 1923 £676,000 had already been collected. Not surprisingly Davies observes (1993, p. 539) that:

> In 1924 when the first handbook of the Church in Wales was published, Archbishop Edwards was able to take pride in the progress of his Church, and he was prepared to admit that the experience of disestablishment had not been as bad as he feared ... By the second quarter of the 20th century, Anglicanism, measured by the numbers attending Easter Communion, was stronger in Wales than in England.

One of the main reasons for the archbishop's upbeat assessment is suggested by C. Harris and R. Startup (1999, p. 6) in their sociological study of the Welsh Church:

> In spite of Disestablishment, the Anglicans held to the principle that they had a responsibility to parishioners in their entirety. Indeed, as they retained possession of the parish churches and cathedrals, they continued to look like the Establishment—and to a considerable extent to be treated like one.

This is borne out by the fact that in areas like prison, hospital and armed forces chaplaincies, as well as in municipal events and celebrations, it was the Anglican clergy who still performed the main roles and enjoyed the principal positions of public honour and recognition within the Principality. They also continued to be the largest group of routine officiants at municipal cemeteries and crematoria and remained the registrars of all weddings held within a parish church, precisely as they were in England.

creating new dioceses

Disestablishment was seen as a golden opportunity to make episcopacy more acceptable and accessible within what had become a highly critical Welsh culture. The most obvious first step was to divide Llandaff and St. Davids and create the two new dioceses of Monmouth (1921) and Swansea and Brecon (1923) to serve the populous industrial areas of the South Wales mining valleys. The former was given for its cathedral the fine Norman church of St. Woolos in Newport, the biggest town of the see. The choice of cathedral for the other new diocese was not quite so felicitous. The major seaport town of Swansea possessed no great mediaeval pile and therefore the choice fell upon the 13th century priory church at Brecon, suitably grand for the great diocesan occasion, but handy neither for Swansea, nor for the mining towns and villages strung closely together up the Tawe valley. The fact that the Westminster politicians had excluded the Welsh diocesans from having seats in the House of Lords might have been an act of vindictiveness, and might indeed have irked the occupants of those sees back in 1920, but there is little doubt that Welsh Churchmen quickly came to see how, without the constant legislative calls of Parliament to distract their energies, Welsh bishops could, at least in theory, be more likely to give their undivided attention to the pastoral needs of their own clergy and laypeople.

The four ancient Welsh sees were enormous in area, reflecting the four ancient princedoms of Gwnedd, Powys, Gwent and Dyfed, but prior to Disestablishment, they had only their one diocesan bishop each to do the work. The Tudor expedient of creating suffragan sees in large rural dioceses remote from London, as had happened, for example, between 1537 and 1539 at Penrith (for Carlisle), Hull (for York), Nottingham (for Lincoln) and Berwick (for Durham) and far more extensively in Victorian and Edwardian times for the industrial urban dioceses of England, had only once been tried in Wales at Swansea (for St. Davids). It has been tried only once since Disestablishment, creating the short-lived suffragan see of Maenan for St. Asaph in 1928 (Price, 1990, p. 60).

Price considers that the Church was left too poor to contemplate such comparative luxuries, although the Cardiff Convention of 1917 did permit diocesan bishops to choose an assistant bishop if they wished to do so, provided that the appointment was subsequently confirmed by the rest of the bench. The bishop who bears the additional responsibilities of governing the Province has on occasion had the services of an episcopal assistant and it may be that if Llandaff becomes the permanent archiepiscopal see, the diocese may have the permanent services of a suffragan with enhanced powers. Since 1993, there has also been a permanent provincial assistant to care for the small minority of clergy and people who have not been able to acquiesce in the ordination of women to the priesthood, although interestingly, Wales happened to be the first UK province to vote in favour of admitting women to the diaconate. However, there has been no replacement for Bishop David Thomas since his retirement in 2008 and the bench have made it clear to *Credo Cymru* that their decision not to provide a new assistant bishop must be considered their final word.

the Welsh electoral college

The Constitution of the Church in Wales (2010, Part III, 10) lays down the precise composition of the electoral college set up to fill diocesan vacancies. N. Doe (2002, pp. 130-31) explains the detail of this complex and cumbersome system. The basic building blocks are the six diocesan conferences. The clerics and laity of each newly elected diocesan conference choose six of each of their houses to membership of the college, and at the same time appoint a supplemental list of nine of each category to fill casual vacancies. They serve in order of their position on the list, the age limit being set at 70.

Internally the electoral college for the province is composed of three classes: the archbishop and bishops; six clergy and six lay people from the vacant diocese; and three clergy and three lay people from each of the other five dioceses. The archbishop or the bishop next in precedence takes the chair.

The Constitution (V, part III, 16.1-26.2) lays down that the college must meet in private after a Communion service in the cathedral of the vacant see, which is then locked. The college is empowered to lay down detailed regulations for its own procedure, but voting must be by ballot and the whole body must vote together, rather than in separate houses of bishops, clergy and laity. A decision must be reached within three consecutive days. The nomination must then be approved separately by a majority of the bench of bishops. If, within the time scale allowed, no candidate obtains a two thirds majority of the votes cast in the college, the right of appointment passes automatically to the episcopal bench, acting alone. This is widely rumoured to have happened most recently in 2004, when a stalemate between the two main candidates for the Bangor vacancy led the house of bishops to appoint Anthony Crockett, Archdeacon of Carmarthen, and the unsuccessful finalist in the previous year's episcopal election at St. Davids. It seems that his name had not been previously considered for the vacancy by the Bangor college of electors.

There can be little doubt that the Welsh electoral system has been very carefully thought out, as it contains a rigorous machinery of checks and balances which can be clearly seen to be fair to all interested parties. Every bishop and diocese of the province participates, thereby ensuring that the appointment involves not merely a diocesan, but a genuinely provincial perspective. Doe considers that by making the college vote together as a single body, rather than by separate houses, a cohesion of purpose is created that militates against any easy blocking mechanisms by cabals of bishops, clergy or laity. There might indeed be a possibility that such cohesion could be weakened if a secret ballot, rather than just a mere ballot, were specified in the Constitution's procedural rules.

However, some aspects of this collegial system deserve critical examination. In the first place, the members of the college are sworn to confidentiality, which means that they are effectively debarred from engaging in wider consultations once collegial deliberations have begun. Secondly, it might be fairly argued that the vacant diocese should be given the constitutional right, not merely to make an initial statement of its character and needs, but also to initiate the nomination of candidates. Thirdly it might be considered that by the bishops being both involved in the deliberations of the college and then being able to discuss its decision afresh on their own before they ratify it, they are allowed to exercise far too much influence in the process. Finally, it might be justifiably queried whether this intentionally provincial procedure accords the representatives of the vacant diocese sufficient numerical clout in making the final decision.

The vacant see's combined clerical and lay voting strength amounts to twelve, compared to the aggregate of thirty five from the other five dioceses and the bishops. This means that the vacant diocese commands just one quarter less one of the total votes of the college, or as Jones points out (2000, p. 343), that the electors of the other five dioceses can impose a bishop on the vacant see against the wishes of its own representatives. This is totally unsatisfactory.

It is perhaps a virtue of such a unified provincial system that it appears to produce relatively low key, poorly contested and uneventful elections. There is little evidence of vacancies producing anything like an exciting range of candidates and in many cases the final choice seems to fall between just a couple of archdeacons from within the vacant diocese, one of whom goes on to win the election, while the other discreetly retires from parochial and archdiaconal office, as is widely rumoured to have happened in the case of Bryan Jones, the unsuccessful finalist in the St. Asaph election of 1999.

Since a change in the Constitution in 2007, the archbishop has appointed a *facilitator* the moment an episcopal vacancy arises, so that the diocese can be given help in drawing up a profile of its needs and being made aware of the names of possible candidates. This could mark the start of a wider field of choice, but it might also run the risk of being considered yet another evidence of undue central manipulation in the election process. The inevitable question will arise as to whether the house of bishops is itself briefing the person who has the task of making a diocese aware of the names it should be considering and what hidden agenda might be perceived to lie behind his intervention.

However this development turns out, such a long Welsh tradition of predictable appointments might be considered by critics to contribute to the perpetuation of a lacklustre and highly conservative bench of bishops, by its very nature ill-equipped to face the contemporary challenges of numerical and financial decline. And yet there is a good case for arguing that this type of secret conclave, invariably limited to the candidateture of prominent and widely known senior diocesan clergy possesses some merit. Without the cheap razzmattazz of rival campaigns, or the sense of disillusionment left among beaten candidates and their phalanx of hyped-up supporters, this system may make a genuine contribution to a Church famed for its orderly government and the genuine respect it accords to its episcopate.

Welsh bishops from 1905 to 2005

The first decade of the 20th century was a significant one for Wales. In 1906 the Trades Disputes Act reversed the notorious Taff Vale judgement of 1901, which had left the railwaymen's union liable for losses incurred by the Welsh railway company as a result of a strike. In 1908 the Old Age Pensions Bill was put on to the statute book and the following year the new Chancellor of the Exchequer, David Lloyd-George, MP for Caernarfon declared in his budget that he intended *to wage implacable warfare against poverty and squalidness (Owen, 1954, p. 171)*

In 1905 the Crown was still appointing the Welsh bishops in exactly the same fashion as it did the English, although, as we have seen, the pressure for Disestablishment had made it far more aware of the need to be attuned to Welsh desires and aspirations. *Crockford* and *Who was Who* present a fairly clear picture of the Bench, although there is a noticeable reticence in the personal details that the four bishops cared to provide, which appears, somewhat surprisingly, to have persisted right up to the present day.

In 1905 all four bishops were Oxford graduates, half of them from Jesus College. Three had been involved with Llandovery College, then perhaps the most prestigious public school in South Wales, one as a pupil, the other two as headmasters. W. Williams of Bangor had been educated at Westminster School, but J Owen of St. Davids at Botwnnog Grammar School. Three had extensive Welsh parochial experience, two were members of the Athenaeum and one had aristocratic connections. Two had been consecrated in their early forties, one in his early fifties and the other in his late fifties. None recorded hobbies or interests.

In 1925, five years after Disestablishment, and with the General Strike only a year away, the bench of six bishops still contained five Oxford graduates, two of them from Jesus College, the remaining D.E. Davies of Bangor holding a Durham theology degree. Only two divulged the schools they attended, one an English public school, the other a Welsh grammar school. Only C.A.H. Green of Monmouth had aristocratic links, but two had been headmasters of Llandovery College and J. Owen of St. Davids Principal of St. David's College, Lampeter. Four of the six had good Welsh parochial experience, Davies of Bangor as Vicar of the strategic parish of Swansea. Two had been Welsh archdeacons and one a Welsh Dean, while only one recorded membership of the Athenaeum. Two were appointed bishops in their early 40s, two between the ages of 45 and 54 and two in their later 50s.

In 1945 five bishops were still Oxford graduates, but two had previously studied at a Welsh university college, while the solitary Durham graduate was still at Bangor. Only two recorded their place of schooling: one had attended Llandovery College and the other Westminster School. Three had academic or theological college experience, A.E. Morris of Monmouth as Professor of Hebrew at St. David's College, Lampeter and E.W. Williamson of Swansea and Brecon as Warden of St. Michael's College, Llandaff. None had aristocratic links, but instead three had served in the Army during the First World War, W.T. Havard of St. Asaph winning a Military Cross in 1917. Four had extensive Welsh parochial experience, two as Vicars of Swansea. Only one, Morris of Monmouth, reported having hobbies, in his case gardening and oil painting. Of the five giving their ages, four were appointed between the ages of 45 and 50 and the other in his early 50s.

In 1965 five bishops were still Oxford graduates, three of them from Jesus College, but now three had previously graduated from one or other of the Welsh university colleges, while J.R. Richards of St. David's had his first degree from the University of Wales. Of the half who divulged details of their schooling, W.H.G. Simon of Llandaff had been to Christ's College, Brecon and two to Welsh grammar schools, one at Llanberis and the other in Aberystwyth. Five had taught in theological colleges, three had taught theology at University College Bangor and G.O. Williams of Bangor had been Headmaster of Llandovery College. Only two had any length of Welsh parochial experience, J.J.A. Thomas of Swansea and Brecon as Vicar of Swansea, but Richards of St. Davids had served for eighteen years as a CMS missionary in Iran. Two had served as Welsh cathedral deans and another as a Welsh archdeacon, but none as chaplains to the forces. The only hobbies recorded were fishing and walking by Williams of Bangor. Only Williams had been consecrated in his early 40s: all the rest became bishops in their early to middle 50s.

By 1985 there had been considerable change on the bench. Only two bishops were now Oxford graduates, although B.N.Y. Vaughan of Swansea and Brecon had obtained a Welsh degree first. A. Rice-Jones of St. Asaph had also obtained a Welsh degree before going up to Cambridge. The remainder had gained Welsh degrees. All had recorded the institutions where they trained for the ministry. Two had attended Wycliffe Hall, one Westcott House, one Salisury, one Wells and Rice-Jones St. Michael's College, Llandaff. Three had taught in Welsh theological colleges, including Vaughan, who had also taught at Codrington College, Barbados before becoming Bishop of Belize. J.R.W. Poole-Hughes of Llandaff had spent 19 years in Africa, ending up as Bishop of South West Tanganyika. Only half the bench had extensive Welsh parochial experience, including G. Noakes of St. Davids, who had been Vicar of Aberystwyth. D.G Childs of Monmouth and Rice-Jones had both been Church bureaucrats, but Childs also spent seven years as Principal of Trinity

College, Carmarthen, which was at that time the only Church teacher training establishment in the Principality.

By 2005, the year when devolution of government to Wales finally arrived, things had changed dramatically. Of the five bishops divulging their schooling, two had attended minor English public schools, Anthony Crockett of Bangor Pontypridd Grammar School, Barry Morgan of Llandaff Ystalfera Grammar School and Anthony Pierce of Swansea and Brecon a Welsh comprehensive, Dynefor School, Swansea. Only Pierce was now an Oxford graduate, Cambridge having two and London three, although the three Oxbridge men had previously graduated at one of the Welsh university colleges. Two had trained for the ministry at Westcott House, two at King's College, London, one at Ripon Hall and the other at Wycliffe Hall. Two had taught in Welsh theological colleges. John Davies of St. Asaph was unique in having worked as a journalist in Africa.

The entire bench now had good parochial experience. Pierce had been Vicar of Swansea, Morgan Rector of Wrexham and Dominic Walker of Monmouth successively Vicar of Brighton and Suffragan Bishop of Reading, the only bishop to possess no obvious previous links with the principality. Significantly, five had served as archdeacons in Welsh dioceses, three of them in the same dioceses to which they were subsequently appointed diocesans. Carl Cooper of St. David's was consecrated at 42, two in their late 40s and three in their late 50s. The spread of hobbies and interests was wide among the three who recorded them. Walking was mentioned by two, as was the theatre, reading and music, but Crockett also mentioned the eisteddfodau, fly fishing and even fly tying! The university backgrounds of Welsh bishops over the entire century are summarised in fig. 5.

the power of Welsh bishops

Reviewing the results of Disestablishment, Brown (2007, p. 260) observes that *patronage was, by and large, vested in episcopal hands. Although patronage was vested in diocesan and provincial boards in turns with the bishop, in reality the bishops normally got their own way.*

In the same vein, Price admits with candour (1990, p. 6) that *since the Cardiff convention of 1917 bishops have had very great power within the Church and could ensure the rejection of any proposal before the Governing Body.* Moreover, since the diocesan bishops appoint their own deans and archdeacons, from among whom most bishops will be subsequently drawn, the Welsh episcopate is left vulnerable to a wide front of criticism, not least that of perpetuating an incestuous appointments system with its inevitable democratic deficit. This situation has been exacerbated by the recent creation of the archbishop's *facilitator,* whose very existence seems designed to help guide a vacant diocese towards obliging the wishes of the House of Bishops.

Not surprisingly, Brown's study of Welsh bishops during the Victorian era leads him to say (2006, p. 3) that *a tentative conclusion … may be that Prime Ministers have made a better choice of men for the episcopate than the electoral college.*

The methods of the Welsh episcopal election system may however, be a shade more democratic than those of the parochial appointments system. Disestablishment destroyed the old haphazard patchwork of private patronage, which so notably encouraged a variety of church styles and personalities. In its place came the introduction of a four-handled mechanism whereby the diocesan bishop, the diocesan board of patronage, the provincial board of patronage and the diocesan board for a second time each take their turn at appointing an incumbent.

Although the vacant parish is asked to draw up a profile of its needs, it is permitted merely to send two representatives to the meeting of the diocesan appointing committee—only one if it is part of a larger grouping of parishes. In the case of an appointment falling by turn to the diocesan bishop or to the provincial board, the parish has no statutory representation at all. With the lay parochial view therefore either non-existent or vastly outnumbered by diocesan big guns, and without subsequent PCC discussion of an appointment or the

Fig. 5

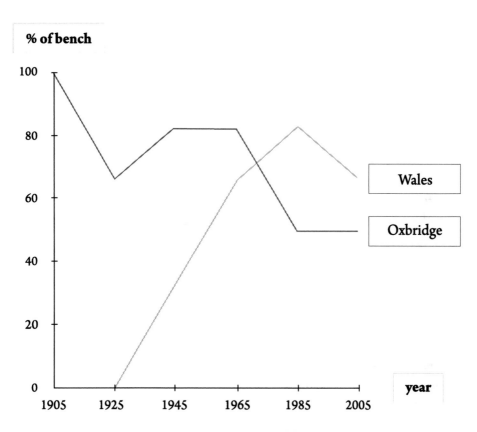

CHURCH IN WALES DIOCESAN BISHOPS 1905 – 2005
university of first degree

Wales includes St. David's College Lampeter

lay representatives' power of veto that obtains in England, it is no surprise that many Welsh lay people are dismayed to find the position of their parishes so precarious and their voice so constrained. In practical terms the diocesan bishop possesses total control of all his churches and can appoint virtually anyone he pleases without any meaningful local consultation, whether his candidate is acceptable to the parish or not.

This democratic deficit is even more starkly underlined by the way in which the elections for the Welsh Governing Body are conducted. Members are elected to represent their dioceses for a three year term and each year one third of the members retire by rotation, which makes elections appear to involve little more than filling routine vacancies upon a committee. Whereas in England there are usually spirited public meetings which allow candidates to be quizzed by the deanery electors and their publicity material and opinions to be thoroughly discussed, in Wales the sending out of election addresses has never been a custom and would, at best, be severely frowned upon. This means that most electors, especially lay people, find themselves left in the dark, with few facts about candidates and even less information about policies to guide their choice. The much-discussed powerlessness of the Welsh Governing Body clearly stems from the stifling limitations that the Constitution places upon any genuine sense of democratic accountability The Welsh have effectively been left stranded in a governmental time-warp of the 1920s!

the reasons behind Welsh monochrome churchmanship

This Welsh episcopal election system and that for appointing incumbents, taken alongside the single provincial theological college of St. Michael's in Llandaff (since the cessation of ministerial training at St. David's College, Lampeter), have done much towards perpetuating the lacklustre nature of much Welsh churchmanship. It is all too evident that card-carrying *Credo Cymru*

Anglo Catholic parishes, although present in Cardiff and the industrial South, are largely conspicuous by their absence across vast swathes of the nation.

Longstanding links with Oxford, brought about through Hugh Price of Brecon's founding of Jesus College in 1571, says Jenkins (1992, p. 106) gave many Welsh clergy and gentry the only opportunity of a university education and therefore doubtless played a part in a wide but, as it has turned out, probably superficial dissemination of Oxford's Tractarian ideals around the country. Bishop David Thomas estimates that perhaps only 43 incumbents across the six dioceses are members of *Credo Cymru*, the Welsh counterpart of *Forward in Faith*, an English organisation set up to maintain the position of Traditional Catholics opposed to the ordination of women to the priesthood.

Because of their dependence, says Brown (2007, p. 260), upon patronage trusts like the Church Pastoral Aid Society and Simeon's Trustees, who lost their rights of presentation to the new Welsh diocesan and provincial patronage boards set up under the terms of Disestablishment, Evangelicals have now all but disappeared from the Welsh scene. Yet the tiny number of established Evangelical parishes that still function, like St. Michael's Aberystwyth and St. Mark's Gabalfa, Cardiff, are undoubtedly hugely successful and wealthy by comparison with most parishes of other traditions.

The result of all this seems to have been the emergence of a self-consciously upper middle-of-the-road churchmanship, tending towards the Catholic in externals, but until very recently traditional in liturgy, and quietly, though unmistakably liberal in belief and doctrine. This sort of stance may have done much to hold together the Welsh Church in the first half century since Disestablishment, but its depressingly monochrome nature has probably weakened its attractiveness in the aftermath of the massive sociological and philosophical shifts in society during the closing decades of the twentieth century—a period characterised for the Church in Wales by what Evans (2000, p. 281) calls *unremitting decline*.

Significantly, the 1995 *Welsh Churches Survey* found that 53% of Church in Wales congregations described themselves as *broad*, with another 10% calling themselves *liberal* (chapter 4). The only other useful statistic revealed that although *broad* churches gained two people in five years, *catholic* churches gained six and *charismatic* churches seven. Here the survey failed to understand the subtler nuances of Anglican churchmanship such as the considerable distribution of charismatic phenomena among traditional Catholics in Wales and the heavy preponderance of the liberally minded among the large Affirming Catholic constituency. There were no statistics that revealed whether growth or decline had characterised the *evangelical* sector, although this happens to be a very tiny element within the Church in Wales. The Survey concluded in an odd and muddled fashion (chapter 6) that:

> *The growth of Broad and Anglo-Catholic churchmanships, may be viewed as a response to change which is a positive choice towards a traditional expression of the Christian faith. The second, the growth of Charismatic churchmanship, may be viewed as a response to change which is a positive response towards new expressions of the Christian faith.*

The *Welsh Churches Survey* makes the valid point that while the Church in Wales had lost only 9% of its people since 1982, the least of all the mainline Protestant denominations, this statistic compared with a 12% gain in the numbers of Roman Catholics. However, this still left the Anglicans as the largest Church in the Principality, with 28.4% of attendances, compared with 21% for the Roman Catholics and 10.4% for the Presbyterians (chapter 3). This could certainly be seen as an encouragement for the Church in Wales, were it not for the accumulating anecdotal evidence of almost exclusively elderly congregations and an almost total collapse in church attendance among the under 21s.

CHAPTER EIGHT

The Scottish Episcopal Church: An Early Exercise in True Democracy

the nature of the Scottish Reformation

On the very eve of the Scottish Reformation in 1550, Scotland had as many as 14 dioceses catering for a population of perhaps only three quarters of a million people (Linklater, 1968, p. 138). Here in the remote far north the Reformation proceeded somewhat differently from the English, occurring in two main spurts, being largely independent of its own monarchy and exhibiting in its early years much more in the way of lay leadership by preachers like George Wishart and the tightly-knit cellular structures known as *privy kirks*. The Roman Catholic hierarchy, led by Cardinal James Beaton, Archbishop of Glasgow, continued in office alongside the new local churches and local preachers, and for two decades there was an uneasy standoff between the two. The Scottish Church historian James Kirk (1989, p. xii) points out that Archbishop John Hamilton of St. Andrews may even have been willing to concede that some of the main demands of the Reformers were fully justified.

Kirk goes on to say (xviii-xix):

> *There was throughout a curious combination, on the one hand, of radical-*
> *ism and revolution, so evident in doctrine, in defiance of authority, and*
> *in the new patterns of worship and church government, and, on the other*
> *hand, of continuity, so marked in the recruitment of personnel from the*
> *old to the new kirk, in the survival of the old financial machinery . . . or*
> *indeed until 1573, of the dispossession of benefice holders for declining*
> *to accept the Reformation. Again, the religious houses survived as legal*
> *entities and as financial corporations; admittedly they were no more than*
> *relics of the past, but the monks and nuns for the most part continued*
> *to live within the precincts as before, supported by their 'portions' . . . as*
> *retirement pensions; the monasteries were not dissolved, as in England;*
> *only the religious observances had ceased or were suppressed. Regardless of*
> *the Reformation, Catholic prelates retained their right to sit in parliament*
> *and vote as the ecclesiastical estate, at a point when the reformers declined*
> *to make new arrangements for the ministry to assume this lordly role.*

Michael Lynch (1992, p. 199) points out that the Reformers of 1560, headed by John Knox, had intended to undertake a complete overhaul of the system of oversight by rationalising the untidy structure of the fourteen mediaeval dioceses into ten districts, each with its own superintendent minister. But then three Catholic bishops changed to the Reformed side and were allowed to remain in their sees, so that in the finish, the Lords of the Congregation appointed only five. Lynch adds (1992, p. 199)):

> *When the General Assembly in 1576 embarked on the task of the*
> *wholesale revision of the polity of the Kirk, it recognised no less than five*
> *offices exercising oversight: archbishops, bishops, superintendents, com-*
> *missioners and visitors . . . superintendents never had the sacramental*

function of bishops, but were cast in the role of New Testament bishops
as watchmen of their flock . . .

From the outset the Scottish Reformers set out to separate ecclesiastical from temporal jurisdictions. They also declined to take the Anglican option of retaining the main elements of the ancient liturgy or maintaining its catholic order. Kirk explains (1989, pp. xvi-xx) how in the 1550s and 60s, under the influence of the French Reformers, some of the local churches took the law into their own hands and opted for what really amounted to a congregational system of government, whereby the local church chose its own minister, whether ordained or lay, and paid him out of their own resources. Alongside the bishops, who were left in office, with their cathedrals and chapters intact, there developed the Genevan notion of the superintendent minister, who slid naturally into many of the old episcopal functions and might on occasion be consecrated to that office in proper episcopal fashion.

Worried by the steady erosion of the old order, with its inherent threat to the Scottish crown, James VI and I set out to bolster the bench and by 1606 he had effectively restored a network of diocesan episcopacy in the Highlands. In 1603 he appointed John Spottiswoode to the Archbishopric of Glasgow, but had him consecrated in London by English bishops seven years later. Spottiswoode may have started as a titular bishop to give him a place in the Scottish parliament, but he was a nonetheless a convinced episcopalian and looked to his ancient predecessors as holy, learned and simple men, although he was as anxious as most of his contemporaries to strip them of the fables and fictions woven around them by mediaeval monks. About this royal initiative to revitalise a dying episcopate Kirk says (1989, p. 479):

The appearance of protestant bishops . . . to whose appointment the
general assembly had accorded its recognition, turned out to be a mixed
blessing for the kirk. Instead of providing energetic leadership within their

dioceses, as the commissioners who preceded them had sought to do, the new bishops, being the Crown's nominees, too frequently appeared as careerists more intent on squandering episcopal revenues than acting as effective pastors of pastors.

There were some notable exceptions. Drawing attention to the eirenic example of the Calvinist presbyter William Cowper, who, after much personal heart-searching, allowed himself to be appointed Bishop of Galloway in 1610, Margo Todd considers that the anti-episcopal polemic of some early Presbyterians does not necessarily reflect the true situation. Using in particular the records of the Perth Presbytery, which sought help from the Bishop of Dunkeld and the Archbishop of St. Andrews for clerical recruitment and ordination, she maintains (2004, p. 301) that:

In fact, the manuscript records of Reformed kirk sessions, presbyteries and synods reveal that presbytery within prelacy actually worked quite well in Scotland from the Reformation until the rise of Arminian and ceremonialist bishops in the 1630s.

Apart from dealing with the appointment of bishops, King James's involvement with the affairs of the Scottish Church declined with his departure for London in 1603 to take over the vastly more influential English throne. His sense of relief at leaving behind the ecclesiastical chaos of Caledonia was palpable and he found himself far more able to indulge his ecclesiastical interests and whims within the more congenial atmosphere of the Church of England, which guaranteed the monarch his position as Supreme Governor and thereby gave him the *de facto* role of chief participant in the appointment of the bench of bishops.

James's son Charles I translated William Laud from the see of London to be his Archbishop of Canterbury in 1633 and under their joint influence several of Todd's *Arminian and ceremonialist bishops* were appointed to Scottish sees and the 1637 Prayer Book, doctrinally far more akin to 1549 than 1559, was foisted upon the Church. This led to popular reaction against episcopacy, which culminated in Jenny Geddes reputedly slinging a stool at the preacher in St. Giles Cathedral, Edinburgh.

the rebirth of the Episcopal Church in Scotland

Throughout the 17th century the currents ebbing and flowing within the Scottish Church pulled it hither and thither, sometimes towards full blown Presbyterianism, sometimes towards Congregationalism and, under the influence of Charles II, firmly towards Anglicanism. However, as J.R. Mackie, Bruce Lenman and Geoffrey Parker show (1978, p. 76), by the end of the Jacobite Rebellion in 1715 the last vestiges of the Anglican way had been expunged, and the Church of Scotland had completed its transformation into a fully Presbyterian shape and organisation. Anglicans north of the border who still wished to remain faithful to the old episcopal ways were forced to organise themselves quite separately. Because of their longstanding relationship with the Crown, this meant that they became increasingly perceived as somewhat English and alien in their nature and culture. This became especially evident after 1688, when the Scottish bishops declined to take the oath of allegiance to William III because of their continuing loyalty to the Stuart dynasty and found themselves reduced to having to minister in meeting houses. Their situation became worse still after the 1715 Jacobite rebellion.

Robbed of any links with the established Scottish Kirk, deserted by the Church of England, isolated from the Hanoverian Crown by their non-juror bishops and reduced to little more than a tiny rump, the Episcopalians were entirely bereft of influence or endowments to help them on their way. In effect, they were forced to organise themselves *de novo*, and therefore the geographical distribution of their churches was almost entirely dependent upon local support, either from a few established landowners in the countryside or from expatriate members of the English and Ulster business communities in the major cities of Edinburgh and Glasgow. F. Stewart (1981, p. 6) notes how the Episcopalians were forced to find meeting places in the recesses of obscure towns, stable lofts and sheds built of stone or peat:

> *The general practice, however, was for the clergyman to take advantage of the goodwill of such of the gentry as were staunch to their traditions and, in the character of a private chaplain, to discharge his office in the mansion of the estate, a select few of the worshippers being present in the room where the service was held, the rest standing in the lobby or hall adjoining.*

Yet for all these persecutions and difficulties, Mackie, Parker and Lenman (1978, p. 299) are right to deduce that *a Church which included in its members many nobles and gentlemen had the power to survive*.

The Presbyterian Kirk possessed all the ancient cathedrals like Dornoch, Kirkwall, Dunkeld and Aberdeen, but the Episcopal Church, even though it could use none of these buildings, chose to perpetuate the old diocesan names and areas, amalgamating most of them into large and often unwieldy units that reflected the widely scattered nature of their own churches and worshippers and the fact that their dependence upon current income provided barely enough money to maintain even a handful of bishops.

Meanwhile the Church of Scotland had settled into a groove of its own. As Christopher Smout explains (1986, p. 185):

> *The Kirk . . . was an ecclesiastical and political establishment whose dominance over the Church in the 1790s had finally been assured by their political subservience to Henry Dundas, into whose hands the Westminster cabinet entrusted the political management of Scotland.*

It was a . . . rational, impersonal and unenthusiastic religion, entirely
orthodox in Calvinist doctrine, yet tolerant of intellectual deviation, and
overwhelmingly polite and conformist in social tone.

The nineteenth century brought about an ideological struggle between this moderate majority and the more forceful Evangelical element led by men like Thomas Chalmers. Matters came to a head when the General Assembly voted in favour of local congregations being able to veto local ministerial appointments, but the judiciary prevented the majority from having their way. As a result, Chalmers seceded with two fifths of the Church's ministers in 1843 to form the Free Church of Scotland.

Alongside these squabbles amongst the Presbyterians and the huge influx of Irish Roman Catholics to work in the new industrial areas of the Central Lowlands, the Episcopalians managed to make some modest progress. After the Napoleonic Wars they had become a popular county Church in the North East. Later, under Anglo Catholic influence from England, they made strenuous attempts to extend their congregations into the cities and larger towns, although many of their churches in the urban slums of Glasgow and Edinburgh were more replete with the beauty of their architecture and fittings than they were with worshippers to enjoy them.

how democracy came to be the Scottish way of appointing bishops

It comes about that by historical accident and because of their tiny size, the Scottish Episcopalians have the only truly elective episcopal appointment system among the three self-governing Anglican Churches in the British Isles, and until 1979, the only one where the entire procedure took place within and at the initiative of the vacant diocese. Neither was this procedure entirely modern: as early as 1727 the four bishops of the Church, meeting together in

Edinburgh, passed six canons, one of which allowed the clergy to elect their own bishops, while the General Synod of 1863 widened the franchise to allow laity to take part as well.

In this Scottish episcopal appointments system, as laid out in the Code of Canons (1952), the clerical electors within a diocese consisted of all the incumbents and presbyters licensed as at the date of issue of the mandate. The lay electors were those who had been directly elected to represent each incumbency, independent or dependent congregation, mission and private chapel within the diocese, however large or small. The dean of the vacant diocese took the chair at the electoral meeting in the cathedral.

The procedure (Code of Canons, IV, p. 4) was as straightforward as was the electorate. At the behest of the chair, nominations were made and seconded in public at the meeting. In the case of more than one name being submitted, a vote was taken on each name in succession. No person could be declared elected unless he had received a simple majority of the votes of the clerical electors present and a simple majority of the lay electors present. The name of the successful candidate would then be submitted to the house of bishops for its approval or rejection.

At first sight, this procedure seems thoroughly transparent, democratic and free from unseemly behind-the-scenes gerrymandering or undue influence from outside the vacant diocese. Yet the real question was whether such a straightforward mechanism could work as well in practice as it did in theory. According to the anonymous preface of the 2005 canons (p. 26) there was a growing uneasiness about it during the 1970s, probably among the heirarchy rather than among the churches themselves:

> The problem was, at heart, a matter of finding the right balance between the proper concern of the diocese for its freedom of election and the equally proper concern of the College of Bishops to witness to and safeguard the role of a bishop in the world-wide Church.

The result was a considerable change to these procedures. Firstly, in 1972 the preliminary meeting of the electors was made obligatory, at which a committee of not more than seven was to be chosen to receive from the electors the names of persons they considered worthy of consideration. This committee was then empowered to compile and circulate a dossier of factual particulars about each of them for the information and guidance of not just the electors, but also the primus and his brother bishops. The bishops were also permitted to submit not more than three names of their own to the dean. Even at the electoral meeting, it would still be possible to bring forward a new name if the nomination had the support of at least a fifth of the electors, but in this case there would be a postponement of the election to allow for the circulation of the relevant particulars. All deacons were admitted to the electorate in 1991.

the Scottish appointments system today

A second and considerably more radical change to the election procedure came by change of canon in 1993. The provincial dimension was introduced through the creation of a preparatory committee, which was given the responsibility for preparing the electoral meeting. Membership of this committee was to include the primus, a further representative of the college of bishops, five mixed clerical and lay representatives of both the province and the vacant diocese and four further clerical and lay members chosen by the diocesan synod of the vacant diocese.

Through the provisions of the 2005 Canons this committee's deliberations are confidential and wide-ranging. It is empowered to receive suggested names from any source, but it is given free rein to consult the vacant diocese's standing committee and the college of bishops, while also being allowed to interview prospective candidates, prepare statements from each and explain why it has included their names on the list of candidates. The Preparatory Committee must then consult the college of bishops before drawing up its final list to ensure that all the names are acceptable to it. This committee is then given the task of preparing and distributing to electors information about each proposed candidate and inviting them to meet the candidates prior to the vote (Canon 4, paras. 8-10).

The electoral synod commences with a celebration of Holy Communion, at which the primus presides. After the vote, the candidate who achieves a simple majority within both the houses of clergy and laity is declared elected. If no candidate reaches this target, the process is repeated. Should this too prove inconclusive, there is a third vote by first preference. Should this too prove inconclusive, those with least preferences are eliminated. (Canon 4, paras. 13-24).

One particular element distinguishes the Scottish procedure from others. There is a separate *none* voting category for those who cannot give their vote to any candidate on the list. If the *none* category amounts to more than one third of the total votes cast, then the election is declared void.

At the episcopal election for Moray, Ross and Caithness, held in Inverness in 2001 to fill the vacancy left by the death of Bishop George Sessford, several candidates were initially nominated. However, the final choice lay between a senior diocesan priest, Canon John Crook and a pharmacist non-stipendiary minister from Lairg, Alexander Gordon (information from Miss A. Francis, Lairg, Sutherland). The village pharmacist lost by only a modest margin and after a short interval as Anglican Chaplain in Strasbourg, returned to Moray, Ross and Caithness as Provost of St. Andrew's Cathedral, Inverness. It is hard to imagine this sort of situation arising in England under the Crown Nomination system. It would be no more likely to happen in Wales with its heavily circumscribed electoral procedures.

The comparatively democratic form of episcopal election process in Scotland is perhaps a reflection of excellent democratic practice at congregational level. Incumbents are generally appointed by the vestry, a council of elected lay representatives established to govern every place of worship. This equivalent of the English and Welsh parochial church council has its own constitution which empowers it to advertise its own vacancy and to receive applications direct from candidates. It is then able to freely discuss them with the diocesan bishop, who although entitled to chair the appointment committee, does not always do so, although he has the power to refuse ratification of the vestry's appointment if he sees fit. The one factor which will always prevent a bishop from confirming such an appointment is if the vestry is incapable of providing the amount of money required to pay an entire clergy stipend.

Since the Scottish 1637 Prayer Book more closely resembles the English 1549 version than it does the 1662, and since the Scottish nobility have traditionally been closely associated with Episcopalianism, the Church has always had a more Catholic feel to its liturgy than the other UK Anglican bodies, but today its overwhelming stance is much more liberal than it used to be, almost exclusively so in some dioceses. *Forward in Faith* churches in Scotland can be counted on the fingers of one hand. However, since local vestries have the power to call a priest who meets their own particular inclinations, it is now no longer unusual to see Evangelical ministries established here and there. By far the most successful of these is St. Paul and St. George's in the heart of Edinburgh, which has been forced to remodel its Regency Gothic building in the last couple of years to accommodate regular congregations that frequently reach a thousand.

Since the Scottish dioceses are so small in terms of churches, congregations and numbers, the diocesan bishops have a much more obviously pastoral function to perform. It could perhaps be said that if their ecclesiastical responsibilities were more onerous and their civic significance greater, maybe a different episcopate would emerge, and with it, a more sophisticated electoral system to service it. The yearbooks show that in 1905 the entire Scottish Episcopal Church had a total membership of only 134,155, with 47,939 communicants spread among 365 churches and serviced by a clerical workforce of 329. In 1975 the total membership had dropped to 81,750, but interestingly, actual communicants were down only to 46,288 spread among 341 churches with 257 active clergy to support them.

Scottish bishops from 1905 to 2005

Although the Scottish Labour Party had been founded in 1888 and its first MP returned to Westminster in 1906, in 1905 four of the seven Scottish bishops still had aristocratic connections, while four were members of the Scottish Conservative Club and one belonged to the Athenaeum.

Three had degrees from Cambridge, two from Oxford and one each from Durham and Trinity College, Dublin. Only four mentioned the schools they had attended, but their variety was wide—Eton, Durham, King William's on the Isle of Man and Glenalmond. Three had taught in theological colleges, both J. Dowden of Edinburgh and A.J. McLean of Moray, Ross and Caithness holding the Pantonian Chair at Edinburgh.

All seven had gained extensive parochial experience, W.J.F. Robberds of Brechin as Vicar of the strategic Bristol parish of St. Mary Redcliffe, but only two had exclusively Scottish experience, both of these becoming bishops for the most rural dioceses in the country. Three had previously been deans or provosts of Scottish cathedrals, while G.H. Wilkinson of St. Andrews, Dunkeld and Dunblane had started his priestly career as curate of the fashionable London Church of St. Mary Abbots, Kensington and his later episcopal career as Bishop of Truro. Two had been consecrated in their early 40s, three in their later 40s and the others at 56 and 60 respectively.

In 1925 four of the bench had degrees from Oxford, three alone from Keble College, while two had graduated from Cambridge and one from Glasgow. There were still two bishops with aristocratic family links and among the four mentioning the schools they attended, Eton appeared again, but the rest were Scottish public schools—Loretto, Fettes and Glenalmond. Six had good parochial experience, four of them in Scotland, while five had served as deans or provosts of Scottish cathedrals. MacLean of Moray had spent five years as a missionary in Assyria, while C.E. Plumb of St. Andrews had been Chaplain in Cannes. For the first time hobbies and recreations were mentioned: two were golfers, one being, not surprisingly the Bishop of St. Andrews, while there was also an early motoring enthusiast and an angler. Three were consecrated in their early 40s, two in their later 40s, one at 56 and the other at 60.

In 1945 three of the bench had degrees from Oxford, two from Cambridge and one from Aberdeen. Only four divulged their schooling: three had attended minor English public schools at Sherborne, Pocklington and Cheltenham, but H.W. Hall of Aberdeen and Orkney had attended a Scottish state school in Pitsligo, where he had subsequently become a teacher. None now had aristocratic family links, but J.C.H. How of Glasgow had served as a Chaplain to both King George V and the VI. Three had served as chaplains to the forces, K.C.H. Warner of Edinburgh winning the Distinguished Service Order with the Royal Air Force in 1919. E. Jordan of Brechin had been Principal of Cuddesdon, T. Hannay of Argyll and the Isles Principal of Mirfield and How Lecturer in Hebrew at St. John's College, Cambridge. Four had chalked up good parochial experience, but only two exclusively in Scotland. How had been successively Vicar of Brighton and Rector of Liverpool and he was alone among the bench in itemising his interests—walking and doing odd jobs. J.L. Barkway of St. Andrews, Dunkeld and Dunblane had started off as a Presbyterian minister, but become Suffragan Bishop of Bedford after a long parochial ministry in St. Albans diocese. One had been consecrated in his early 50s, five in their later 50s and one at 60.

In 1965 two of the bench had graduated from Oxford, one from Cambridge, one from Durham, one from Glasgow and the other from St. Andrews, while D. MacInnes of Moray, Ross and Caithness was unusual in being a non-graduate. Two still possessed aristocratic family links and K.M. Carey of Edinburgh was a Chaplain to the Queen. Six divulged their schools: Haileybury, Shrewsbury, Marlborough and Pocklington appeared, along with an obscure private establishment in a West London suburb, but E.F. Easson of Aberdeen and Orkney had attended Morgan Academy in Dundee. Three had taught in theological colleges, two in Edinburgh and Carey as Principal of Westcott House, Cambridge. MacInnes had been a chaplain to the forces and won a Military Cross in 1944 while Easson had been chaplain to Peterhead Prison and F.H. Moncrieff of Glasgow chaplain to Edinburgh Prison. J.W.A. Howe of St. Andrews, Dunkeld and Dunblane had spent four years in Ghana as a school chaplain. Only R.K. Wimbush of Argyll and the Isles registered any hobbies, his being gardening and walking, while only five bishops divulged their ages. Of these one was consecrated in his late 40s, three in their early 50s and one in his late 50s.

The 1980s were a time of growing economic prosperity and national self-confidence for Scotland as oil production from the Forties and other offshore fields gathered pace. Not only did Aberdeen boom with rig-related industries, but so did the financial sector based in Edinburgh. By now only one bishop, Michael Hare-Duke of St. Andrews, Dunkeld and Dunblane was a graduate of Oxford. Two held degrees from Durham, one from London, another from Leeds, but only one from a Scottish university, in this case St. Andrews. Frederick Darwent of Aberdeen and Orkney was a non-graduate banker, Ted Luscombe of Brechin a graduate accountant. Alistair Haggart of Edinburgh had been Principal of Edinburgh Theological College, the only bishop to have worked in ministerial training. Five had good Scottish parochial experience, but Derek Rawcliffe of Glasgow had worked overseas for 23 years and Hare-Duke had worked exclusively in English parishes, ending up as Director of the Clinical Theology Association and then Archdeacon of Westmorland. Not a single bishop mentioned hobbies or pastimes. Two had been consecrated in their early 40s, three in their early 50s, one at 56 and Haggart at 60.

The new Scottish Parliament held its first session in 1999 and with it came a noticeable increase in national independence of thought and action. Not surprisingly, the episcopal picture by 2005 had become surprisingly varied. Only four of the six bishops recorded their educational details: one had attended Glenalmond, while of the other three, John Crook of Moray, Ross and Caithness had attended Manchester's William Hulme's Grammar School and John Mantle of Brechin and Bruce Cameron of Aberdeen and Orkney had attended Scottish state institutions, the first Grove School in Broughty Ferry and the second Eastwood Secondary in Glasgow. Six of the seven were university graduates, one from Edinburgh, one from Glasgow, one from St. Andrews and three from outside Scotland—none from Oxbridge, but two from St. David's College, Lampeter and another from Trinity College, Dublin. Surprisingly, only four had any significant Scottish parochial experience, while three had taught in theological colleges and Brian Smith of Edinburgh had come from the English suffragan see of Tonbridge. Michael Henley of St. Andrews, Dunkeld and Dunblane had been a curate at London's fashionable St. Marylebone Parish Church and afterwards Chaplain of the Fleet and a Chaplain to the Queen. All but one recorded hobbies and pastimes: four were golfers, three music fans, two film enthusiasts and Smith a short-wave radio ham. None had reached the episcopate in their forties: four had been appointed in their early 50s, two in their late 50s and one at 60. The academic background of Scottish bishops over the entire century is shown in fig. 6.

Fig. 6

the international ripples of the Scottish system

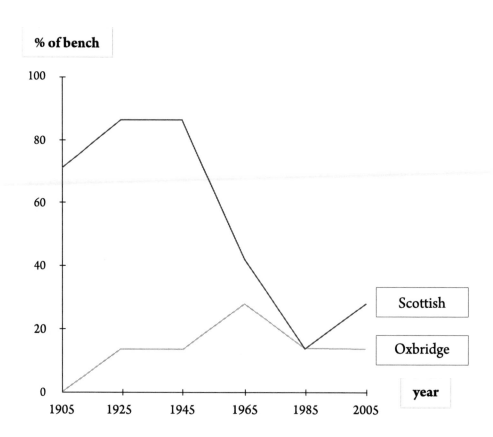

SCOTTISH EPISCOPAL CHURCH DIOCESAN BISHOPS 1905 – 2005
university of first degree

The Scottish appointments system has had a significant impact upon the rest of the Anglican Communion, primarily through the direct involvement of the Scots at a defining moment in the early history of the Episcopal Church in the United States of America. As the numbers of Church of England members grew throughout the 18th century in the old colonial states like Pennsylvania, Maryland, Virginia and the Carolinas, so the need grew for confirmations and ordinations. Since 1701 the colonists had been making repeated requests for episcopal assistance to the Bishop of London, who had official oversight of the American settlements along the eastern seaboard, but nothing happened. The Archbishop of Canterbury was as dilatory about providing practical help for the fledgling American Church as he was over dealing with similar problems which had arisen for John Wesley and more than 15,000 Methodist converts across the Atlantic, probably because any bishop appointed would invariably become an officer of the British state with a seat in the House of Lords and certain powers of coercive jurisdiction. This might prove highly offensive to those of the American colonists whose ancestors had left Britain at least partly to escape from bishops.

After a short war with Britain, the American Colonies broke free. With the Declaration of Independence in 1775, the situation for Episcopalians grew desperate, more especially as they were viewed as opponents of the new regime on account of their support for King George III and the British Army. Samuel Seabury, a High Church Tory S.P.G. missionary from Staten Island, who had served as a British Army chaplain during the War of Independence, sailed over in person with a mandate for his consecration signed by ten out of fourteen of his clerical colleagues back home (Addison, 1951, p. 58). He met with nothing but frustration and indifference after spending more than a year in London, being told that he could not be consecrated without an act of Parliament, as well as making an oath of allegiance to King George III and receiving the endorsement of the Connecticut state legislature. In desperation Seabury travelled north to see if he could drum up more sympathy in Scotland for the plight of the Americans. There he met with a more sympathetic reception.

As the Scots bishops were leaders of a semi-private unofficial Episcopal Church that had never taken an oath of allegiance to William of Orange or his successors, but nonetheless possessed impeccable orders, they were all the more free to help Dr. Seabury, since, like them, he had been elected by his brother clergy. J.P. Lawson (1843, pp. 327-328) describes how he was duly consecrated Bishop of Connecticut in the second floor rooms of a back-alley house chapel in Aberdeen on November 14th, 1784 by three Non-Jurors, the Bishop of Aberdeen, his Coadjutor Bishop and the Bishop of Ross and Moray.

However, only a month before Seabury's consecration, William White of Philadelphia had presided over a representative meeting of clergy and laity in New York, which included participants from Virginia, Maryland, Delaware, Pennsylvania, New Jersey, New York, Connecticut and Massachusetts. They adopted a set of principles, which included, amongst others, giving the Protestant Episcopal Church full power to regulate its own affairs, adopting canons made jointly by clergy and laity, organising the Church by state conventions and aiming to place functioning bishops in every state.

J.T. Addison (1951, pp. 59-60) records how in September, 1785 the first General Convention of 16 clergy and 24 laity of the Protestant Episcopal Church took place at Philadelphia, with seven states being represented. Connecticut did not attend as it objected to the principles set out at the New York meeting and North Carolina and Georgia were too weak to respond officially. An address from the convention was presented to the archbishops and bishops of the Church of England by John Adams, the American Minister to Great Britain. In the aftermath of the Philadelphia convention, three bishops were elected—Samuel Provoost, Rector of Trinity Church, Wall Street for New York, William White, Rector of Christ Church, Philadelphia for Pennsylvania and David Griffiths, Rector of Fairfax for Virginia.

The English hierarchy responded to the American address by asking them to make some changes to their proposed Prayer Book. Then, since news had come that Parliament had passed the necessary enabling act, White and

Provoost sailed for England. As the Virginians could not afford to pay Griffiths's passage, he never actually embarked. Nonetheless, after their consecration in Lambeth Palace Chapel on February 4th, 1787 by Archbishop John Moore of Canterbury, Archbishop William Markham of York, Bishop Moss of Bath and Wells and Bishop Hinchcliffe of Peterborough, an entirely elected episcopate of the requisite canonical three had unexpectedly and belatedly appeared to take the helm of the developing North American situation (Addison, 1951, p. 61).

As Addison says (1951 p. 72-3), quoting S.D. McConnell:

> The introduction of the laity into the place assigned to them was a momentous step ... From government by bishops, themselves the creatures of the King, to government by a convention made up of popularly elected bishops, priests and laymen, is a tremendous leap.

American historian Allen Guelzo (1994, pp. 18-19) observes that before the Revolution, the Church of England had been the Established Church in six out of the thirteen North American states. With neither the British Crown nor the new revolutionary government being involved in any official fashion with the Episcopalians after independence, it was no surprise that the Americans should come to use the democratic election system of the General Convention that had produced two of their three long-sought-for prelates. The Church's bishops were henceforth to be chosen at a meeting of each state convention, the assumption being made that each state and diocese were coterminous. But at the insistence of Seabury and his fellow Connecticut High Churchmen, they were to constitute a separate House in their own right and as there were now three of them, new bishops could be validly and conveniently consecrated in America for America by Americans.

Paul Marshall (2005, pp. 553-554) records how the Scottish Episcopalians came to the rescue of abandoned members of the Church of England a second time in 1825 when Primus George Gleig and his associates consecrated the British Embassy Chaplain in Paris, Matthew Luscombe, a missionary bishop to serve numerous small congregations scattered across continental Europe—a bishop *to go abroad,* as Lawson (1843, p. 584) lists him.

bishops for a worldwide empire

Bishop Stephen Neill (1977, pp. 225-227) shows how one unexpected consequence of the American War of Independence was the expulsion of many Episcopalian clergy from their churches for continuing to use the state prayers for the British royal family. They and many thousands of lay people fled across the border into Canada. It was for their pastoral care that the Archbishop of Canterbury consecrated Charles Inglis as Bishop of Nova Scotia in 1787, to be augmented by James Mountain's consecration only six years later as Bishop of Quebec. These were the first bishops of the Church of England with a specifically *colonial* episcopate. As immigration from the United Kingdom continued, especially into Upper Canada, the Church grew, dioceses multiplied and a separate Province was created in 1862, five years before the Dominion of Canada itself gained a measure of independence from the mother country.

In India, largely on the back of the trading settlements of the East India Company, a small band of Anglican Christians had been developing since the beginning of the 17th century., helped by British chaplains, Lutheran missionaries and the two London-based Societies for the Propagation of the Gospel in Foreign Parts and the Promotion of Christian Knowledge. Neill records (1977, p. 216) that the SPCK's annual report for 1791 contains a similar grumble to that of the American Episcopalians before the Declaration of Independence:

> How long it may be within the power of the Society to maintain
> missionaries ... is beyond our calculation ... we ought to have suffragan
> bishops in the country, who might ordain deacons and priests, and secure a

regular succession of truly apostolical pastors, even if all communications
with their parent Church should be annihilated.

In a belated response to this request, the Church of England appointed Thomas Middleton Bishop of Calcutta in 1814, but because of the arrival of the first convict ships at Botany Bay in 1787, he found himself saddled with a huge jurisdiction which encompassed not only the whole of India, but the continent of Australia as well! However, in 1833 an Act of Parliament established new dioceses based upon Bombay and Madras and that same year the Bishop of Calcutta was given the title of metropolitan, but this did not lead to full provincial self government until 1930.

In 1836 Australia gained its own bishop, followed by Tasmania in 1842, but so rapid was the growth in immigration that the principal diocese was subdivided only five years later into the sees of Sydney, Adelaide, Newcastle and Melbourne, with the Bishop of Sydney automatically holding the title of Metropolitan, but although some embryonic steps towards creating a separate province were taken in 1872, full self-governing status did not follow until 1962.

The Bishop of Calcutta had originally also been given the responsibility of looking after the needs of British colonists in South Africa, since any ship going to India from the mother country would have to pass the Cape of Good Hope anyway! The sheer numbers of Anglican people finally forced the appointment of Robert Gray as Bishop of Capetown in 1847. He was the first bishop for foreign parts to be consecrated outside a very private ceremony held within the mediaeval confines of Lambeth Palace (Neill, 1977 p. 303). In 1853 the further dioceses of Grahamstown and Natal were created, with the South African Province coming into being that same year.

Much the same pattern of events occurred in other British colonies. In the West Indies the freed slaves gained their first bishop in 1824 and their second in 1842, with the province being established in 1882. Successful missionary work in West Africa led in 1864 to the consecration of Samuel Crowther as the first Bishop of Sierra Leone by the Archbishop of Canterbury in Canterbury Cathedral, the first black African to reach the episcopate. The Church spread through the Gambia, the Gold Coast and Nigeria and the province was inaugurated in 1951 (Neil, 1977, pp. 339-341). This grouping has been subdivided again since and Nigeria is now far and away the largest Anglican province in the world, with over 19 million members and three archbishops.

In 1857 George Selwyn, the first Bishop of New Zealand, called a conference of himself, the Bishop of Christchurch, eight priests and seven laymen to draft a constitution for a British dominion given a measure of autonomy from the mother country five years earlier. Crown lawyers, by a slip of the pen, had defined his diocese as extending from Latitude 50 South to 34 North instead of *South,* thereby giving him 4000 miles of extra oversight! Once a further two bishops had been sent out from England, the New Zealand prelates consecrated William Williams as Bishop of Waiapu, followed in 1862 by John Patteson as Bishop of Melanesia, the first Anglican bishop to suffer martyrdom since the Reformation. In both these cases no consecration could take place until letters patent arrived from the Crown and the Archbishop of Canterbury gave his consent (Neil, 1977, pp. 287-292).

Inevitably, as these new provinces gained their freedom from control by the Church of England, so the Crown was forced to relinquish its role in episcopal appointments. In almost all cases the new provinces opted for some version of democratic electoral system, whereby the vacant see uses either a simple majority or a system of proportional representation at a special diocesan assembly to decide upon its new bishop, although nowadays in most cases there is some safeguard written into the electoral procedure whereby the name of the winning candidate is submitted to the other bishops of the province for their agreement, a not unreasonable requirement since it will inevitably fall to these very bishops to co-consecrate and then work alongside such a person.

CHAPTER NINE

Recent Thinking on Episcopal Ministry in the Church of England and Elsewhere

the effect of synodical government

Since setting up a comprehensive system of Synodical Government in 1970, the Church of England has been forced to do a lot of rethinking of its time-honoured procedures and practices. This major event signalled a fundamental shift in thinking away from the episcopal and clerical domination that had gone with the long-established voice of the bishops and clergy meeting together in Convocation, towards a genuinely constitutional lay involvement in every element of decision making at national, diocesan and deanery levels. Such lay involvement had already been foreshadowed in the 1919 enabling legislation which set up the Church Assembly. This body had comprised the diocesan bishops, the clerical members of the two Convocations and an elected freestanding House of Laity, which could meet separately when it so desired, but did not have the same right as the Canterbury and York Convocations to itself initiate major business nor to be included as an equal voting partner in matters of faith, doctrine or church order (Welsby, 1984, p. 146).

The coming of the General Synod marked a significant departure in procedure from an episcopal point of view by including for the first time elected representatives of suffragan bishops alongside the diocesans, although not conferring upon them *per se* membership of the House of Bishops.

the arrival of the Crown Appointments Commission

One of the immediate consequences of creating a more democratic General Synod was an increasing feeling among its members that the procedures for the appointment of bishops should be overhauled. There has always been in England an understandable reticence to question the doings of the Crown, more particularly since the Church of England itself was so obviously a creature of King Henry VIII, but nonetheless pent up frustrations have their mysterious ways of reaching the front door of Number Ten Downing Street as well as penetrating the castellated towers of Lambeth Palace, which face it across the Thames.

In response to these sentiments, the Crown Appointments Commission was set up in 1977 under James Callaghan's Labour administration to propose names to the Crown for senior ecclesiastical appointments. Podmore (2001, p. 137) shows how Prime Minister Callaghan was not willing to cede the Crown's entire involvement to the Church since he felt that if the Queen were still required to make the actual appointment of new bishops, then as a constitutional monarch, she should be entitled to consult her ministers for advice, not least because some bishops would in time gain their place in Parliament as members of the House of Lords.

However, the constitution of the new Crown Appointments Commission made it a body that was, for the first time, clearly seen to be chosen by the Church itself, its members comprising the two Archbishops, three clergy and three laity elected by General Synod from among its members, four representatives elected by and from the vacancy-in-see committee of the vacant diocese and the Archbishops' and Prime Minister's Appointments Secretaries, neither of these last two being voting participants (Welsby, 1984, p. 223).

When a diocese lost its bishop, there was now extensive consultation about the vacancy, involving civic as well as ecclesiastical interests, while particular attention was paid to the views of the diocese. Through what subsequently became known as the Crown Nomination Commission, the Church effectively determined the field of choice and within this field the Commission placed candidates in order of preference. Under this arrangement the Crown could not introduce names of its own into the final nominations, but via the Prime Minister's Appointments Secretary, it was perfectly capable of entering names of its own into the discussions at a far earlier stage. The Crown ultimately, on the Prime Minister's advice, made its choice from the two names forwarded by the Commission. Nonetheless, in the hallowed traditions of Britain's unwritten constitution, the Church accepted that the Crown's agreement to this convention was purely voluntary, and could, at least in theory, be repudiated at any time (Cameron Group, 1990, para 507).

Chadwick (1990, p. 144) records Archbishop Michael Ramsey's acerbic response to these new arrangements when he is quoted as saying on his retirement from Canterbury, *They don't get any better bishops and it takes them much longer to get them.*

The difficult circumstances in which the Crown Nomination Commission operates and which to some extent overarches its actual freedom of manoeuvre, are frankly acknowledged by the Cameron Group, (1990, para 505):

> *The disjunction remains, and perhaps must now remain, between the interaction of the ecclesial relationships which must come into being to create a bishop; and the practical processes of selection, which must answer to many other requirements. What bridges the two is the Church's responsibility to the nation, which, deeper than its public expression of the nation's formal Christian alignment, has to do with the necessity laid upon*

the Church to proclaim abroad the good news of God's Kingdom. The bishop to be appointed has to win souls as well as care for them: the souls of everyone in the diocese, Church-connected or not, are in his cure.

All this is now about to change. Under proposals made in 2008 in response to Prime Minister Gordon Brown's wish to end the Government's direct involvement in the choice of the episcopate, the Church will in future submit only one name to Downing Street for appointment by the Queen. The constitution of the Crown Nomination Commission will be altered in order to make it more akin to the electoral college which makes episcopal appointments in Wales, although the Church remains keen to have the continued involvement of the Prime Minister's Appointments Secretary as a non-voting adviser, apparently to maintain some sort of continuing state link.

the anomaly of the suffragan bishop

Although Henry VIII's experiment with suffragan bishops was short-lived, the inherent usefulness of the concept was rediscovered by the Victorians as they faced the twin tasks of caring for the burgeoning urban populations and mass building of new churches brought about by the Industrial Revolution (Cameron Group, 1990, paras 407, 415). New dioceses like Ripon, Manchester, Wakefield and Liverpool had been created from 1836 onwards and there was a further spurt of new sees during and after the First World War, mostly in the sprawling new suburbs of the South and Midlands, such as St. Edmundsbury (1913), Chelmsford (1914), Coventry (1918), Guildford (1927) and Portsmouth (1927). The coming of some of these bishoprics had already been foreshadowed by their previous existence as suffragan sees of a larger parent diocese.

Although Henry's suffragans were directly appointed by him, the procedure changed significantly with the Victorian revival. Despite being technically still a Crown prerogative, the appointments came to be made at the initiative of the sponsoring diocesan, who would submit two names to the Archbishop for transmission to Downing Street. In most cases the first name would then be appointed.

In 2005 *Crockford* listed no less than 64 suffragan bishops serving in the provinces of Canterbury and York, only five dioceses, Newcastle, Bradford, Leicester, Portsmouth and tiny Sodor and Man being without them. Manchester had three—Hulme, Middleton and Bolton; Southwark three—Kingston, Woolwich and Croydon: and even rural Exeter had two—Crediton and Plymouth. London, as the Church of England's third see by precedence, but premier by population, boasted no fewer than five; Stepney, Kensington, Fulham, Willesden and Edmonton. This huge expansion in suffragan numbers has taken place piecemeal, without there ever having been a concerted review of the ways in which a diocesan bishop's multifarious duties should be reserved to himself, shared or delegated. It was entirely up to the diocesan to decide how many or how few of his episcopal functions he might be willing to delegate to a suffragan.

Bogle (2002, pp. 15-16) recounts how Mervyn Stockwood wrote to Archbishop Geoffrey Fisher soon after his appointment as Bishop of Southwark in 1958 about the suffragan vacancy he needed to fill at Woolwich. Stockwood summed up the capabilities of his existing provost, two archdeacons and his suffragan bishop at Kingston, but went on to explain to his primate why John Robinson, Dean of Clare College, Cambridge was the person he was seeking as his new episcopal colleague:

> *I want as Bishop of Woolwich a man (1) who understands what I am trying to do; (2) who has the intellectual competence and theological knowledge to advise me; (3) who is accustomed to dealing with and teaching ordinands; (4) who, while his special concern will be for experimental work, can at the same time do the normal pastoral and routine duties of a suffragan bishop. At Southwark there is a strongish team at the centre ... and I know they will be a great help to me. But all*

*of them are essentially conventional churchmen . . . Within the existing
framework they will be friends and guides to me and I shall be able to talk
things over with them. But in addition to these . . . I want a new Bishop of
Woolwich who . . . will appreciate the need for a new approach in places
like Rotherhithe and Bermondsey . . . how to win to Christ the thousands
and thousands of people . . . to whom Christianity means nothing.*

The *Dioceses Measure* of 1977 attempted to tidy up this messy situation
(Cameron Group, 1990, paras 410,417,442). Section 10 allowed a diocesan
bishop to temporarily delegate to his suffragan in particular the two functions
of administering confirmation and holding ordinations, this being done by
instrument and therefore not requiring the consent of the diocesan synod.
This instrument was personal to the suffragan concerned and temporary only
if a particular period of time was specified. Otherwise it continued for as long
as the suffragan held office under his diocesan.

Section 11 of the measure went much further and made provision for
permanently dividing a diocese into episcopal areas, binding not only upon the
bishop of the diocese in office at the time the scheme was made, but also upon
his successors. The diocesan could choose to exercise his episcopal ministry
within a geographical area of his own alongside that of his area bishops, but
whatever organisational method was adopted, because area bishops had a
clear demarcation of responsibility, the diocesan bishop had an opportunity
to develop his own special role as the unifying force within the whole see, a
function with solid historical precedent.

This system had not changed in principle since 1977, although the two
names now found their way to the Prime Minister via the Crown Nomination
Commission rather than directly through the Archbishops. As with diocesans,
after 2008 the Church will submit only one name to the Crown, but the
appointment will be made by the Commission rather than by the bishop of the
diocese with the vacancy that needs to be filled. The Pilling Report *Talent and*

Calling (2007) suggests that, since the appointment of any suffragan bishop has a much wider significance than the purely local (para 5.3.2), the intention should be for the diocesan bishop with a vacancy to assemble a pool of those considered particularly able and gifted from whom a suitable appointment might be made (para 5.6.5.2), with his clerical and lay diocesan advisory group playing a significant part in the proceedings.

the further anomaly of flying bishops

One of the unintended consequences of the Church of England's decision to ordain women to the priesthood in 1992 was the need to cater for the not insignificant minority of mainly traditional Catholic clergy who might find themselves in a state of impaired communion with any diocesan who had participated in a practice they felt to be both unscriptural and at variance with the unchanging tradition of the Church Catholic over nearly two millennia, particularly as expressed through the invariable practice of the vastly larger Roman Catholic and Orthodox communions.

Considerable Parliamentary pressure was brought to bear upon the Church as a result of a sustained campaign by the pressure group *Cost of Conscience* and in the finish three Provincial Episcopal Visitors were appointed to care for those clergy and parishes whose parochial church councils passed what became known as resolutions A, B and C, the last a request for alternative episcopal oversight to that of the diocesan bishop having geographical jurisdiction. These three so-called *flying* bishops occupy the specially created suffragan sees of Ebbsfleet and Richborough in the Southern Province and Beverley in the North. They may cross diocesan boundaries almost at will to meet the requests of their clientele, but do not possess as of right all the powers normally devolved upon area bishops.

Despite a growing impatience among the vast majority who are perfectly happy with the principle of women and men sharing one priesthood, the

Provincial Episcopal Visitors have been a great success with those who use them. They have, after all, been chosen by the Archbishops for the express purpose of offering an acceptable ministry to those clergy and congregations who request them. Therefore not only are they highly esteemed for their traditional Catholic approach to Christian doctrine and the episcopal teaching function, but also because they offer a level of personal pastoral care and oversight to their relatively small constituency that majority clergy and parishes can only dream of.

report of the Archbishops' Group, 1990

A comprehensive milestone was the publication in 1990 of the ground-breaking report of the Archbishops' Group on the Episcopate. Surprisingly, this group's original remit had not been to look exhaustively at the entire subject of bishops, but purely to investigate, at the instigation of General Synod, the questions of theology involved in the possible consecration of women to the episcopate. In her foreword, Sheila Cameron, the Group's Chair, explains that prudence and desirability quickly widened its terms of reference into a more general study of the nature and function of the episcopate in the Church. As the members of the group had been appointed by the two archbishops specifically to ensure that both proponents and opponents of women bishops were given an equal bite of the cherry, the tone and content of the report can probably be taken as a more reliable barometer than most of where the modern Church of England as a whole stands upon the questions of the nature and purpose of its consecrated leadership.

Perhaps the main contribution of the Cameron Report is to articulate for the first time a coherent Anglican *three planes* philosophy of the episcopate, a diversity in unity which it sees as a mirror of the Holy Trinity and much of which it claims to have distilled from the writings of Ignatius of Antioch, Augustine of Hippo and Irenaeus of Lyons, which have already been considered in an earlier chapter. Cameron admits quite candidly (para 7) that:

A major theme of the report—and indeed, its governing principle—is
that these three planes intersect in the person of the minister with special
responsibility for oversight of the unity and common life of the people
of God.

In this connection, the report quotes with approval the Orthodox theologian Lossky's (1957, p. 43) description of the bishop as the *polypletheia* or
multitude—the truly *corporate* person.

Cameron sees the *first plane* as the bishop exercising a ministry of unity in
relation to his local community, the Christian one in particular, but also the
wider one. As the focus of that community's worship and life and in protecting
it as the guardian of its faith and order, he stands in a relationship to it which
enables him to act on its behalf.

Cameron sees the *second plane* as the bishop maintaining regular two-way
contact and discussions with the leaders of other local Christian communities
so that the local church is constantly in touch with other local churches. On this
plane, it sees the bishop's function as maintaining the unity of the local with
the wider Church, although whether its inevitable identification of the *local*
church with a typical modern English diocese rather than with the properly
functioning grass-roots parish, must be open to question.

Finally Cameron sees the *third plane* as the bishop maintaining through
the succession of bishops from generation to generation since Apostolic
times the unity of the Church down the years, the outward continuity in their
consecrations being a visible sign of their inward continuity in teaching and
doctrine.

Having covered such a immense breadth of matter, the report finally drifts
into the ecumenical considerations involved in being a modern diocesan,
touching with evident approval on the *shared* ministry of the Anglican bishop,
the Roman Catholic archbishop and the Chair of the Free Church Federal
Council on Merseyside. However, quite unlike most other reports of General

Synod commissions and working parties, its final chapter makes no specific recommendations for the future of the episcopate—almost as if it is forced into a coy admission that here alone, among all the matters of moment affecting the future of the Church of England, this has to be one territory that it dares not invade.

For all that, in its final three pages the report does at least come close to making its position crystal clear on one matter of crucial significance, which it seemed to have overlooked in setting out its *three planes* of the bishop's role. Of all the various episcopal functions it might have highlighted, it chooses to focus upon the teaching role alone and declares unequivocally in para 672:

> *We believe that it is of the first importance that our bishops should be strong teachers of the faith who are both deeply engaged in the continuing education of the people of God . . . and powerful defenders of the faith and winners of souls in the world. Such evangelism and guardianship of the faith involves a diversity of gifts, not all of which can be looked for in every bishop, but which we must seek to ensure are present in their fullness in the episcopate as a body.*

Two paragraphs later the report goes even further and states bluntly that the bishop himself *must be a teacher,* who is capable, not only of looking forwards along the line of time in a prophetic fashion, but backwards through Christian history to its apostolic origins to discover the lessons from the past that will inform and invigorate the Church in its presentation of Christ to the world of today.

the episcopal consecration service in the Alternate Service Book

The Alternative Service Book (1980) was intended, according to its preface, (p. 9) *to supplement the Book of Common Prayer, not to supersede it.* It nevertheless contains an order for consecrating bishops which makes some major changes from the 1662 rite in both the content and the emphasis of the service, reflecting what the preface calls *rapid social and intellectual changes, together with a world-wide reawakening of interest in liturgy.*

Cranmer's seven point interrogation of the episcopal candidate has been extended to eight points, but the content considerably abridged. In the second and third questions the episcopal teaching function is less orientated towards the Scriptures as towards *the doctrine of the Christian faith as the Church of England has received it* and Cranmer's feisty call to *banish and drive away erroneous and strange doctrines contrary to God's Word* is reduced to to an anodyne request to *uphold the truth of the Gospel against error.*

The prayer of the archbishop before the actual consecration has within it an echo of the modern eucharistic thanksgivings and omits the Cranmerian petition that the bishop-elect should *use the authority given him, not to destruction, but to salvation; not to hurt, but to help,* a weakening of emphasis matched by the loss of 1662's blunt *be to the flock of Christ a shepherd, not a wolf.* Instead there is a somewhat banal reference to the bishop's guardianship of the sacraments and his role as president at the worship of the people of God.

completing the remodelling in Common Worship

Common Worship 2005 builds upon the changes made in 1984 to construct what is virtually an entirely new liturgy. The archbishop now introduces the service, not with prayer, but with an explanation of what the Church perceives itself to be and how the episcopate encapsulates and services that perception. The dominating picture of the Church is not so much the flock of Christ as the royal priesthood, to which, in Cameron's *three planes* fashion:

> ... they are to gather God's people and celebrate with them the sacraments
> of the new covenant. Thus formed into a single communion of faith and

love, the Church in each place and time is united with the Church in every place and time.

Before the *Declarations*, as the examination of the candidate is now called, the archbishop returns to explaining the functions of the 21st century episcopate. With a much more heightened sense of pastoral awareness than in 1662, he declares that bishops are . . . *to love and pray for those committed to their charge, knowing their people and being known by them* . . . while with an eye to the modern upsurge in lay and collaborative ministry, *They are to discern and foster the gifts of the Spirit in all who follow Christ, commissioning them to minister in his name.*

The consecration prayer is now renamed the *ordination prayer*, maybe an indication that the Church of England has finally come down on the side of the episcopate being a separate and higher order of ministry rather than an ornamental but largely supervisory extension of the presbyterate. The prayer has an even more marked eucharistic feel than that in the ASB and after the laying on of hands, it asks God to fill his servant:

> . . . *with the grace and power which you gave to your apostles, that as a true shepherd he may feed and govern your flock, and lead them in proclaiming the gospel of your salvation to the world. Make him steadfast as a guardian of the faith and sacraments, wise as a teacher and faithful in presiding at the worship of your people.*

Teaching the faith therefore now appears to rank only third among the episcopate's prime functions, while the essential quality of that teaching is marked out as wisdom rather than content or courage in its delivery.

The giving of the Bible to the new bishop still features in the service, but it may now be detached from its traditional place immediately after the consecration proper and left till the *sending out* section after the communion of the people has ended, in which case it will be combined with the presentation of the pastoral staff, itself the restoration of a practice abandoned in 1552.

Rubric 13, states that if the delivery of the Bible is left till the end of the service, *It is important that the Giving of the Bible is clearly distinguished from any subordinate ceremonies.* The Liturgical Commission said that it felt that by placing the delivery of the Bible here, at the point of blessing that marks the finale of the service, the significance of Scripture in the ministry of the newly consecrated bishop would be heightened. However, when the rite is viewed as a whole, it becomes fairly obvious that by visibly disclocating the consecration prayer from the delivery of the Bible, emphasis has shifted away from the primacy of the episcopal teaching function with its Scriptural focus that was such an obvious feature of the 1662 order.

Roman Catholicism and Orthodoxy

According to A. Black (1980, pp. 67-72) the milestone Second Vatican Council proclaimed the collegiality of the universal episcopate by instituting a periodic international synod of bishops, together with national bishops' conferences, whose decisions were to have juridically binding force under certain conditions. However, Black considered that the promotion of the collegial ideal downwards to the clergy and laity had turned out to be somewhat patchy. He suggests that the appointment of Catholic bishops should combine diocesan preferences with the views of clergy and laity, along with advice and consent from the national hierarchy, there being no need for Rome to be involved at all.

The Cameron Report (1990, paras 51-54) however, is considerably more upbeat and notes some major changes of emphasis in Roman Catholic thinking since the Second Vatican Council. *Lumen Gentium* places a much greater emphasis upon the local diocese, however small, declaring that it represents in microcosm the entirety of the Church. Its clergy constitute, with their bishop, a unique sacerdotal college, with the laity also sharing the priestly, prophetic and kingly office of Christ.

At the same time, *Lumen Gentium* has also brought the Roman Catholic position on the nature of the episcopate into sharper focus. Consecration is now called episcopal ordination and through it is conferred a threefold gift of teaching, sanctifying and governing, the first being a clear recognition of the New Testament priority accorded to the episcopal teaching function.

A striking note is provided by the new Catholic Catechism inaugurated by Pope John Paul II in 1992 on the 30th anniversary of the opening of the Second Vatican Council. In para. 1560 (p. 349) it states that a newly consecrated bishop *becomes collegially with all his brother bishops the solicitude for all the Churches*. At the same time para. 1562 (p. 350) makes the surprising assertion that *priests are co-workers of the episcopal order for the proper fulfilment of the Apostolic mission entrusted to it by Christ.*

In another surprising change of emphasis Cardinal Cormac Murphy-O'Connor (2004, p. 71) has commented that *in fact a Roman Catholic bishop, while faithful to the Holy See, is completely autonomous in his own diocese.*

The Cyprus Statement agreed with the Anglicans in 2006 makes it clear that for the Orthodox the New Testament does not offer a blueprint for church order, but rather a source that may be elaborated upon by the decisions of ecumenical councils (Reid, 2005, p. 190). Orthodox bishops can only be chosen from among monks and since its many national Churches are geographically dispersed across wide and culturally contrasting areas, there are few signs of any real changes in thinking about the episcopate. The bishop is seen primarily as the representative of the local church and the bishop in communion with the faithful as an eschatological representation of Christ himself among his people. Fouyas (1972, p. 151) sums up the current position thus:

> While the Roman Church is monarchical and authoritarian, the structure
> of the Orthodox church is hierarchical and conciliar. The Orthodox

> *Church admits that each particular Church, in both the East and West*
> *is self-governing . . . the bishops are independent of each other, and each*
> *entirely free within his own bounds, obeying only synodical decisions,*
> *sitting as equals in synods.*

Kallistos Ware (1982, pp. 4-5) emphasises that for the Orthodox, Ignatius of Antioch remains a type for the episcopate: like him, *the bishop is not primarily a teacher or administrator, but the celebrant who presides at the Sunday liturgy . . . the local pastor whom they all see Sunday by Sunday at the Eucharist,* but then he goes on (p. 8) to describe the Greek diocese of the 1940s as:

> *. . . by English standards, very small and sparsely populated; in some*
> *respects more akin to a rural deanery . . . The bishop retains a far greater*
> *measure of direct personal responsibility and delegates comparatively*
> *little . . . The Greek bishop is commonly the most approachable of men;*
> *the sheer accessibility of the generality of the bishops is a matter for*
> *wonder and rejoicing . . .*

Alfeyev (2002, p. 237) makes the significant point that for the Orthodox, only an ecumenical council can have the authority to change anything significant, but as this has not occurred in the East for twelve centuries, there is little likelihood of it happening again, especially in view of the large number of autonomous national churches and the hugely different social and political environments within which they are now set.

Anglican orders were pronounced *utterly invalid and altogether void* by Pope Leo XIII in his epistle *Apostolicae Curae* of 1896, largely, it seems, because the words used in the ordination of priests according to the 1662 Prayer Book did not contain a clear and unambiguous reference to the Eucharistic offering and therefore cast doubt upon both the form and intention of the rite (Bettenson, 1943, pp. 382-83).

The force of this denunciation has neither lessened with the passing of the years, nor after the lengthy deliberations of the Anglican/RC Unity Commission. Those Anglican bishops who accepted the Pope's offer and joined the Ordinariate in 2010 were re-ordained priests in Westminster Cathedral the following year, but not until they had first been re-confirmed. It may well be that such blatant Roman triumphalism and public devaluation of the long ministries of many good and devoted Anglican priests will limit the attractiveness of the Ordinariate to merely that small minority who were temperamentally and liturgically Anglican Papalists already.

By contrast, an Encyclical from the Ecumenical Patriarch to the Presidents of the Particular Eastern Orthodox Churches in 1922 takes a totally different and more conciliatory line towards Anglican orders. It begins by accepting the consecration of Matthew Parker as Archbishop of Canterbury by four bishops in 1559 as *a fact established by history* and then goes on to state that . . . *in this and subsequent ordinations there are found in their fullness those orthodox and indispensable, visible and sensible elements of valid episcopal ordination—viz. the laying on of hands, the Epiclesis of the All-Holy Spirit and also the purpose to transmit the charisma of the episcopal ministry.* As far as the Orthodox are concerned, Anglican orders have never been in doubt. (Bettenson, 1943, pp. 444-45)

the growing band of extra-mural Anglicans

With the establishment of the Reformed Episcopal Church in the United States in the 1870s as a response to the perceived increase in ritualism within the Protestant Episcopal Church (Addison, 1951, pp. 211-213), there was a return to the idea that bishops were more of a supervisory category of presbyter rather than a separate order in their own right. This was expressed not only by including representative presbyters alongside bishops in performing the laying on of hands at episcopal consecrations, but also by ensuring that new bishops should not necessarily be shorn of any previous parochial charge.

The Reformed Episcopal Church happens to have a recognised UK counterpart in the Free Church of England, a tiny body which also owes its origins to the anti-Tractarian feelings of the 19th century and whose Prayer Book and Ordinal are almost an exact replica of the 1662 rites.

A number of new extra-mural Anglican Churches arrived on the American scene in the wake of the Episcopal Church's proposal to ordain women priests. The Continuing Anglican movement took proper shape at a big congress held in Missouri in 1977, out of which came the *Affirmation of St. Louis* (website of the Fellowship of Concerned Churchmen, www.anglicanchurches.net). Three men were elected by the congress to lead the new Church.

These three *St. Louis* bishops were originally consecrated by two retired Anglican bishops and the written consent of a bishop of the Philippines Independent Church unable to be present, which made their orders appear somewhat irregular. All three subsequently broke ranks and each bishop then went on to lead his own Church, out of which came the Anglican Church of America, the Anglican Catholic Church and the United Episcopal Church. Because of unhappy public perceptions in the wake of the break-up, the biggest body, the Anglican Church of America, had its own bishops reconsecrated at the hands of Robert Mercer, a retired Bishop of Matabeleland and a Mirfield monk, along with the retired Bishops of Namibia and New York, so that all those consecrated and ordained by them since that date actually possess valid Anglican orders, which makes their situation quite different from those obtaining in the other Continuing Churches.

Although the *Affirmation* did not enshrine the principle that all bishops should care for a parish alongside their episcopal duties, lack of resources originally forced this solution upon the three Churches that grew out of the *St. Louis* consecrations, Since then they have found good pastoral reasons for continuing the practice in many of their dioceses, even now that their memberships are much stronger and their finances less strapped.

The Anglican Church in America has a tiny sister body in the UK called the Traditional Church of England, which has no bishops of its own but uses the services of American bishops as and when required. The reason for this is because the membership is considerably more diverse in churchmanship than in the USA and the election of a bishop might have caused sufficient internal dissension for a split to occur. In fact, when Leslie Whiting, a former West London vicar of impeccable Catholic pedigree, was unanimously elected to lead the UK affiliate, his appointment was blocked by the American hierarchy and he had to be consecrated by two other American Continuers with the help of a retired African Anglican bishop.

Since the tone of these new American Continuing Anglican bodies is unashamedly Catholic in faith and order, it may be something of a surprise to find that their common espousal of parish priest-bishops might be taken to suggest a certain ambivalence in their attitude towards a separate episcopal order. The development of these bodies may however be placed in jeopardy by the decision of the largest, the Anglican Church in America, to end its separate ecclesiastical existence and instead be absorbed into the Ordinariate that Pope Benedict inaugurated in 2010.

Alongside the practical outworking of the episcopal ideal in these new bodies, it is worth noting in passing that Pritchard (1991, p. 283) shows that the smallest Episcopal Church dioceses like Western Kansas, Utah and North Dakota number only between 25 and 35 parishes apiece, which approximates to roughly the same number as in many of the dioceses in the major Continuing Anglican Churches (information from UECNA Bishop Peter Robinson, Prescott, Arizona). The modest size of these dioceses allows the development of a close and mutually supportive pastoral relationship between a bishop and his clergy and people, which may have played a significant part in explaining how swift has been the growth of church numbers and congregational size among the more vibrant Continuing Church bodies.

The American situation has grown more complicated still in recent years with the departure of many key orthodox Anglican parishes from the Episcopal Church as liberal bishops have sought to impose their doctrinal and moral views upon all the parishes within their dioceses. Several sizeable and wealthy congregations have decided to seek episcopal oversight from among the GAFCON orthodox African provinces of the Communion, but although they have thereby remained technically Anglican, they have almost all been forcibly ejected from the Episcopal Church and discovered that their church properties and finances are legally vulnerable and capable of seizure by the diocese within which they are situated.

At an inaugural meeting held in Bedford in 2009 these scattered congregations, including those of the Reformed Episcopal Church and some Anglicans in Canada, established a formal constitution as the Anglican Church in North America, with Pittsburgh's Bishop Andrew Duncan as its first primate. At Bedford the new Church also made two key decisions. It incorporated into its canons the provisions that congregations should hold the legal title to their own property and that the episcopate should remain open to males only (canon 8, section 3).

In June, 2011 the GAFCON primates promised their support to those in England who have been forced out of conventional Anglican structures because of their opposition to the Church's equivocal witness to Christian marriage and its increasingly tolerant approach towards clergy in same-sex relationships. This group, the Anglican Mission in England, includes Christ Church Wyre Forest, Christ Church Sheffield Central and Christ Church Durham, some of them already large congregations. A panel of five English bishops, one of them Dr. Michael Nazir-Ali, will oversee English developments in association with the council of GAFCON primates, with one of their key concerns being to instigate a vigorous campaign of church-planting, presumably in areas where liberal dioceses have eliminated orthodox parishes and Christian witness needs to be urgently re-established (Anglican Mission in England press release, 23/6/11).

The total of people active within ACNA is growing steadily and had already topped the 100,000 mark by 2010. Their aim is seriously ambitious—to have a thousand active congregations within five years. The province of 28 dioceses in the USA and Canada is now officially recognised as such by the orthodox primates of the Global South, whose provinces now form the majority of the Anglican Communion's membership. However, as ACNA currently ordains women to the priesthood, along with some of the African provinces with which it is linked, relations between itself and the *St. Louis* jurisdictions have not developed quite as quickly as might have been envisaged, despite the fact that they hold largely common theological positions and are equally opposed to the secular humanist agenda, especially in regard to marriage and homosexual practice.

CHAPTER TEN

The Statistical Survey and Its Results

finding out what clergy and laity really think about the episcopate

Apart from one or two pieces of research like D.W. Turton's (2003), dealing with particular aspects of the episcopate within a narrow Church context, there does not appear hitherto to have been any comprehensive, systematic study that uses empirical methods to discover what the perceptions and expectations of the bishop's office may be among clergy and key lay people on the one hand and among the episcopate themselves on the other.

Over the past half century or so the Church has made much of the rediscovery of its own essentially theological nature as the Body of Christ alive and at work in his world, which Paul taught so vividly and systematically in Romans 12 and Ephesians 4. Through works like J.A.T. Robinson's *The Body—a Study in Pauline Theology* (1952), the Church has now become far more attuned to seeing the necessity of all that Body's constituent parts working together in a harmonious, creative and effective partnership. It therefore becomes vitally important to assess exactly how the episcopate, as one major organ of this Body, views its own purpose and character and how that purpose and character are seen and felt by those myriad other Body parts that seem to be inextricably linked to it by this uniquely divine biology.

There is a considerable literature available today on the subject of how to plan sociological surveys, together with a growing body of material specifically related to the methods of discovering the opinions of Christians about matters that closely affect them, particularly within the settings of ecclesiastical institutions and the personnel and apparatus that service them. The ground-breaking *Church Times* Survey of 2001, spearheaded by Professor Leslie Francis of the University of Wales, Bangor, revealed the complexity and huge potential of data obtained by the questionnaire method over a wide variety of topics. Their study and analysis has now established empirical theology as a significant and respected discipline within the larger body of the subject.

what characteristics the four chosen dioceses have in common

The main factor in choosing which dioceses should represent each of the three Anglican Churches on the British mainland was that they should be broadly comparable in character. All four dioceses were to have a spread of genuinely rural and inner urban parishes, with the inevitable belt of suburbia between the two. The rural areas were to be overwhelmingly agricultural in character and the urban areas were to have at their core Victorian residential neighbourhoods originally built around major manufacturing industry, whether these still survived intact, or whether they had been rebuilt in the slum clearances of the 1960s or were now in the process of renewal and redevelopment. The bishops were to work their dioceses without having any official suffragan, although this did not preclude those who enjoyed part-time help or the services of retired assistants.

---

the two chosen English dioceses

The large Northern diocese of Bradford is in the York province and centred upon a city of some 467,000 (2001) which grew to its present size on the back of 19th century woollen and worsted manufacture and local coal mining which fuelled it (Smith, 1953, pp. 433-461). The diocesan boundaries stretch from the densely populated City of Bradford, with its considerable Asian population, westwards onto the open sheep grazing moorlands of the Yorkshire Pennines and across the Dales to the Cumbrian borders. There are two archdeaconries, Bradford being predominantly urban and Craven overwhelmingly rural. The *2007/08 Diocesan Yearbook* lists 150 clergy to care for 177 parish churches, other worship centres and *fresh expressions* ministries. The diocesan bishop has no suffragan, but enjoys the help of four retired bishops.

The Midland diocese of Leicester is in the Canterbury province and relatively small in area, but focused upon a city of 280,000 (2001) originally devoted to textile manufacture and engineering and close to what used to be a small but productive coalfield (Smith, 1953, pp. 302, 536-537). The archdeaconry of Loughborough is an area of semi-rural villages and former mining communities stretching westwards towards Burton-on-Trent. The Leicester archdeaconry contains the city proper with its Victorian terraces and later estates and its large and well-established Asian community, but beyond lies an undulating lowland area of large arable farms and dairy herds stretching eastwards towards Melton Mowbray and Grantham. The *2007/8 Diocesan Yearbook* lists 183 clergy to care for 318 parish churches and worship centres. Although the diocesan bishop has no suffragan, he does enjoy the help of one part-time and one retired bishop.

the Welsh diocese

Monmouth, centred upon Newport, is by area the smallest of the Welsh dioceses. The coastal city itself has a population of just over 137,000 (2001), with tongues of dense urban development creeping up the steep-sided valleys behind, the industrial base of the whole area being originally built around coal mining and steel manufacture (Smith, 1953, pp. 289-292). The diocesan boundaries stretch from the Bristol Channel in the south up to the open tops of the Brecon Beacons in the north and from the English borders in the east, westwards towards Cardiff, spread across two archdeaconries, Newport being predominantly urban and Monmouth predominantly rural. The *2007/08 Year book* lists some 135 clergy to serve a total of 188 parish churches and other worship centres. The diocesan bishop has no suffragan and, indeed, had no other episcopal help save that of the Provincial Assistant Bishop, who happened to live within the diocese at Abergavenny.

This Assistant Bishop, who retired in 2008, served not only Monmouth, but every one of the six Welsh dioceses and was appointed by the Welsh Church in 1997 to care for the specific needs of those opposed to the ordination of women as priests. Although this might be only a minority constituency, it nonetheless totalled just over 80 active parish clergy in 2006, which, together with another 50 or so retired priests, gives it a clerical strength in excess of a smaller diocese like Bangor.

the Scottish diocese

Edinburgh is a large diocese centred upon the capital city of Scotland, extending from the Firth of Forth eastwards to the North Sea, westwards towards Glasgow and southwards towards the Northumberland border. It exhibits most of the normal industrial and commercial development of such a national centre, but grew to its present population of 448,000 (2001) not just upon its status, but also because of considerable processing industries associated with the port of Leith and the resources of the Midlothian coalfield (Smith, 1953, pp. 284-286). Away from the crowded streets of the Georgian and Victorian city, the ground rises towards the sparsely populated Southern

Uplands and the thriving rural economy is sustained by either livestock or arable farming, depending largely upon altitude. The *SEC 2007/08 Yearbook* lists some 107 clergy to serve 64 incumbencies and other worship centres. The bishop has no help apart from two retired diocesans who happen to live within the diocese. The Scottish Church has no archdeaconries.

the context of the questionnaire

It was decided at an early stage that the entire survey should be conducted by post and centred round a wide-ranging core of questions common to all three sets of respondents, whether bishops, clergy or laity. This core of questions was intended to discover what were each group's perception and evaluation of all the main aspects of a bishop's public and private diocesan functions, particularly his pastoral, teaching, disciplinary, administrative, legal, public and political responsibilities. They also sought to tease out what were each group's opinions about the qualities needed among aspiring episcopal candidates and what were their feelings about existing and alternative episcopal appointment procedures.

It had originally been intended that alongside all bishops being requested to answer the same core questions as the clergy and laity in the postal survey, extra questions could be inserted to explore more specifically their own special responsibilities and interests. It soon became clear that with such a modest total of potential episcopal respondents, a great deal more might be gained by offering them the chance to provide their own selection of interesting or unexpected details in their work experience and thereby provide an enhanced bank of qualitative information about a key group very rarely researched and still less published.

choosing the clergy to participate

In order to try to achieve a clerical response rate of at least one from each benefice in the four chosen dioceses, it was decided to send questionnaires to all full-time incumbents and assistant curates and to all non-stipendiary clergy. All chaplains engaged full-time in extra-parochial ministry, whether in hospitals, schools or prisons, even if they were without any parochial involvement as honorary curates, were similarly included. However, it was decided to exclude most retired clergy, however active they might still be in ministry, largely because the sheer weight of their numbers might skew the findings and also because many might have served their entire ministry outside the diocese where they now had permission to officiate, perhaps even in a totally different province of the Anglican Church.

It is important to clarify the position taken with regard to the non-stipendiary clergy. In all three Churches, non-stipendiaries are generally licensed to parishes as assistant curates. Because of the Scottish Church's low level of financial endowments, non-stipendiary clergy have perforce been more extensively used in parochial front-line positions of responsibility than in England. However, even in England and Wales, tightening budgets now make it no longer unusual for a non-stipendiary minister to have the pastoral charge of smaller, weaker parishes, in the inner cities as much as in the countryside. It was therefore felt vitally important to ascertain the opinions of this particular sector within the scope of a wide-ranging clergy questionnaire.

The house-for-duty principle, whereby parishes are cared for part-time by working non-stipendiaries or by active retired priests in return for a rent-free house, is now well embedded in English rural dioceses, such as Gloucester, Exeter and Salisbury and is beginning to appear in Wales as well. Seeing it has become a more significant element among diocesan personnel and in deciding ministerial strategy, and since its clergy have a regular ministerial function, this particular category of retired priest alone has been included within the scope of the questionnaire.

choosing the laity to participate

When it came to deciding which lay people should be asked to complete the questionnaire, different arrangements had to be made for each country.

In England and Wales it was felt most worthwhile to employ one of the two churchwardens, who are the main office bearers in each parish. In the event, it was decided to choose the second of those listed in each diocesan yearbook. In Scotland, where there are no churchwardens as such, the nearest equivalent seemed to be the alternate lay representative to the diocesan conference from each congregation listed in the *SEC Yearbook*.

These particular officers would be most likely to have had working contact with their bishop through being leading lay figures and his legal representatives within each parish and therefore of necessity being consulted over appointments and parochial strategy. They would also have met their bishop through attending confirmations, visitations and other formal diocesan, deanery or parochial occasions and thereby perhaps have given some thought to the work involved in being a bishop and to the personal, pastoral, liturgical, theological and managerial attributes and skills that they perceive might be necessary for the episcopal role.

After considerable thought and consultation, it was decided not to include within the survey those holding parochial Reader licenses, since unlike other laity, these folk were already likely to have given some mature consideration to the episcopate and its role and, like the clergy, to have encountered their bishop at closer quarters during their training and at their formal admission.

As detailed PCC records are not held centrally by the dioceses, it was felt that trying to involve sidespeople and others in the survey, although worthwhile in itself, might place too great a burden upon incumbents and allow some element of self-selection to creep in since they might find themselves naturally inclined to look for a person they would consider articulate enough to return a completed questionnaire. In addition, by trying to involve a wider cross-section of the laity in each parish, there might be a serious risk of presenting questionnaires to those who had never actually met or had any other direct dealings with their bishop and could therefore fall victim to the easy temptation of importing second hand opinions and prejudices culled from elsewhere, rather than causing offence to their vicar by returning a form full of blank spaces.

difficulties involved in choosing which bishops to participate

When it came to choosing bishops to participate in the survey, there were considerably more delicate considerations to be weighed. At a very early stage it was decided, in consultation with Canon Jeremy Martineau, that there would be no purpose in attempting to use the questionnaire in face-to-face interviews with the serving diocesan bishops of the four sees from which the clerical and lay respondents came. Requesting this sort of meeting would probably be asking too much of such busy men, while of itself, such a tiny total would provide an almost valueless statistical sample.

Serving bishops might also be exposed to an unfair risk of adverse publicity or even personal disaster if they were willing to be open and candid in expressing their opinions. Or else, more likely, it was felt that they might be driven into being almost totally and defensively uncommunicative in the face of a stranger whom they had no way of checking for the veracity of his motives and who might indeed be legitimately suspected of being a potentially malicious whistle-blower.

It was also considered that a bigger statistical sample of bishops was needed if the episcopal part of the survey was to have any real value. There needed to be a conscious attempt to achieve a balanced number of Catholics, Evangelicals, Liberals and maybe Charismatics and also a fair spread of those with urban and rural episcopal experience. Alongside these criteria, there would need to be a proper representation amongst the English, not merely of diocesans, but also of those suffragans who had gained personal experience of using area powers devolved from their diocesan bishop.

In the event, it was decided to approach retired bishops instead, using the same postal questionnaire. Those approached were to be every English diocesan and suffragan bishop and every Welsh and Scottish diocesan who had retired between 2000 and 2008, making a grand total of 60. It was felt that this sort of geographical distribution might be valuable in offering episcopal respondents a level of representation very roughly commensurate with the comparative strengths of the three mainland Anglican institutions from which they came. The exercise, however, depended entirely upon whether those bishops invited to participate would actually agree to do so. There was no way of knowing beforehand if they would!

matters covered in the core questionnaire

In order to safeguard the guarantee of confidentiality offered to survey participants, the only details entered onto their forms before dispatch were gender, a basic lay or clerical classification and the researcher's own estimate of the rural, suburban or inner urban nature of their parish. Finally, in an attempt to ascertain their precise churchmanship, all respondents were asked to choose which of fifteen options they felt might best represent their own personal theological viewpoint, the statements used being a modified version of those used by H.N. Malony (1995).

The first section of the questionnaire proper looked at the public and administrative aspects of a diocesan bishop's work, asking all respondents to grade by the Likert scale what they considered ought to be a bishop's priorities in terms of his known functions, such as handling clergy discipline, attending the House of Lords (in England), chairing diocesan and other committees and representing the Church within the wider spheres of civic, academic and social life.

The second section turned the spotlight upon the diocesan bishop's pastoral responsibilities towards his clergy and congregations, focusing in particular upon his special role in teaching, defending and interpreting the Christian faith, making himself personally accessible to incumbents, assistant curates and their families, caring for ordinands and their dependents and spending time among local parishes and their people, as well as acting as the local focus of Christian unity. By using the Likert scale the questionnaire asked respondents to indicate their own perceptions of what should be a bishop's priorities among these varying functions.

The third section asked respondents to rate their preferences among five possible episcopal appointment systems practised around the Anglican Communion, with alternatives ranging from appointment on the nomination of a national Church committee, as presently practised in England, through an electoral college system like that in Wales to a fully independent system of electoral democracy within the vacant diocese, common in many parts of the Anglican world. A final question in this section asked what the attitude of respondents would be to the extension of the episcopate to women or practising homosexuals, with both those for and against these developments being probed further to see if their agreement or objection were based primarily upon personal, sociological or theological factors.

additional questions for each group

Annexed to the core questionnaire were one or two extra questions aimed specifically at either the lay, clerical or episcopal constituencies. The laity were asked to state the frequency of their own contacts with their bishop and the clergy probed about whether they had in the past felt or would in the future feel able to consult bishops about spiritual, personal or parochial matters. In their turn, the bishops were to have been asked at a personal interview if they could look back over their episcopates and identify those elements of their work that they had found the most satisfying or most frustrating. In the event, the expense of travelling around the three countries to meet them face to face proved prohibitive and so this element was instead included as a supplementary item attached to the core questionnaire.

Both the core questionnaire and the supplementary material devised specifically for episcopal, clerical and lay respondents are printed in their entirety as Appendix One. Although most of the material from the questionnaires has been analysed for this publication, considerably more information was obtained, especially on the churchmanship of respondents. This presents opportunities for further research and analysis in the future.

the results of the survey

The overall results (Table 1) seem to demonstrate an astonishingly good response, despite the main underlying problem inherent in this particular exercise. Conducting a survey about bishops among the serving clergy and leading laity of an episcopally ordered Church is of necessity an extremely unusual and ultra-sensitive proceeding, the more so since most clerics, certainly in Wales and to a lesser degree in England, owe their very employment to their diocesan bishop. Because anonymity had been guaranteed in the covering letter, it was not felt appropriate to write, telephone or e-mail tardy respondents to return their survey forms.

table 1
survey response rates

LEICESTER	clergy sent	184	clergy recd	82	response	44.5 %
	laity sent	304	laity recd	161	response	52.9 %
	total	488	total	243	response	49.7 %
BRADFORD	clergy sent	136	clergy recd	72	response	52.9%
	laity sent	150	laity recd	86	response	57.3%
	total	286	total	158	response	55.2%

MONMOUTH	clergy sent	106	clergy recd	53	response	50.0%
	laity sent	183	laity recd	83	response	45.3%
	total	289	total	136	response	47.0%
EDINBURGH	clergy sent	100	clergy recd	48	response	48.0%
	laity sent	55	laity recd	28	response	50.9%
	total	155	total	76	response	49.0%
BISHOPS	sent	60	recd	25	response	41.7%

Monmouth produced the largest number of blank clergy forms returned to sender, perhaps implying that this diocese had the greatest clerical turnover of the four surveyed, while it also recorded the lowest lay response rate, maybe linked to the exceptionally tiny worship numbers in some rural parishes, which may perhaps have led to the appointment of a token churchwarden here and there.

Although the questionnaire was extensively discussed at successive forums of the Centre for the Study of Rural Ministry and altered at the suggestion of two serving bishops, the final version of the document was not actually tried out upon small groups of clergy or laity before it was rolled out to the four chosen dioceses. Had this simple preliminary been followed, subsequent problems might not have arisen.

section B—concerning a bishop's main roles

table 2

percentage agreeing with a bishop's specific primary roles all countries

Q	laity		clergy		bishops	
	%	valid total	%	valid total	%	valid total
B1 focus of unity within diocese	95	350	94	254	100	25
B2 represent diocese to wider church	90	351	88	255	96	25
B3 represent wider church to diocese	80	346	76	253	100	25
B4 support/encourage local parishes	96	348	94	254	100	25
B5 maintain succession of orders	52	336	53	250	82	22
B6 maintain apostolic doctrine	62	342	72	248	82	22
B7 with clergy first among equals	71	347	80	252	87	24

Table 2 shows that bishops were almost unanimous (97%) in agreeing with the first two of the Cameron Report's *three planes* of episcopal ministry—the bishop acting as the focus of unity within his diocese (B1) and his role in representing his diocese to the wider Church and vice versa (B2 and B3). The laity (88%) and clergy (86%) were not far behind in registering their agreement.

However, when it came to Cameron's *third plane*—the bishop maintaining the apostolic succession of doctrine (B6), the bishops' approval rate dropped to 82%, the clergy's to 72% and the laity's to 62%. Succession of orders (B5) scored marginally less: the bishops' 82% being matched by the clergy's 53% and the laity's 52%.

The bishops were surprisingly sympathetic (87%) to the idea of their being considered first among equals among their clergy (B7), but unsurprisingly the clergy only a little less so at 80% and the laity not much behind at 71%.

The bishops were unanimously in favour of giving their personal support and encouragement to local parishes and congregations (B4), which was virtually mirrored by the laity at 96% and the clergy at 94%. This strikingly strong affirmation of belief in the prime importance of the local church community is highly significant, the more so since many bishops still mistakenly persist in considering a large modern diocese to be the *local* church.

section C—a bishop's priorities

From table 3 it will be seen that the bishops gave a unanimously high priority to teaching and explaining the Christian faith (C6) and interpreting the Christian faith to the needs and challenges of our age (C8). 86% of clergy agreed with the teaching priority, but the lay proportion was even higher at 94%, while interpreting the Christian faith attracted 100% of the bishops, 94% of the clergy and 93% of the laity. Significantly, a hefty 93% of the laity prioritised the defence of the Christian faith against attack (C7), while the bishops scored 84% and the clergy slightly less at 78%.

table 3
percentage giving high priority to a range of
specific episcopal tasks all countries

Q	laity		clergy		bishops	
	%	valid total	%	valid total	%	valid total
C1 attending.national political forums	47	346	48	249	54	24
C2 attending national Church forums	89	352	85	251	88	25
C3 attending diocesan synod/cttees	84	351	86	253	92	25
C4 attending secular public events	62	351	71	253	92	25
C5 handling clergy discipline	83	349	68	254	92	25
C6 teaching/explaining Christian faith	94	350	86	252	100	25
C7 defending Christian faith	93	351	78	251	84	25

C8 interpreting Christian faith	93	348	94	254	100	25
C9 knowing individual clergy	85	350	88	253	100	25
C10 knowing individual ordinands	72	351	80	253	72	25
C11 knowing individual readers	43	352	52	253	48	25
C12 knowing individual churchwardens	33	351	34	254	58	24
C13 knowing groups of teachers	32	352	21	254	40	25
C14 knowing groups of councillors	31	349	32	253	48	25
C15 knowing community groups	47	353	35	254	48	25

The bishops gave a level score of 92% to attending diocesan synods and their committees (C3), attending secular public events within the diocese (C4) and handling clergy discipline (C5). The laity at 84% were slightly less enamoured of the diocesan synod, while the clergy were far less enthusiastic about clergy discipline (68%), whereas the laity were considerably more so at 83%, maybe because they invariably find themselves at the receiving end of most complaints about misconduct and incompetence among the parochial clergy.

In terms of getting to know particular groups of people, bishops were unanimous in giving priority to clergy and their families (C9), with which both clergy and laity concurred to a lesser but still overwhelming degree at 88% and 85% respectively. Ordinands and their families (C10) came next for the bishops at 72% and also for the laity at 72%, but here the clergy were predictably more in favour at 80%.

Among other *people* priorities for the bishops, churchwardens (C12) were rated important by 58%, whereas the clergy were less concerned at 34% and the laity least of all at 33%—the more surprising since they were all churchwardens themselves! 52% of clergy gave high priority to readers (C11) and least to local teachers (C13) at 21%, while a significant minority of laity (47%) prioritised local community groups (C15), where they were pretty well exactly matched by the bishops (48%).

Surprisingly, opinions among all three categories of respondents were evenly divided about the priority that should be accorded to the House of Lords and other national political forums (C1), with the bishops the keenest at 54% and the laity least so at 47%.

section D—some controversial topics

This pot-pourri of statements produced some interesting results about attitudes towards certain topical issues. With regard to those loosely connected with pay and conditions of employment, there was little support for bishops having at least eight weeks holiday per year (D1), bishops themselves proving least impressed at 17%, neither was there much enthusiasm for bishops being paid the same as parish clergy (D6), least of all from the laity at 13%. Bishops having a fixed term contract (D7) registered the support of a modest 34% of the laity, compared to 26% of clergy and only 16% of bishops.

table 4
percentage of those agreeing with certain
statements about bishops all countries

Q	laity		clergy		bishops	
	%	valid total	%	valid total	%	valid total
D1 at least 8 weeks holiday per year	20	350	27	251	17	25
D2 model good work/life balance	84	353	89	253	88	25
D3 media give fair portrayal	25	353	19	254	4	25
D4 work with local media of bps	85	353	79	253	84	25
D5 too much money spent on bps	34	351	24	252	24	25
D6 should be paid same as clergy	13	351	24	252	24	25
D7 appointed for fixed term	34	350	26	255	16	25

D8 delegate all administration	43	351	45	248	33	24
D9 accessible day/night	59	353	47	255	84	25
D10 parish not diocese basic block	86	352	75	254	60	25

Bishops delegating administrative tasks to their archdeacons (D8) attracted 43% of the laity and 45% of the clergy, but only a third of bishops. The biggest surprise was the overwhelming 84% of bishops who were in agreement with their being accessible to clergy day or night (D9). The laity at 59% were also significantly supportive, but the clergy less so at 47%. There were overwhelmingly positive responses by all three groups to the proposition that bishops should model a good work/life balance (D2), but quite how this might be achieved against the heavy demands made by both clergy and laity in other parts of the survey remains an open question.

Not surprisingly, only a tiny 4% of bishops felt that the media portrayed them fairly (D3), but there was a similar lack of satisfaction among the clergy (19%) and not much more among the laity (25%). Laity (85%) and bishops (84%) were overwhelmingly in favour of bishops working with the local media to improve the image of the Church (D4), with the clergy not far behind at 79%.

At 86% the laity strongly agreed with the proposition that the parish, rather than the diocese should be considered the main building block of the Church, with the clergy not far behind at 75% and even the bishops themselves weighing in at 60%.

section E—women bishops and practising homosexual bishops

The proposition that the episcopate should be open to women (E1) was agreed to by an overall 72% of clergy in the four dioceses of England, Wales and Scotland; a healthy but perhaps not overwhelming majority. The laity overall concurred slightly less with the idea at 67%, whereas at 84% the bishops' support was decidedly stronger.

However, when the results are analysed by diocese, it is clear that Edinburgh at 83% for the clergy and 82% for the laity is well ahead of the two combined English diocesan figures of 72% for the clergy and 69% for the laity.

In Monmouth clergy and laity in favour dropped to 63% and 60% respectively, just failing to reach the two thirds majority the proposition would need to marshal if it were to be passed by the Welsh Governing Body.

table 5
section E—those agreeing with women bishops and practising homosexual bishops

E1 women bishops	%	valid total	E2 practising homosexual bishops	%valid	total
Leicester /Bradford			**Leicester/Bradford**		
clergy	72	111	clergy	26	40
laity	69	165	laity	15	38
total	70	276	total	20	78
Monmouth			**Monmouth**		
clergy	60	31	clergy	23	12
laity	63	52	laity	16	13
total	61	83	total	19	25
Edinburgh			**Edinburgh**		
clergy	83	40	clergy	51	24
laity	82	33	laity	41	11
total	82	73	total	46	35
Bishops	84	21	**Bishops**	24	6

When it came to the proposition that the episcopate should be open to practising homosexuals (E2), the response was quite different. Taking together the figures for all four dioceses, those who agreed with this possibility gained only 17% among the laity but a noticeably better 30% among the clergy, with almost exactly a quarter of the bishops agreeing.

Broken down by dioceses, the Edinburgh result was by far the most positive, with a bare majority of clergy and 41% of laity agreeing to the idea. However, the English and Welsh laity were uniformly unenthusiastic, the idea scoring only 15% in Leicester/Bradford and, 16% in Monmouth. However, the clergy were more sympathetic in Leicester/Bradford with 26% and in Monmouth 23% agreed.

The fact that the results from Edinburgh show a much more liberal attitude towards female and gay bishops than those from the other two countries may merit closer examination. The capital city undoubtedly played a pivotal role in the C18 Scottish Enlightenment and its cosmopolitan feel in modern times owes a great deal to its famous Festival and Fringe held there each summer. In recent years it has been presided over by liberal-leaning bishops, among whom Richard Holloway was by far the most controversial and high-profile. Maybe the results might have been different in other Scottish dioceses.

section F—how bishops should be chosen

Respondents were presented with five choices of methods that might be used to appoint bishops, ranging from the existing Welsh electoral college system through to a free and open democratic election as used in most Anglican provinces of Africa, Asia and the Americas. The question asked them to place their preferences *in merit order from 1 to 5,* which might have been expected to produce the requisite figures within the boxes provided for each of them. In fact, because choice 1 was not clearly identified as *most preferred* and choice 5 as *least preferred*, some appeared to think that they should assign a Likert scale number to each alternative. Where respondents' intentions were not clear, their answers have been discounted from the results. In addition a small proportion of lay respondents felt unable to tackle this question because they claimed to have insufficient knowledge to do so. For these reasons, this section of the survey proved the most disappointing, with total respondents down by just over a hundred to 82% of the average rate of replies in the other sections.

In view of the end of direct Crown involvement in episcopal appointments in England, the first choices of method in the two English dioceses were of especial interest (fig 7). Clergy in Leicester/Bradford seemed most comfortable with an electoral college where the vacant diocese held a majority of seats (F2), this option scoring 52, with the other electoral college option gaining 29 and a totally open election 27. By contrast, the Leicester/Bradford laity were most enthusiastic for a totally open diocesan election (F5), which scored 68, a diocesan election with closed candidate list (F3) coming second at 63 and a diocesan election with an open candidate list requiring later episcopal consent (F4) in third place at 39. The Leicester/Bradford laity were not particularly supportive of either two electoral college methods (F1 and F2), which scored only 31 each.

The Monmouth results were also illuminating in view of the fact that option F1 is in fact the existing electoral system in Wales. A fair number of clergy favoured this option (12), but they were well outnumbered by a combination of the 14 who preferred a totally free and unfettered election (F5) and the 10 who favoured an open candidate list with its result subject to later approval by the House of Bishops (F4). Among the first choices of the Monmouth laity, only a paltry 10 favoured the existing Welsh system (F1), whereas 59 preferred one or another of the three diocesan election systems, with F4 just the leader. Thus there appears to be only minority support for the way things are at present handled in Wales.

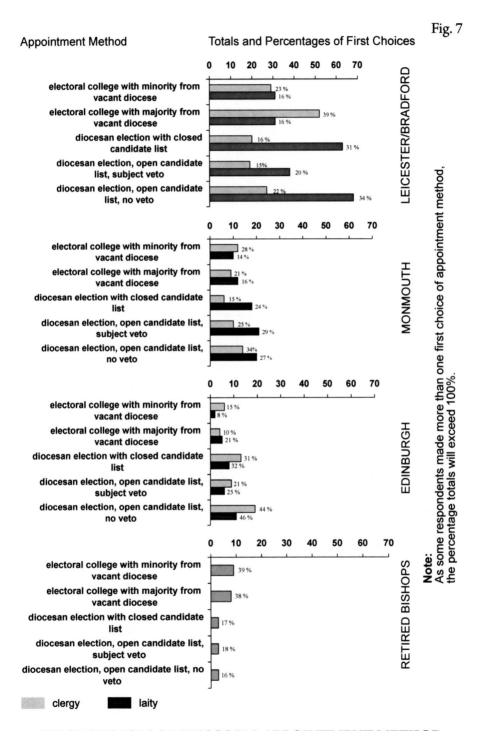

Fig. 7

Appointment Method

Totals and Percentages of First Choices

FIRST CHOICES OF EPISCOPAL APPOINTMENT METHOD

The present Scottish appointment system, which is basically the closed election of F3, proved to be only second favourite among the Edinburgh clergy with 13 first choices. A completely open and unfettered election (F5) came top with 19 and the laity demonstrated a similar preference for F5 with 11, while F3 came second with 8 and F4 third with 6. This diocese certainly seems to favour the more open Scottish electoral procedures that obtained before the steady rise of central interference began in 1973.

Bishops, as might have been expected, showed a marked preference for the electoral college system, with F1 in the lead of first choices at 9, a whisker ahead of F2 with 8, while all the the democratic election options were condemned to trail far behind with only 3 each.

table 6
percentage of combined first and second choices of episcopal appointment methods (F1-F5) by diocese and by clergy, laity and retired bishops

	val. total	top 2	%	val. total	top 2	%
Leicester		clergy			laity	
F1 electoral college minority from vacant diocese	66	30	45	127	35	27
F2 electoral college majority from vacant diocese	70	47	67	131	43	33
F3 diocesan election closed candidate list	65	26	40	132	72	54
F4 diocesan election. open, result later vetted by bps	64	26	41	130	77	59
F5 diocesan election, open, no later vetting by bps	63	15	24	132	58	44
Bradford						
F1 electoral college minority from vacant diocese	61	28	46	67	23	34
F2 electoral college majority from vacant diocese	62	31	50	64	27	42
F3 diocesan election closed candidate list	59	24	41	70	34	48
F4 diocesan election, open, result later vetted by bps	59	28	47	67	34	51
F5 diocesan election, open, no later vetting by bps	59	19	32	69	32	46

Monmouth

F1 electoral college minority from vacant diocese	42	19	45	72	20	28
F2 electoral college majority from vacant diocese	42	25	59	71	27	38
F3 diocesan election closed candidate list	39	14	36	74	41	55
F4 diocesan election, open, result later vetted by bps	40	20	50	72	42	58
F5 diocesan election, open, no later vetting by bps	41	16	39	73	26	36

Edinburgh

F1 electoral college minority from vacant diocese	40	7	17	24	5	21
F2 electoral college majority from vacant diocese	39	10	26	24	5	21
F3 diocesan election closed candidate list	42	19	45	25	13	52
F4 diocesan election, open, result later vetted by bps	43	31	72	24	16	67
F5 diocesan election, open, no later vetting by bps	43	23	53	24	17	71

Bishops

F1 electoral college minority from vacant diocese	23	14	61
F2 electoral college majority from vacant diocese	21	14	67
F3 diocesan election closed candidate list	18	8	44
F4 diocesan election, open, result later vetted by bps	17	6	35
F5 diocesan election, open, no later vetting by bps	17	6	35

When first and second choices are combined (table 6) the trends in opinion are the same, but less marked. Among the Leicester and Bradford clergy the electoral college with a majority membership from the vacant diocese (F2) still comes out on top, whereas F4 comes out slightly ahead of F3 among the laity.

However, putting together first and second choices in Monmouth shows the clergy coming out in favour of the more diocesan weighted F2 and the laity almost neck and neck between the more open F4 and the diocesan election with a closed candidate list (F3)—still demonstrating a clear lack of support for the present system.

In Edinburgh the clergy unmistakeably prefer F4 and the laity F5, the totally open and unfettered diocesan election system, suggesting once again that the change towards a more closed electoral system in Scotland is not where most clergy and laity wish to go.

Fig. 8

LAY PEOPLE'S CONTACT WITH THEIR OWN BISHOP
totals for all four survey dioceses

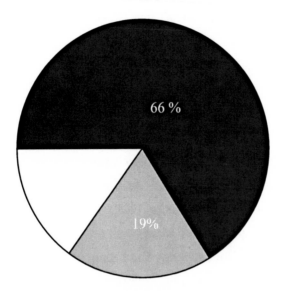

valid total 352

I have met my bishop face to face at least once in a past year
I have met my bishop face to face at least once in a past two years

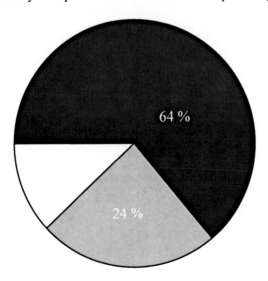

valid total 344

I have heard my bishop face to face at least once in a past year
I have heard my bishop face to face at least once in a past two years

A very small number of respondents complained quite correctly that all the options presented on the survey form presupposed a secret ballot, which they did not feel sat easily with the way such major decisions ought to be made in an institution claiming to be a Christian Church. To them it seemed that the Church should be anxious to embrace more openness, both in its internal affairs and in its response to the guidance of the Holy Spirit.

section F—lay contact with bishops

Fig. 8 shows that across all four dioceses the laity scored a good 66% when it came to reporting that they had met their bishop face to face at least once during the previous twelve months (H1), while almost exactly the same proportion said that they had heard him preach or speak at least once during the previous year (H2). Once meeting the bishop and hearing him at least once were allowed a two year span, the figures rose to an impressive 85% and 88% respectively, suggesting, like the response to C12, that the link between bishop and churchwarden is better than might be expected, especially in Wales, where big distances between parishes and their bishop might be expected to exercise an adverse effect.

table 7

percentage of laity who have met their bishop at least once in the past one or two years (H1) and have heard him preach or speak at least once in those same periods (H2) all countries

H1 met bishop

	valid total	in last yr	%	in last 2 yrs	%	total	%
	352	233	66	66	19	299	85

H2 heard bishop

	344	221	64	83	24	304	88

section I—clergy consulting bishops

Table 9 shows an overwhelming 84% of clergy agreeing that they would be willing to consult bishops on parochial matters (I3), well ahead of 63% on spiritual (I1) and 58% on personal matters (I2).

table 8
Section I—clergy willing to consult a bishop and those helped by doing so
all countries

	valid total	agree	neutral	disagree	% agreeing
I1 would consult on spiritual matter	251	159	45	48	63
I2 would consult on personal matter	250	146	54	50	58
I3 would consult on parish matter	252	212	25	15	84
I4 helped by consulting bishop on spiritual matter	237	80	92	65	34
I5 helped by consulting bishop on personal matter	244	103	73	68	42
I6 helped by consulting bishop on parish matter	243	127	69	47	52

By contrast, the numbers of those clergy who agreed that they had been positively helped by consulting a bishop were considerably less on all three counts, totalling 52% on parochial questions (I6), 42% on personal matters (I5), and only 34% on spiritual concerns (I4), suggesting that clergy expectations of their bishops, although already fairly modest, are not matched by their actual experience at the very times when they need the ear of their bishop the most (see fig. 9).

Fig. 9

CLERGY OPINIONS ON CONSULTING BISHOPS ABOUT PROBLEMS
totals for all four survey dioceses

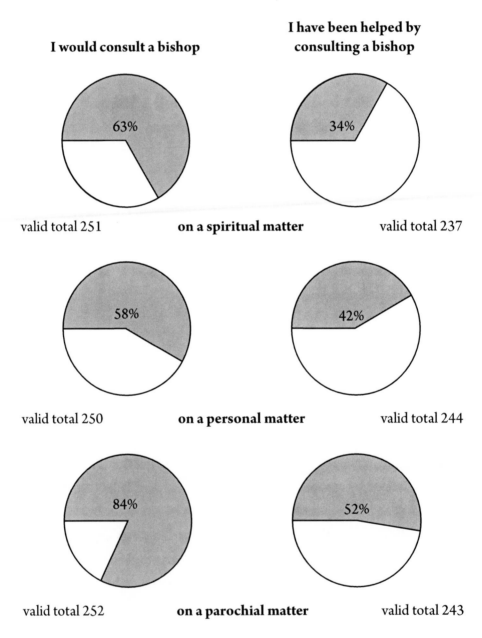

I would consult a bishop

I have been helped by consulting a bishop

63%

34%

valid total 251   **on a spiritual matter**   valid total 237

58%

42%

valid total 250   **on a personal matter**   valid total 244

84%

52%

valid total 252   **on a parochial matter**   valid total 243

A 32% drop between being those willing to consult on a parish matter and those being satisfied with the consultation seems inordinately high and suggests that bishops may be less happy at a managerial level than they are on the more obviously pastoral plane. It is perhaps worth mentioning in passing that a small number of respondents said that they preferred to use the services of a spiritual director in these circumstances.

CHAPTER ELEVEN

Bishops' Views on the Episcopate

the nature of the response

The bishops who completed the common spine of the questionnaire totalled some 24, but 21 of them, not all the same individuals, returned their supplementary sheet, including one who did not return his survey form but sent instead an amazingly comprehensive and detailed evaluation of his episcopal ministry. This means that overall there was a 41.7% response rate, quite a satisfactory result in view of the especially delicate personal nature of the questions and the natural reluctance many must have felt in replying in such detail to someone they did not know and whose personal, academic and ministerial credentials they had no chance of checking, since at that time the researcher had no entry in the Crockford Clerical Directory. As only 19 of all 60 bishops contacted (31.6%) managed to complete both parts of the survey, this weakens the statistical value of the exercise. Whatever is lacking in figures, however, is amply compensated for by the big qualitative value of the responses.

Interestingly, most of the forms were returned very quickly and none arrived long after the exercise should have been completed, as was the case with several clerical and lay responses. Two senior retired English diocesans and one retired Scottish high-profile diocesan declined to take part in any way. This was especially disappointing since their contributions might have been particularly unusual and illuminating.

The questionnaires were dispatched in August, 2008 to all bishops in England, Wales and Scotland who had retired between January 2000 and June 2008. This total included all former diocesan, area, suffragan and flying bishops, including those who had retired abroad. In the finish 22 English, three Scottish and one Welsh bishop responded. The particularly thin result from Wales underlines once again how claustrophobic the Welsh Church appears to have become since Disestablishment. Because free and open expression of opinion has been deemed in the past to somehow betray a destructive and disloyal attitude towards the institution, it is almost impossible to discover reliable information about where the work of the Church is succeeding or failing or what its members may actually be thinking about current issues or where they hope to see new developments in the future.

opinions on women bishops

Despite an overwhelming 84% of retired bishops being in favour of E1, the consecration of women to the episcopate still remains a highly contentious issue, and therefore the precise reasons behind the opinions of bishops in their role as senior churchmen are important to ascertain. In response to the subsidiary question, six respondents failed to give any reasons for the Likert scale they had assigned to this question. Of the remaining 19, nine (47%) gave primarily theological, two (11%) sociological and eight (42%) mixed theological and sociological reasons for their decision. Equality was mentioned by only two, but five made the direct implication that since women could already be ordained priests, they could equally well be consecrated bishops, one English bishop reversing this argument by expressing the historically dubious but nonetheless widely held opinion that *the priest's ministry is an extension of the bishop's.*

One English bishop expressing his support for women bishops said, *what is of salvific importance is Christ's humanity, not his masculinity. Theological reasons for restricting ministry to males (in the capacity of representing Christ to the Church) therefore fail.* Another English bishop explained why it was his duty to support the proposition: *It is the work of the Gospel to do so; the talents and calling are God's gift and a sign that the Church is absorbing the message of all one in Christ.* Yet another English supporter said that *the Church's leadership should reflect the inclusive character of humanity redeemed in Christ,* which was amplified by a northern English diocesan, who said, *The Body of Christ is to be an inclusive community of people, male and female, since God is not merely Father, but the ultimate reality of what all—he, she or it—are part.* However, one Scottish bishop made the extraordinary theological jump of claiming that *women in the threefold ministry is the fruit of Catholic belief!*

Of the small number who disagreed with the proposition, none took the trouble to give their theological reasons beyond merely citing Scripture and tradition, but one English bishop made the practical point that *women would not be able to provide unity in a diocese.* Among those who quoted Christ himself, there were quite opposite conclusions, a Welsh supporter saying that *we need to catch up with Christ's attitude to women* and an English objector replying that *the Lord chose twelve men as his Apostles.* However, two supporters entered caveats, a northern English diocesan stating, *my reservation is that women becoming bishops is likely to further impede cohesion with our Roman Catholic brothers and sisters.* The other supporter also generously suggested that *provision should be made for accommodating those who disagree and a code of practice seems feasible.*

It has since become abundantly clear that opponents distrust this sort of imprecisely expressed goodwill, however charitably expressed. They have now arrived at a situation where they will never be able to settle for anything less than a structural solution embedded within the legislation that will have to be enacted in order to create women bishops.

practising gay bishops

In reply to E2, which requested Likert scale scores on the issue of ordaining practising gays as bishops, the retired prelates were markedly less enthusiastic, with only 24% in favour. Of the 21 responses to the subsidiary question, seven (33%) gave theological reasons, three sociological ones (14%) and one a mixture of the two (5%). The remainder made qualifying observations that could not be classified under any of these three headings, but are important to record for their sheer variety.

Nearly all those who gave theological reasons for their score were against the proposition, three quoting the Ordinal. One English bishop said that *bishops and priests should present to the world the ideal for Christian life and be prepared to live sacrificially, upholding traditional Christian values and standards.* A northern opponent said that he was aware that *sexual practice today is not merely about re-creation—babies,—but recreation—pleasure. I think that we need to hold to the importance of marriage as the normal way of relationships.*

Another English opponent, while admitting that *the moral propriety of active homosexual behaviour, especially in a representative person, is a matter of legitimate dispute,* went on to add that *if it is a part of the bishop's role to be a focus of unity, restraint should be exercised for the sake of unity: Paul's argument in Romans 14 is relevant.* An English bishop who agreed with the proposition, nevertheless interpreted this passage of Scripture the same way, arguing that the needs of the *weaker brothers* called for voluntary restraint where a church was seriously divided on the issue, but in his view this would be *at the cost of injustice to individuals.*

A Scottish bishop pointed out, perhaps mischievously, that *practising homosexuals have for years been made bishops in the Church of England and in the Roman Catholic Church.* He then went on to say that he knows of *no reasonable Scriptural arguments against.* This somehow suggests that for not a few supporters of practising gay bishops, Scriptural evidence can be readily ignored if they judge it to be *unreasonable* when it does not support their own particular point of view.

All five bishops who were neutral on the E2 issue gave broadly similar reasons for their ambivalence. One English bishop claimed that this development would be *inappropriate given current circumstances,* whereas another English prelate said that *the issue for me is whether society or local congregations can receive episcopal ministry from such a person.* Another English bishop cautioned, *I don't think we should be canvassing to have practising homosexuals as bishops,* but another felt that although the general consensus was not yet sufficient to proceed, *public opinion is softening.* An English opponent declared that *the time is not yet ripe for this, nor is it yet certain that homosexual orientation is innate, as opposed to learned behaviour.* The solitary Welsh bishop, who was also against the idea, called it simply *a distraction.*

what bishops found their most satisfying work

The supplementary questions asking respondents about the satisfactions and the frustrations of their episcopal ministry intentionally avoided using a *tick-box* approach. It was deemed especially valuable to allow those who now no longer held major responsibilities but had plenty of time on their hands, the opportunity to put down their own conclusions in their own way, which several made a matter for commendation. Because they had retired sufficiently recently, they would still have clear memories of their experiences in office. One said with some surprise *I've never been asked these questions before.* The wealth of information provided was astonishing in its detail and frankness.

62% of the bishops said that they gained satisfaction in the pastoral care of their clergy, one of the English prelates emphasising that he tried to do it *on a systematic ongoing basis rather than crisis-orientated.* An English rural diocesan reported that as trust was built up between himself and his clerical colleagues *I really felt that in many ways it was like an extended family,* while a Northern diocesan said that *it was a privilege to meet so many clergy—and laity—who are seeking to live and work for the furthering of God's kingdom here on earth: they were a stimulus to my own life and witness and gave me good stories to pass on to other people.*

Spending time in the parishes came second in the score sheet, with 57% rating it as satisfying work. One English bishop called his parish visitations *on the whole a great restorative,* and it was obvious that many bishops used these occasions as a springboard to meet widely differing groups of people, at home, in the workplace and in the school. One English bishop enjoyed holding open forums on his parish visits in order to allow questions and discussion on any topic that parishioners wished to raise.

Maybe intimately connected with time spent in the parishes, community involvement came joint third with 48%. One English rural diocesan said that because of this social component, for him *being a bishop is much less churchy than being an archdeacon.* One English bishop made a point of saying how much he enjoyed being involved with urban regeneration, while an English rural diocesan remembered *making a useful contribution to the world of farming and rural life, especially through the dreadful circumstance of BSE and Foot and Mouth Disease.* Another former diocesan in an English rural diocese of only half a million people felt that his area was *big enough to be really interesting, but small enough to come to know and work with many local community leaders.*

Sharing third place at 48% was leading and being part of a diocesan team. One English bishop praised his *creative senior staff,* while another said that *compared with other bishops we had a happy and harmonious staff meeting.* The unexpectedly high level of satisfaction with this aspect of episcopal ministry may perhaps reflect the fact that bishops are acutely conscious of the dangers of isolation from their fellow clergy because of their position as organs of ecclesiastical discipline. Being surrounded by senior staff like their cathedral dean and archdeacons enables them to confide their concerns and plans to a close circle, so that they can help in setting priorities and share in the episcopal burden of allocating time between the varied demands of so many parishes and individuals.

Conducting confirmations scored rather less than might be expected, coming in at fifth place with 43%. An English rural diocesan explained that *I made a priority of confirmations and pre-confirmation visits to the candidates, which I found to be an excellent teaching opportunity.* One bishop helped to prepare candidates for confirmation himself, saying that he gained particular satisfaction from *stimulating young people.* This milestone occasion of conscious Christian commitment offers a wonderful opportunity of meeting not only the candidates, but also their extended families and friends, both within the formalities of the service itself and in an informal setting afterwards over refreshments. It is therefore something of a disappointment that bishops were such a long way from giving confirmations a unanimous satisfaction rating.

Teaching and preaching came sixth with 38%. Since this is such a prime function of the Apostolate in the New Testament and of the episcopate through-out Christian, and especially Anglican history, this lowish satisfaction score is worrying, the more so since proclamation and explanation are basic methods of communication—very much the buzz word of our age. Sadly, there was not even a hint that a bishop might be an active evangelist or apologist for the Christian faith. However, one Scottish bishop mentioned how much he enjoyed preaching at the Maundy Thursday gatherings of his clergy *and washing the feet of those who were willing to be washed,* while an English bishop enjoyed *preaching across the whole spectrum of churchmanship.*

Caring for ordinands and conducting their subsequent ordinations came well down in the scoring at seventh place, with only 33%. This again was something of a surprise, since looking after this group has traditionally been a principal function of the episcopate. One English area bishop from an urban diocese gained much satisfaction from *bringing on ordinands* and a Scottish bishop enjoyed ordaining clergy *with whom you have shared their preceding discernment.*

Taking services came further down at eighth position with 28%, but here there were some particularly illuminating comments. One English bishop gained satisfaction from *always celebrating the eucharist,* while an English urban suffragan enjoyed *devising and leading worship for special events* and another enjoyed *stimulating excellence in parish worship and liturgy, dispelling clerical slovenliness.* A bishop who had held an ancient English see with a house in the mediaeval cathedral close was glad of the opportunity *to join with the cathedral community for daily worship—much better than a lonely bishop's private chapel!*

Other episcopal satisfactions included visiting schools and colleges (24%), attending synods and committees (19%), dealing with the media (14%) and conducting retreats and pilgrimages (14%). One English bishop was clearly delighted to be able to use these latter occasions *to help folk pray in a prayerless world.*

Attending the House of Lords also scored 14%. Because the survey results included Welsh and Scottish bishops as well as English suffragans, who would not have had the experience of Parliamentary work, this response is probably a little misleading. If all those who had not served as English diocesans had been removed from the arithmetic, a much more positive note might have emerged. One English rural diocesan wrote of his seven years in the Lords, *I enjoyed it very much and thought it a huge privilege. It was important, especially with a government which had a huge majority and little competence in legislation, or even less inclination to subject legislation to proper scrutiny.*

An English diocesan happened to be one of only 14% who gave a satisfaction rating to the development of ministry. For him *lay ministry was a priority in a predominantly rural diocese, which during my thirteen years in office had to accept a steady decline in the number of stipendiary clergy. Drawing on some inspiring examples from the French Roman Catholic Church, we were able to create well-trained, well-motivated teams of lay people, eventually in about half of the benefices.*

Administration had been satisfying for 14% and ecumenical contacts for 14%, but help for the Church overseas and relations with other faiths scored only a disappointing one each. The satisfaction percentages are expressed graphically in fig. 11.

One English rural diocesan, who had enjoyed holding confirmations, leading pilgrimages, visiting parishes regularly and encouraging his clergy to make a habit of themselves visiting their parishioners, made an unexpectedly touching observation—he was astonished at the welcome he received in every parish he visited and *there was a genuine sense of feeling that I was being prayed for by so many people.* This seems to be nothing less than a heartfelt and spontaneous response by clergy and people to his own intense personal commitment to the episcopal role.

the flip-side—episcopal frustrations

Not surprisingly, lack of time came top of episcopal frustrations at 57%, not just because of constant juggling of responsibilities and engagements, but as one English bishop said, because of *trying to find time for extended reflection.* Another English bishop complained of weariness—*at times I really did get very tired by non-stop busyness and expectations,* while another English bishop was frustrated by *having too many demands on the go at the same time—too much of a good thing!*

Right up at second place (52%) came dealing with problematic clergy. Pent-up episcopal frustrations were painfully obvious in the sharpness of some of the comments. One Scottish bishop described the problem as *dealing with lazy, opportunistic and embittered clergy,* while an English area bishop complained of *a lack of urgency, imagination, professionalism, leadership ability and training among some of the clergy.* Another English suffragan battled with *clerical complacency and ineptitude.* For one English diocesan, administering clergy discipline took up *endless time,* while another sighed over the *virtual impossibility (or great difficulty) of dealing with ineffective, idle or immoral clergy who cause scandal to congregations and the wider public.* An English rural diocesan found himself in difficulty *moving on clergy who were obviously in the wrong job and out of sympathy with diocesan policies and priorities, or just not very competent or diligent—but who hung on tenaciously!* An interesting related comment came from an English bishop, who had experienced obvious frustration in *trying to get incumbents and assistant clergy to listen and talk to each other before their working relationship crumbled.*

Fig. 10

PERCENTAGE FRUSTRATION RATES WITH ASPECTS OF EPISCOPAL MINISTRY

Anglican bishops in mainland Britain who retired between January 2000 and June 2008

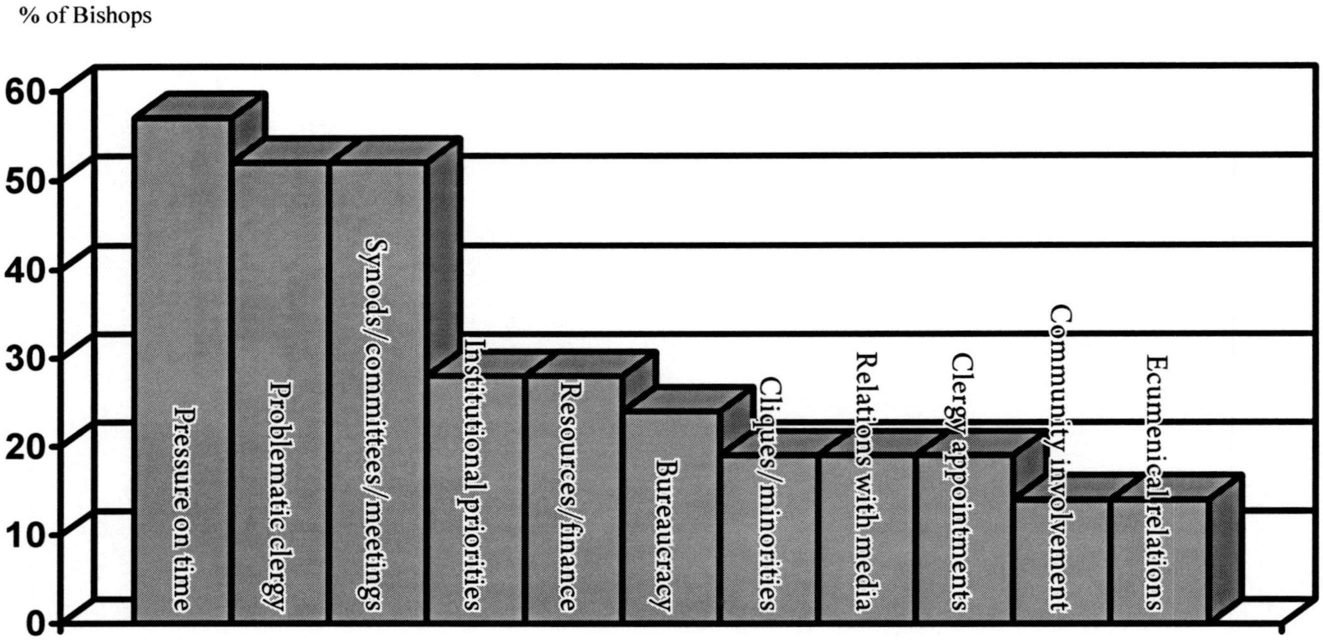

% of Bishops

Ecumenical relations
Community involvement
Clergy appointments
Relations with media
Cliques/minorities
Bureaucracy
Resources/finance
Institutional priorities
Synods/committees/meetings
Problematic clergy
Pressure on time

60 50 40 30 20 10 0

The sheer number and colour of these comments strongly suggests that the problem of unsuitable, incompetent or lazy clergy is far more widespread than is generally recognised and that the mechanisms for handling it are both time-consuming and manifestly inadequate. One Scottish bishop added a worrying dimension of his own when he complained of *inheriting senior people already in post—a football manager takes with him his managerial team when he moves to a new club—quite often a new bishop has people working against him.*

Attending synods, committees and meetings came third in the episcopal frustration table scoring 48%. One English complaint was about having to travel so frequently to London for meetings, whereas for an English Provincial Episcopal Visitor, the natural complaint was finding himself in bishop's staff meetings *where the diocesan and those he had appointed were antipathetic to the traditionalist position.* One English area bishop's frustration arose out of having to attend *meetings which could be badly chaired, lacking in professionalism and go on too long.*

Lack of resources and finance came in fourth at 28%, with marginally more complaints about this from area bishops, one of whom observed that *I did not have sufficient support, financial or practical, for the running of a large area of the diocese—larger than some complete dioceses.*

Sharing fourth place with 28% was a general frustration with the priorities of the Church as an institution. This was expressed most clearly by an English diocesan who spoke frankly of his discomfort at *being part of the leadership of an institution that ignores and overrides the integrity of local communities and individuals and being part of a body that is so concerned with image and success and so anxious about finance—and yet so inadequate in dealing with each other.* An English area bishop spoke of his frustration at *the increasing pre-occupation inside the Church with its own organisational structures and internal life,* while the Welsh bishop gave vent to his feeling that *so many of our discussions in synods and committees are irrelevant to the actual needs of the contemporary world.*

Fig. 11

PERCENTAGE SATISFACTION RATES WITH ASPECTS OF EPISCOPAL MINISTRY

Anglican bishops in mainland Britain who retired between January 2000 and June 2008

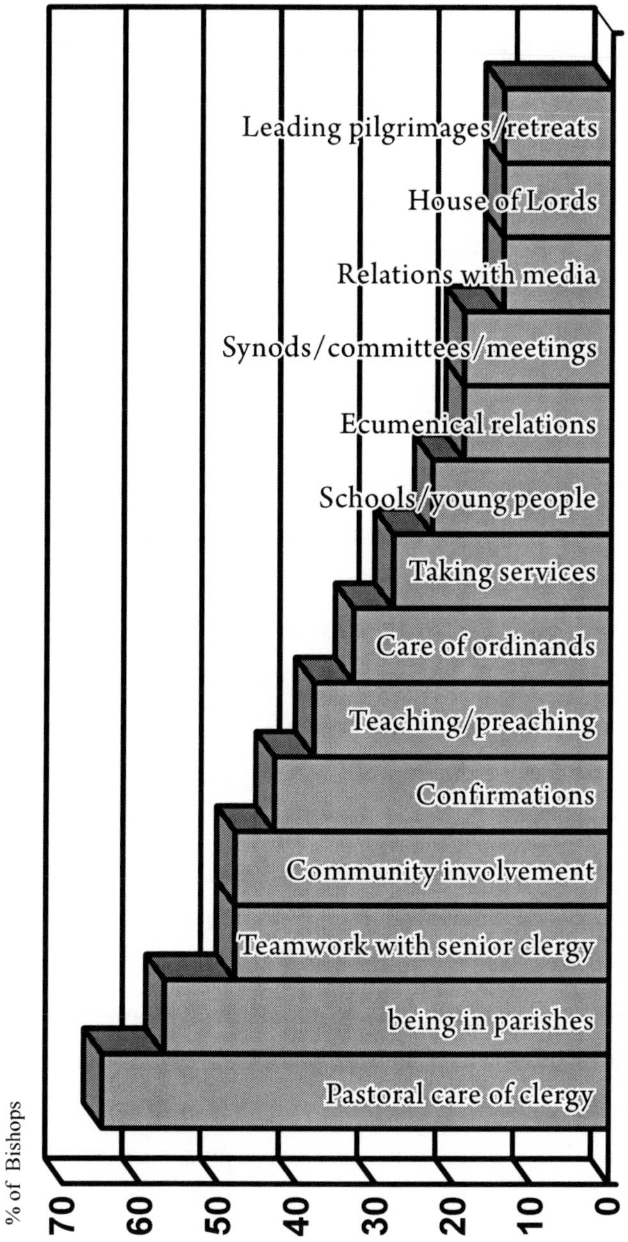

% of Bishops

Leading pilgrimages/retreats

House of Lords

Relations with media

Synods/committees/meetings

Ecumenical relations

Schools/young people

Taking services

Care of ordinands

Teaching/preaching

Confirmations

Community involvement

Teamwork with senior clergy

being in parishes

Pastoral care of clergy

70 60 50 40 30 20 10 0

Sixth place at 24% was given to bureaucracy. One English bishop spoke of *a mountain of paper* while another said that *recent years have seen an increase in bureaucratic expectations without provision of resources to meet them*. Another lamented that he suffered *constant bombardment of correspondence and committee-generated tasks as the Church continually changed the goalposts on finance and staffing*. Yet another was forced to spend too much energy *responding to projects and issues imposed from on high*.

Dealing with cliques and minority pressure groups made seventh place at 19%. One Scottish bishop declared his frustration with *clergy and laity who thought that their way was the only and the right way*, while an English diocesan complained of *having to bear the systematic orchestration of demands by minorities with the Church of England*. This bishop also said that he *bore the abuse and annoyance of people, lay and ordained, at the disturbance of their familiar way of doing church, especially on issues of status, parochial and personal*.

In similar vein, another English bishop spoke of *the entrenched griping of organisations which aim to keep the Church in the past and to press only their own view*. Another English bishop spoke of *dealing with closed cliques with no give and take—or clergy who choose to isolate themselves and then complain of being marginalised!* Party groupings of Catholics and Evangelicals and traditionalists like the Prayer Book Society seem to be the target here, but the question might well be asked whether some bishops, by their offhand and somewhat dismissive tone, failed to accord these legitimate groups the attention they deserved and may themselves have been the authors of at least some of their own frustrations.

The issue of appointments, which are such an important part of a bishop's workload, featured at joint seventh place with 19%. One English rural diocesan expressed his frustration at finding problems in *attracting good and enthusiastic clergy to work in a deeply rural area—jobs for spouses, schooling, transport and the heavy financial strain caused by living on their stipend without having a second income*. Another English bishop was sad at *not being able to give good opportunities for clergy, particularly those in mid-ministry*.

Also sharing seventh place with 19% came relationships with the media. One Northern diocesan felt particularly vulnerable at a time when the organised Church appeared to be in decline and he complained that he was being misunderstood by the media, *thought to be interested only in religion as an activity that competes for public support with politics, work, leisure and so on, whereas my interest is in God, who can make the whole of life more rich.*

14% complained about slow progress on the ecumenical front. One English diocesan was particularly frustrated by ecumenical geography, with the irritation of its overlapping denominational boundaries, while another English bishop graphically described ecumenical work *like wading through mud.*

Some topics were raised by only one bishop each, but are striking enough to warrant separate mention. One English diocesan complained of having to *debrief failed ordinands who cannot see their own blindspots,* while another made the point that while he had enjoyed the job in its totality, he had come to the surprising conclusion that *on the whole the bishop is irrelevant to the daily life of the local church.* Yet another said that his main frustration was *not being able to spend more time in the parishes.* The frustration percentages are expressed graphically in fig.10.

Most touching of all was this comment from a former Northern diocesan. His frustration centred on his *uncertainty about whether I was doing the best that could be done—people were very kind, saying many nice things about me and my ministry, but inevitably one does not hear from the majority of people! Was Sunday's service helpful or merely entertaining?*

The lasting impression given by the enormous scale and variety of these responses is that bishops have their ups and downs like any other occupational group, but that the calls upon their time and energies are increasing endlessly as expectations rise, not just from the local clergy and laity at the bottom, but from the synods and their bureaucracies at the top. The obvious conclusion must be that the bishop is placed uncomfortably between the two like a washer, attempting to defuse criticisms from the one side, which have largely been caused by the insensitivity and inflexibility of the other, while at the same time he is desperately trying to lubricate the institutional machine and be nice to both. Because of their intermediate status between the parish and the diocesan bishop, it seems that area and suffragan bishops suffer the most. The poor old episcopate cannot win either way!

CHAPTER TWELVE

So Where Do We Go from Here?

the modern bishop's dilemma

M odern management techniques in business and commerce mostly revolve around deciding where a company or institution wishes to go and then deciding what should be its priorities in order to get there. The mechanics of this approach are built around creating a trademark mission statement, setting clear goals, adopting strict quantifiable accountability and establishing a comprehensive audit culture (Gill and Burke, 1996, pp. 12-70). It is within these demanding confines that modern executives must fashion their leadership and make their decisions.

Against this attractively straightforward secular model can be placed Jeremy Begbie's view of the problems faced by a modern bishop, quoted by Ian Cundy and Justin Welby, (2000, p. 26):

> *The bishop's power is rightly constrained. He operates within a framework*
> *of legal measures, synods, boards and committees; he rarely has the*
> *support of an infrastructure comparable with those who hold similar*
> *responsibilities in other organisations and professions; his ability to*

243

manage and shape the spiritual life of a diocese is eviscerated by the
vagaries of the freehold, which breeds a culture of clerical and parochial
independence. He is at the beck and call of unreasonable expectations:
constant availability and divine competence to solve all problems and
right every ill of society. If he seeks to be an efficient manager, he is told
that his is a spiritual role; if the diocese lacks cohesion and direction, he is
to blame. He may well reflect that giving a lead in the Church of England
is like trying to take the cat for a walk.

All this vividly corroborates Hugh Melinsky's description of the bishop being ostensibly placed in the diocesan driving seat and yet tugged around constantly by the merciless pull of varying demands and massive expectations— *the bishop's authority swathed in impressive impotence* (*1992, p. 157*).

Section B of the survey did at least confirm that all three sections of the church—bishops, clergy and laity—largely agree about the main planes of a bishop's role and purpose, a clear affirmation that across the three mainland countries at least, the episcopal system is both well understood and highly valued. Nonetheless, the response to B7 indicates that among clergy especially, there is something of a nostalgia for the less hierarchical ways of the Celtic Church—a feeling that, in modern terms at least, the episcopal role should more nearly approximate to that of a senior partner in a professional practice like law, accountancy or medicine, rather than to a high-powered chief executive in the business world.

back to the parish

In this connection it is worth noticing that according to Teresa Morgan (2011), the Self-Supporting Ministry, which by 2009 had risen to a considerable 27% of the total clerical workforce of 15,680, still feels itself largely neglected by the Church, and therefore, by implication, by its bishops. In very few senses have the members of this dedicated body of priests and deacons been treated as equal partners in parochial ministry and strategy, even though the Church would find itself in desperate straits without their generous contribution. There is abundant anecdotal evidence that the bishops' prime concern still lies with the interests of the full-time paid clergy and the development of their careers and that the talents, skills and enthusiasm of the SSMs remain relatively under-utilised in the parish and the workplace because to allow them to be gainfully exploited might cut across the privileges and preserves of the full-time professional clergy.

Instead of being enablers and encouragers of every variety of ministry, many bishops are still behaving like the union shop stewards of the old closed-shop trades like dockwork and printing, keeping all the best tasks for people in possession of the right *ticket,* to the exclusion of many capable priests who are still too often considered merely well-meaning amateurs. If bishops could bring themselves to stop peddling their mistaken confusion of the diocese with the local church and cut their links with old-fashioned restrictive practices, they could unleash this bank of ministerial expertise, together with the talents and enthusiasm of what is now a vast army of over 10,000 Readers. Cumbersome, unwieldy and stress-inducing groupings could be dismantled, allowing every parish in England and Wales to be once again adequately, maybe even generously staffed at no extra cost. Such a move would parallel the Cameron Government's moves towards increased localisation in the running of public services. The Church could then finally turn its back on demoralising pastoral reorganisations and instead move forward with all guns firing to make a serious and sustained effort to reclaim Britain for Christ.

The response to B4 among bishops, clergy and laity produced resounding agreement for the idea that local parishes and congregations, rather than the diocese, should be the focus of a bishop's personal interest and encouragement, a finding underlined in D10, where there was heavy support for the idea that the parish rather than the diocese is the main building block of the Church and might therefore be expected to feature at the top of both episcopal and diocesan priorities. *The Church of England has always been territorial,* said Hinton (1994 p. 139). The findings of this survey suggest that at ground level the parish still matters the most, however hard bishops may try to sell the deanery and the diocese.

Clergy and laity, perhaps churchwardens especially, need to know that their parishes and its local ministries matter most to their bishop. The lack of such assurance, especially when pastoral reorganisation proceeds in diocesan offices far away from the routine needs and aspirations of the parishes, must play a significant part in the loss of morale that seems to pervade so many sections of the Church today.

The perception that the bishop is a member of a separate and superior order of ministry, an idea actively encouraged by the modern Ordinal, appears to go against both the natural instincts of the Church at large and the strongly pastoral *episkope* of the New Testament epistles. It may be that the growing Anglican obsession with the distinct authority of the episcopate is nothing more than an unconscious response to the Roman Catholic collegial notions of the episcopate fostered by Vatican II and amplified in the final report of ARCIC, which were in themselves a genuine endeavour to dispel lingering mediaeval ideas about the primacy of the Papacy. Journalist Monica Furlong (2000, p. 181) takes a sideswipe at the collegiality of bishops by saying, *they vote, and even speak, with worrying unanimity, as one man* ... and then dismisses the notion as merely *borrowed clothes from the Roman Catholic Church, which do not quite fit, since the Church of England is a very different organisation.*

When it came to assessing what should be the *people* priorities in terms of the allocation of a bishop's time and energies, it soon became clear that in a setting where he is involved in the competing claims of extensive local and national committee work, maintaining clergy discipline, caring for his clergy and their families, being the official spokesman to the media, and acting as the repository for any other problem that cannot find a home, he is on a hiding to nowhere. A retired English diocesan bishop wrote, *I could only be a bishop once—I would love a second chance with a mentor guiding, directing, assisting and assessing the next time!* Small wonder that Bishop Colin Buchanan wrote in despair with his returned survey form, *we are a much misunderstood class!*

The survey results in Section C do at least provide some clear guidance on how a bishop might find his way through the minefield of competing pulls on his ministry. The responses show that the laity in particular are anxious for their bishops to be teachers and interpreters of the Christian faith and to be its defenders against the multitudinous attacks it receives from an increasingly sceptical and hostile world. Maybe they sense that there might be more than just a grain of truth in Clive James's quip quoted in the Oxford Dictionary of Humorous Quotations, (1985, p. 276)—*the crisis of the Church of England is that too many of its bishops, and some would say, of its archbishops, don't quite realise they are atheists, but have begun to suspect it.*

The Prime Ministerial diaries of the fictitious Jim Hacker, so hilariously acted out by Paul Eddington, Nigel Hawthorne and Andrew Fowlds in the BBC TV series *Yes Minister* in the early 1980s are reckoned by almost all politicians to be an uncannily reliable picture of how governmental decisions were made at that time. In *The Bishop's Gambit* we get a chance to sneak a look inside the Crown Appointments system as it seemed to the participants at the Downing Street end. The Cabinet Secretary, Sir Humphrey Appleby is giving the Prime Minister a review of possible candidates for the diocese of Bury St. Edmunds and mentions one South London incumbent who has designed a new church where there were *places for dispensing orange juice, and family planning, and organising demonstrations—but no place for Holy Communion.* Jim Hacker asks his two officials if they approve of this design, to which Sir Humphrey breezily replies, *Oh yes, you see the Church of England is run by theologians.* In response to Hacker's bewildered face, he smiles knowingly and says, *Well, theology's a device for keeping agnostics within the church* (Lynn and Jay, 1986, pp. 221-22).

setting episcopal priorities

All this suggests that in planning the allocation of his time, a bishop might do well to give top priority to his travels around the diocese performing confirmations, since here he has an opportunity to publicly teach and proclaim the Christian faith and coach, encourage and enthuse the Church's newest recruits, while at the same time affirming those players who have spent long years getting muddy on the pitch and are desperate to see new talent thrive and succeed. In this connection it is worth recalling what Peter Jagger (1982, p. 148) writes of the Victorian Bishop of Oxford, Samuel Wilberforce:

> *To read through his diary during his episcopate reveals how this part of his duties was anything but a tiresome chore; for him it was a responsibility of great privilege and one which made a deep impression upon him and upon those present at his confirmations, both candidates and observers.*

Should bishops remain in the House of Lords?

So much of the clutter that bogs down the modern bishop is the residual thinking of an Established Church that is frightened it might lose its purpose and grip in national life if it abandoned the privileges and status it has inherited from the Middle Ages. Top of these demands comes attendance at the House of Lords by 26 of its bishops; Canterbury, York, London, Winchester and Durham as of right, and the remainder by seniority. In addition, Canterbury, York and London have the valuable extra privilege of a seat on the Privy Council, which advises the monarch on constitutional matters.

The possibility of major changes in the way the House of Lords is at present constituted were considerably enhanced by the publication in 2000 of the report of the Royal Commission which sat under the chairmanship of Lord Wakeham. This was itself a response to the commitment made to Lords reform in the Labour election manifesto of 1999. Wakeham accepts that the entire range of faith communities should be represented in the Upper House, but he nonetheless recommends that the total Christian representation from all denominations should remain at 26, stipulating that 21 of these seats should be reserved for England and the remaining 5 for Scotland, Wales and Northern Ireland. He further specifies that of the English total, 16 should be reserved for the Church of England, but that the Church might wish to reconsider its existing form of representation. The selection of representatives from the Muslim, Jewish, Sikh and other faiths would be in the hands of the Appointments Commission (2000, paras 108-111).

To avoid becoming enmeshed in political controversy it has become customary that the bishops should confine their contribution in Parliament largely to educational and social matters (Pennington and Bickley, 2007, pp. 40-43), but even this becomes more difficult as the content of legislation in these fields possesses increasingly moral and religious overtones and consequences.

Bishops' contributions to Lords' debates are not frequent, but when they do take to their feet, they make considerable and skilful use of arguments based upon facts, statistics and advice from academics and professionals in order to influence opinion through the presentation of well-informed and credible assessment of the issues under discussion. However, because they are apparently too busy with diocesan commitments to indulge much time in informal lobbying and friendships around the bar and recreational areas, they miss the opportunity to play an important part in influencing policy-makers.

When it comes to their specifically Christian contribution towards debates, it turns out that in the 1980s explicit reference to the Bible was made in only 7% of their speeches and Biblical material explored in detail in only 1%, so that it might well be asked whether they offer anything recognisably distinctive or particularly Christian beyond the overwhelmingly liberal terms of public discourse (Pennington and Bickley, pp. 46-47).

In this connection it may perhaps be significant that the only Asian on the bench, Michael Nazir-Ali, who had been robust in his defence of the Christian faith in the public arena as much as the ecclesiastical, should find it necessary to resign his see of Rochester in 2009 so that he could have the freedom to defend the Judaeo-Christian cultural tradition he considered fundamental to the history and identity of Britain. He clearly felt straight-jacketed by being expected to follow an episcopal line in the House of Lords which consistently failed to challenge the dominant agnostic and humanist consensus that has become one of the intellectual hallmarks of the modern Establishment.

The results of the survey proved tantalisingly inconclusive on the question of Lords attendance. Attending national political forums attracted the support of just 48% of all respondents, with 30% being neutral and 22% according it low priority. Attendance at national church bodies and diocesan synods gained overwhelming support, but only personal knowledge of clergy and ordinands was given such high priority, with groups of local teachers and councillors attracting only 28% and 32% respectively. All this suggests that a bishop might more easily avoid criticism if he concentrated his pastoral activities more tightly and perhaps left the development of wider community contacts to his clergy and laity.

As the bishop is the Church's public face within his diocese, it is no surprise that clergy and laity, as well as bishops themselves, should feel so uniformly dissatisfied with the portrayal of the Church by the media. Only 22% of total respondents agreed that they give it fair coverage and a large 82% wished bishops to work more closely with local media to present a better image. This implies that in the search to fill any vacancy in the episcopal leadership team, considerable weight should be given to discovering candidates with proven media communication skills. In its simplest sense, this is merely to underline yet again, but perhaps in more contemporary terms, the importance attached to effective teaching by the Apostles, the Early Church and the Anglican Reformers.

Appointing bishops

Section F of the survey, which dealt with episcopal appointment methods, was not entirely conclusive, partly because of the lower level of response, especially by the laity. However, perhaps the most telling constant was the feeling among clergy and laity in England, but also in Wales and even in Scotland that the vacant diocese should play a much greater part in the appointments process. The totally open diocesan election proved marginally the most popular first choice overall at 31%, followed by a diocesan election with a closed candidate list at 25% and the electoral college with a built-in majority from the vacant diocese next at 22%. Slightly less popular was the open diocesan election subject to later veto by the House of Bishops at 20%. Bottom of all came the electoral college with a built-in minority from the vacant diocese, which collected only 19%. Thus a considerable 77% of all 523 respondents gave their top preference to some sort of internal diocesan election system.

The Archbishops' Secretary for Appointments compiled an official briefing document in 2009 for the benefit of vacancy-in-see committees. This sets out current arrangements for filling episcopal vacancies in the light of the Perry Report (2001), the recommendations of which preceded Gordon Brown's announcement that the Prime Minister no longer wished to be directly involved in the process. The Crown Nominations Commission is now constituted 50:50 between six representatives of the clergy and laity elected from the vacant diocese and six members of the clergy and laity elected from the General Synod, along with the two archbishops and the Prime Minister's and Archbishops' Appointments Secretaries, the last two being non-voting members. The briefing highlights in what ways it perceives the wider needs of both Church and State should inform its consultations with the vacant diocese.

These are spelt out on p. 9:

> *The diocesan bishop is not only the bishop of his diocese, but also part of the collective leadership of the Church of England as a whole and a member of the House of Bishops, and, in most cases, a potential future member of the House of Lords. The Archbishops will prepare a statement which will set out the needs of the Church of England as a whole with particular regard to the range of skills, perspectives and experience of existing members of the House of Bishops.*

This survey suggests that such priorities do not genuinely reflect the mind of the Church at large and might indeed perpetuate that tendency to drown out the direct voice of the vacant diocese in the interests of wider political and ecclesiastical considerations, which was such a major criticism of Crown appointments before 1977.

The indirect influence of the liberal Establishment upon the selection process may be gauged from the theological colleges attended by the English bench at the end of April, 2011, when there were just two vacancies among the 43 posts.

The dominance of Cuddesdon was obvious: twelve of the diocesans (28%) had trained there, but added to the four alumni of Westcott House, this gave the liberal Catholic bishops a considerable 40%. This compared with just five (12%) from the more orthodox Catholic colleges of Mirfield and St. Stephen's House.

A similar picture emerged from the Evangelical side. Ridley and Wycliffe Halls dominated with 9 bishops, but added together with the six from Cranmer Hall, St. John's Nottingham and Trinity Bristol, this gave the open Evangelical colleges 35% of the bench, whereas the conservative Evangelical Oak Hill contributed only one.

This suggests strongly that the tried and tested Crown policy of trying to ensure some balance in making episcopal appointments between various schools of thought in the Church has all but gone. There is now an obvious bias against conservatives from the Evangelical school and a lesser prejudice against orthodox Catholics, which shows little appreciation of the financial strength and spiritual vitality displayed in so many of their parishes.

Using the opportunities presented by pastoral reorganisation, many liberal bishops are neutralizing trust patronage and making liberal parochial appointments in traditionalist parishes. This is bound to cause cause ill feeling, uncertainty and decline, which may well cost the Church dear in terms of drastic falls in diocesan incomes as dissatisfied worshippers leave for the attractions of Evangelical independency or a more sympathetic Ordinariate. Liberal Anglicanism may do relatively well in major city centres and in prosperous suburbs and wealthy villages through presenting a largely secular programme of good music and intellectual discussion around social, moral and political themes. It has little power to convert unbelievers to Christ or to foster close Christian fellowship in an age of strident atheism and general apathy towards organised religion.

two defining issues—women bishops and gay bishops

In terms of the two major issues of controversy confronting the Church in the new millenium, the results of the survey are clear. There is strong support for women bishops among 70% of all respondents. However, with over fifteen years now passed since the legislation to ordain women succeeded in England in 1992, it is clear that a stubborn 30% still remain either against or uncertain about this development, a feeling which is, after all, in line with the feelings of the world's two greatest Christian communions, Rome and the Orthodox. The answer to this dilemma may be easy to find if the weight of both the survey's majority and minority views are taken seriously into account.

If democracy and synodical government are to have any real meaning, then the majority must surely be accorded the right to proceed as soon as possible with the consecration of women bishops. This would serve the pastoral needs of not only an increasingly female priesthood, but also the many parishes who have embraced the new perspectives and possibilities that they bring with them.

However, the Church must face equally the unpalatable fact that opponents of women priests and bishops are not going to disappear. Both among *Forward in Faith* and *Reform* parishes are some of the most numerically strong, financially successful and youth-orientated churches in the UK, particularly in England itself. Up till now, the Anglo Catholic constituency has been contained within the Church by having its own *flying* bishops, who both understand what their parishes require of them and have most of the specific powers to provide it. Conservative Evangelical parishes have as yet received no *flying bishop*, almost certainly because their Parochial Church Councils have not been willing in sufficient numbers to take what is considered the extreme step of passing Resolution C. Their unhappiness is nonetheless both real and deep.

While the majority quite rightly enjoy their democratic prerogative to have the women priests and bishops they want, so indeed should the minority be allowed to manage without them. Each side ought to subscribe conscientiously to this fundamental principle of fairness and brotherly respect and be willing to act upon it with generosity.

The Church could then proceed to establish at least one extra non-geographical diocese in each of the four provinces of Canterbury, York, Wales and Scotland to allow potentially difficult dissidents to remain full members of the Anglican Church, which would invariably entail allowing their bishops sufficient liberty by statute to develop the life of both their parishes and their dioceses as they saw fit.

When it comes to consecrating practising gays as bishops, the survey produced a clearly negative result. Overall only 22% were in favour, with 43% declaring strong disagreement. Despite the growing demands and increasing influence of equal rights and diversity legislation, majority feelings on this matter, especially among the laity, seem still to be in line with Christian moral teaching since the earliest days of the Church that the sexual instincts of the human race can only find their God-given fulfilment within the context of heterosexual marriage. This position is forcefully and publicly held by both Rome and Orthodoxy. The survey results suggest that there is no serious demand for the Anglican Church in the UK to change its stance in this particular area. For this reason alone, it seems odd that the Church's legal opinion should have advised members of General Synod in June, 2011 that a bar on appointing bishops in a civil partnership would be illegal (Daily Telegraph, 20/6/11). The Church shows increasing signs of panic whenever such an orthodox counter-cultural stance might run the risk of offending the liberal Establishment, whatever might be the majority opinion of church members or the general public.

the political, financial and social background

The Church and its structures cannot operate in a vacuum. How it envisages its mission and how it organises itself to further that mission must inevitably revolve around how it responds to the challenging issues of the day, whether these are political, economic or social.

One of the dominant political issues of the new millenium is the growing danger to the world posed by global warming, whether it is seen to be the result of the industrialisation and urbanisation of the world economy or the latest in a long line of climatic shifts in the span of geological time. Either way, the search must now be on to discover and develop renewable sources of energy for an electricity-hungry world, which is already beginning to realise that petroleum and natural gas stocks are running out fast and that business, commerce and even living itself may have to be more locally focussed once the days of cheap and ubiquitous energy recede into just a memory. Small and local may once again be beautiful. For the Church that will mean refocussing upon the parish or local congregation.

The financial state of the world is becoming as critical as its climate. With individual, corporate and national debt spiralling out of control, confidence and trust has necessarily become weaker. Whether the effects of the *credit crunch* turn out in the long term to be predominantly deflationary or inflationary, investment incomes are certain to be static or dropping and the Church will become even more dependent upon current, rather than upon investment income, particularly as interest rates seem likely to hover just above zero for the foreseeable future. For the Church as an institution this may well mean looking to the parish for its very survival, but even at this local level, severe pressure upon domestic incomes is sure to make life increasingly difficult.

Society is moving away from being moulded and sustained by predominantly Christian influences to instead being built around the philosophical frameworks of humanism and post-modernism, with their elevation of the individual and their depreciation of absolute moral values and social cohesion. The Christian Church finds itself increasingly on the back foot, trying to defend its views of the sanctity of human life, of the family, of care for the poor and needy and decency in human affairs against a noisy onslaught of those who would shut its schools, remove its tax privileges, silence its moral voice and sideline its work and witness. As it finds itself increasingly squeezed off the national stage, so the Church will need to look back to its local roots—in the parishes of the cities, the suburbs and the countryside.

a new type of bishop for a new age

In essence then, this survey shows that clergy and laity, even the retired bishops themselves, are keen to see a return to the pastoral focus of the episcopal task—which for Anglicans has always meant, not the diocese, but the local parish. The survey demonstrates that clergy have learnt to have certain expectations of their bishop's advice and support in spiritual, personal and parochial crises which are often not matched by reality. Yet laity and clergy alike look to the bishop for encouragement and support in planning and bringing about the health and vitality of the local Christian community as well as providing intellectually strong leadership and proven skills in diplomacy.

Furlong (2000, p. 245) quotes with manifest approval Cardinal Basil Hume's inaugural homily at Westminster Cathedral in 1976, where he talks about his understanding of the episcopate:

> It is a function of leadership, but of a leadership that is different. It is characterised by service and devotion. A bishop ought not to impose himself on others. Rather, he should seek to draw out from others what is best in them. He should not stifle but release spiritual energies.

One of the unexpected consequences of the Church of England's creation of *flying bishops* in the wake of the legislation authorising women priests has been the accidental rediscovery of what the episcopate is really about. The relationship between the Catholic Provincial Episcopal Visitor and his constituency is a close one: he regularly meets his parish priests, individually as well as corporately; he is always on hand to ornament and enrich the special occasion; he plays a big part in the nurturing and training of ordinands and he has the oversight of a manageable number of parishes. Small wonder that Catholics are so anxious at his possible demise and that many others, perhaps motivated by a touch of jealousy, would be delighted to see him disappear!

If a bishop is to properly know his clergy, parishes and people and, as Hume says so aptly, release and not stifle spiritual energies, then the Church must abandon the large dioceses of the Saxon kingdoms and their piecemeal subdivision to accommodate the population bubbles of the Industrial Revolution and the period after the First World War. This survey shows that legitimate clerical and lay expectations of their bishops are both considerable and spread over a very wide field of activity. Now may be exactly the right time to transform the neglected deanery unit into a small diocese, not only to make the episcopal task more realistic and manageable for bishops themselves, but also in order to give practical demonstration to the pastoral care and warmth of the episcopal shepherd, who is meant to mirror none other than the Good Shepherd himself, who both knows his sheep and is known by them (John 10:14).

The Church has become mesmerised by the mediaeval trappings of prelacy—an episcopal throne in a grand cathedral, with its dean and chapter, rows of inscribed canons' stalls, bewigged chancellor, choir school, diocesan coat of arms and all the bureaucratic apparatus that goes with them. Even newer dioceses like St. Edmundsbury, Portsmouth and Bradford have not been content with a big parish church become pro-cathedral, but have insisted instead on lavish extensions and plush furnishings in an attempt to mimic their mediaeval forbears.

What is here suggested is that the bishop's chair should reside in the main church of the deanery and that from here the bishop should embark on easily accessible pastoral and supervisory work in, say, between twenty five to thirty five parishes, while remaining a fully functional parish priest himself. This would involve a minimum of expensive travel, emotional fatigue or bureaucratic complication and would require only the most modest secretarial help. His principal task would be to seek out the talents of clergy and laity alike and hone them to be of maximum benefit to both the Church and the world—collaborative ministry brought to life at a truly local level.

By continuing to be a parish priest himself, and being paid the same stipend as his clergy, but with adequate clerical support to sustain his own charge, he would not run the risk of becoming disconnected from the routine round of his priests and parishes. This is no new idea. In the 1640s Archbishop James Usher of Armagh proposed suffragan bishops for deaneries in his *Reduction of Episcopacy unto the form of Synodical Government received in the Ancient church* (Benn, 2002, p. 22). Such a move could indeed be seen as nothing more revolutionary than a return to something like the original function of the episcopate in the city dioceses scattered across the Roman Empire of the 4th century.

It would match the small Orthodox dioceses of Greece, but also many of the dioceses in rural Italy. Citta di Castello in the Upper Tiber Valley of Umbria has a population of only around 60,000. In 2007 Bishop Pelegrino Ronchi had oversight of 55 priests, 24 religious and 11 permanent deacons. He spent a weekend in each of his 60 parishes on a regular basis, telling his clergy, *You make the programme—I'll follow.* While there, he would make a point of joining the parish priest in visiting and welcoming people who had newly moved into the village (information from personal interview, 2007). Such an intimate level of pastoral involvement is possible only if today's unwieldy dioceses are systematically broken up and remodelled with this sort of pastoral objective in mind.

Recently there have been hints that the Church might be softening up opinion for a change in the diametrically opposite direction. Because of relatively low numbers on parish electoral rolls, the Chadwick Report (2010, pp. 52-63) suggested that Bradford, Ripon/Leeds and Wakefield dioceses should be amalgamated into a single grand West Yorkshire see, with its main cathedral in Wakefield, but its diocesan administration based in Leeds. Parishes in Cumbria would be transferred to Carlisle diocese, those in Lancashire to Blackburn and those in the North Riding to York, but the three cathedrals would remain with most of their existing functions intact. This suggestion has been brought forward largely to save money on diocesan administration, which seems fair enough. However, if it actually limits the number of suffragan posts to only the existing ones at Pontefract and Knaresborough, together with the two former diocesan posts which would then be reclassified as suffragan, a timely opportunity for a return to a more practical and effective episcopate would be missed.

In Acts 1:21 Peter is recorded as reminding his fellow believers that *the Lord Jesus went in and out among us* and there is a great deal to be said for encouraging spontaneity, familiarity and unpredictability as essential elements in this renewed oversight. If the bishop is to model an authentic Apostolic ministry and yet demonstrate a good work/life balance, as an overall 86% of respondents clearly wished him to do, then his witness must be essentially incarnational and therefore involved in every aspect of parish life, including the everyday and purely humdrum, with far less emphasis upon his having to occupy centre stage on every conceivable occasion.

As the Church loses an increasing proportion of its investment income through poor yields in bonds, shares and property and has to rely almost exclusively upon the direct giving of the people in the parishes, the trend towards the rationing of fewer full-time clergy established by the Sheffield Formula (Welsby, 1984, p. 255) will inevitably accelerate. More and more pastoral and liturgical work will have to be undertaken by non-stipendiary and ordained local ministers, retired clergy, readers, pastoral auxiliaries, worship leaders and the like, who will perforce need regular access to local specialist training. In this context the new local bishop could expect to play a major role. It might well be argued that a necessary qualification for episcopal leadership in this new deanery-become-diocese might be the Apostolic ability to teach and train. Indeed, it might well happen in the course of time that all those offering for full-time stipendiary ministry should expect, as a major part of their selection process, a careful assessment of their aptitude to become such local *teaching* bishops, since they would be needed in large numbers and probably soak up almost the entire availability of full time clergy.

The respected Charismatic leader David Watson wrote tellingly (1978, p. 19):

> . . . the renewal of the Church must begin with the local church, and not
> with an ever-increasing proliferation of para-church structures. If there
> is a failure here, there can be no significant renewal at all.

However, as such a remodelled and more local episcopate would utilise and build upon the parochial structures that already exist, it might be considered merely a development of what might be called an *institutional* episcopate.

Within the diocese of London are two Evangelical churches—one charismatic and the other conservative—which have quite unintentionally opened a window upon what might be called a *dynamic or organic* episcopate. Holy Trinity, Brompton, at the heart of fashionable Knightsbridge, devised the *Alpha* course to attract enquirers to explore the claims of the Christian faith. *Alpha* was an immediate success and helped by London's excellent bus and underground network, HTB has attracted a huge following over the years, which it has in turn urged to go back to their home parishes to help revive moribund churches.

The result is a considerable network of rejuvenated parishes in West and South West London, who look to Holy Trinity as their spiritual home. At the beginning of 2011 the church had a staff of no less than seventeen curates. Maybe because of this, Bishop Richard Chartres of London felt that he would like its Vicar, Prebendary Sandy Millar to become a bishop to deal particularly with mission situations like theirs. However, this could not be achieved through the usual channels as it would invariably have cut across normal Crown protocol, so it seems that he arranged for the Ugandan Church, who already had links with Prebendary Millar, to consecrate him as one of their bench instead, thus opening the door for him to return immediately to England and be legitimately appointed an Assistant Bishop in the Diocese of London, while simultaneously having charge of the Holloway parish of St. Mark's Tollington Park (Diocese of London press release, 21/10/2005).

A parallel situation has arisen at St. Helen's, Bishopsgate in the heart of London's Square Mile, where longstanding outreach efforts built around informal lunch hour services for the business population have been hugely successful. In the same way as at Brompton, new Christians have been encouraged to return to their home parishes to resuscitate flagging churches and as a result there are now several other congregations in the City and Inner East London who look to St. Helen's as their mother church and to its Rector, William Taylor for a degree of oversight (information from the Revd. Andrew Jones, Hackney, London). At the beginning of 2011, St. Helen's had a staff of thirteen curates. In this case it has not led to the consecration of a new bishop.

Something similar may be happening in the North East of England, where the respected Evangelical leader David Holloway exercises a degree of unofficial oversight over Jesmond Parish Church's new congregational plant on the opposite bank of the Tyne at Holy Trinity, Gateshead, which actually lies within Durham diocese. Because of the Clayton Memorial Church's big numerical following and the serious dearth of other Evangelical parishes in the Newcastle diocese, Jesmond might in time find a compelling need for other such church plants elsewhere in the city. However, the situation here is still very fluid and not a little complicated, since Jesmond has for some time capped its financial contribution to the diocese and been out of communion with its liberal bishop over a number of issues, mostly concerned with Christian beliefs and morality.

The work of the Church Army and many other pioneering agencies in developing *Fresh Expressions* to create new churches in new ways for the huge proportion of the unchurched in modern society will no doubt bring about a need for more such experiments in *dynamic or organic* episcopacy in the years ahead. This has already been foreshadowed in the official report *Mission-Shaped Church* (2004, p. 145), which recommended that an appropriate member of senior staff in every English diocese should be allocated to cater for what Bob Jackson (2002, p. 170) calls *new non-geographical parishes to cater for the emerging postmodern world of relational community.*

should bishops dress to kill?

In the light of the ever-growing chasm between the Church and most of the British public and the urgent need to bridge this gap and re-establish meaningful communications, it might be considered worthwhile to ask whether the now universal habit of bishops wearing mitres is really appropriate. These strange hats seem to contribute a great deal towards making bishops the convenient laughing-stock we cannot afford for them to be.

Mitres have been worn only since Randall Davidson's time at Canterbury and albs and other eucharistic embellishments of various hues are even more recent innovations. It is certainly interesting to note that most young males—and those not quite so young, rarely dress in garish colours, whatever their social class. Even when it comes to leisure wear on the streets, they clearly prefer black, blue or white. The *episcopal habit* defined in the 1662 Consecration service consists of white rochet, black chimere, black scarf and maybe the hood of the university degree a bishop has earned. Not only is this *magpie* habit still the official garb of the Anglican bishop, which he wears at his consecration and whenever he attends sessions of the House of Lords, but it is far and away the most dignified. The modern substitution of a red chimere for the black does not greatly diminish the dignity of the episcopal attire, but it must surely be high time to ditch the mitre—a ridiculous piece of headgear which, so it is rumoured among many irreverent Catholics, is so restricting on the wearer that it may be the cause of serious malfunctions in neurological impulses within the episcopal brain!

Since it seems now to have become common practice for Roman Catholic bishops to wear black clerical stocks with their suits, perhaps it is time to ask Anglican bishops to forgo purple shirts with their hint of ecclesiastical superiority and copy their Roman counterparts in a display of clerical humility. If bishops must wear pectoral crosses, it might be apposite to ask why they should find it necessary to display the chain but hide the actual cross away within an inside pocket. The cross is a potent symbol of the Lord's ultimate sacrifice to win our salvation from sin and death and our chief pastors should surely be willing to wear it with confidence and the right sense of pride.

towards a Spirit-filled episcopate

One of the characteristic features of modern society is its instability, subject as it is to so many pressures, stresses and cross currents, both internal and external. A firmly based local church and episcopate will be much better placed to weather whatever storms may batter Church and society in an uncertain future and to provide people with what they so desperately need—a divine ark of stability, peace and hope in a confused and suffering world.

In similarly turbulent times, Peter and his colleagues grappled with the responsibilities of setting up an infant Church against all the odds. Luke (Acts 2:42-47) records of the Jerusalem church that:

> *They devoted themselves to the apostles' teaching and fellowship, to the breaking of bread and to the prayers. Awe came upon everyone, because many wonders and signs were being done by the apostles. All who believed were together and had all things in common; they would sell their possessions and goods, and distribute the proceeds to all, as any had need. Day by day, as they spent much time together in the temple, they broke bread at home and ate their food with glad and generous hearts, praising God and having the goodwill of all the people. And day by day the Lord added to their number those who were being saved.*

Rediscovering these ancient priorities must surely be an attractive proposition for the entire 21st century Church as it faces challenges not unlike those it was forced to confront during the first century of its existence, when twelve working men were called by Jesus to leave the the familiar shores of Galilee and go out in his name to make disciples of the whole world.

However, we should never lose sight of the fact that, like the New Testament *episkopos/presbuteros,* his modern successors, the bishop and priest, cannot allow themselves to set up in competition with the every-member ministry which God gave to the entire body of his people by settling tongues of fire upon the heads of each one of them on the Day of Pentecost (Acts 2:3).

Instead, those who have been ordained are there to shepherd this universal outpouring of God's Holy Spirit, making sure that the Body of Christ never lacks the solid Biblical teaching and effective pastoral oversight that are essential to both its character and effectiveness. The varied gifts of the Holy Spirit are there for every individual Christian to discover and employ, but they will need to be developed and honed by those who have been specifically called by God and publicly ordained within the Church to deliver this enabling ministry of the living Word and effective sacraments. Such is the Apostolic way and with it goes the Apostolic challenge.

In facing this challenge a renewed episcopate must play a central role, since the office of a bishop has the solid back-up of Apostolic origins, a noteworthy and continuous past and an easily recognisable public face, perhaps as much so today as at any time in its long history. Echoing almost exactly the words of Paul writing his second letter to Timothy (1:6-7), the 1662 rite accompanies the laying of hands upon the new bishop's head with these challenging words:

> Receive the Holy Ghost for the office and work of a Bishop in the Church
> of God, now committed unto thee by the imposition of our hands; in the
> Name of the Father, and of the Son, and of the Holy Ghost, Amen. And
> remember that thou stir up the grace of God which is given thee by this
> imposition of our hands; for God hath not given us the spirit of fear, but
> of power, and love, and soberness (or self-discipline).

The three qualities that should characterise the episcopate—power, love and self-discipline—are the particular gift of the Holy Spirit for the performance of this special office. They may indeed come with the laying on of hands at the consecration, but if they are not being stirred up every day by fervent prayer and careful meditation over the Scriptures, the work of a bishop will become flaccid, lacking in emotion, unfocussed and ultimately ineffective. The spirit of fear, which Paul is warning Timothy about here in his second epistle, may well be unconsciously embedded within the ethos of the modern Anglican Church, moving quietly and invisibly around the episcopal bench. It inflicts its damage by closing down the miracle of divine energy by dealing only in the purely rational and routine, replacing the loving shepherding of clergy and lay people with the deadness of bureaucracy and breaking down a man's self-discipline by demoralising him through the sheer weight and indiscriminateness of the demands made upon his finite time and energies.

It is a supreme irony that at the very moment a man is being ordained and commissioned for what is probably the most important job the Church has to offer, the consecration prayer in *Common Worship* should omit the words of the second part of this wonderful prayer. They encapsulate both the opportunities and the pitfalls of the episcopate, that ancient pinnacle of sacred ministry that everyone seems so ready to respect and desire, but so few seem willing to help blossom and flourish.

APPENDIX

UNIVERSITY OF BANGOR

SCHOOL OF THEOLOGY AND RELIGIOUS STUDIES

Bangor,
Gwynedd,
Wales,
LL572PX

My own telephone: 01691 830010

I am doing important doctoral research within this department, under the supervision of the Revd. Professor Canon Dr. Leslie Francis of Warwick University on the subject of clerical and lay perceptions of the English, Welsh and Scottish Episcopates.

I think you will agree that this is especially important work now that Gordon Brown has decreed that the Crown no longer wishes to play a direct part in the appointment of English bishops and the Church has started thinking about how to do the job itself.

Could you please help me by taking care in answering this questionnaire and then return it to me as soon as possible in the stamped addressed envelope provided? I have included on your form only male/female, full-time/NSM and inner city/urban/rural classifications. I do urge you to participate. Your views are vital since the results of this survey will be communicated to the Church authorities and made widely available.

Remember that no names or addresses are wanted—the answers should be entirely anonymous.

Thanks very much indeed.

Yours sincerely,

The Revd. Mike Keulemans

BISHOPS—A STATISTICAL SURVEY

What do you feel about the main roles of a bishop?

AS—Agree Strongly   D—Disagree

A—Agree   DS—Disagree Strongly

N—Neutral

	AS	A	N	D	DS
He should be the focus of unity within his diocese.					
He should represent his own diocese to the wider Church.					
He should represent the wider Church to his own diocese.					
He should give personal support and encouragement to local parishes/ congregations.					
He should maintain the ancient succession of apostolic orders.					
He should maintain the ancient tradition of teaching apostolic doctrine.					
Among his clergy he should be considered as first among equals.					

What priority should a bishop give to the following tasks?

VH—Very High   L—Low

H—High   VL—Very Low

N—Neutral

	VH	H	N	L	VL
Attending national political forums like the House of Lords.					
Attending national Church forums like General Synod.					
Attending the Diocesan Synod and its various committees.					
Attending secular public events within the diocese.					
Handling clergy discipline within the diocese.					
Teaching and explaining the Christian Faith.					
Defending the Christian Faith against attack.					
Interpreting the Christian Faith to the needs and challenges of our age.					
Getting to know individual clergy and their families.					
Getting to know individual ordinands and their families.					
Getting to know individual readers.					

	AS	A	N	D	DS
Getting to know individual churchwardens.					
Getting to know groups of local teachers.					
Getting to-know groups of local councilors.					
Getting to know local community groups.					

What do you think of these statements?

AS—Agree Strongly   D—Disagree

A—Agree   DS—Disagree Strongly

N—Neutral

	AS	A	N	D	DS
A bishop ought to take at least eight weeks holiday per year.					
A bishop ought to model a good work/life balance.					
The media generally give a fair portrayal of bishops and their opinions.					
A bishop should work with local media to present a better image of the Church.					
Too much money is spent on bishops and their staff.					
Bishops should be paid the same as parish clergy.					
Bishops should be appointed for a fixed term of years.					
A bishop should delegate all administrative tasks to his archdeacons.					

	AS	A	N	D	DS
A bishop should be readily accessible to his clergy day or night.					
The Church's main building block is not the diocese but the parish/local congregation					

What do you feel about these issues?

AS—Agree Strongly   D—Disagree
A—Agree   DS—Disagree Strongly
N—Neutral

	AS	A	N	D	DS
Women should be able to become bishops.					

What main reason do you have for your view?

	AS	A	N	D	DS
Practising homosexuals should be able to become bishops.					

What main reason do you have for your view?

_____

_____

_____

_____

_____

How should bishops be selected?

Bishops appointed in secret by the Church's own Appointments Committee, which would contain a built-in minority of members chosen by the vacant diocese.	
Bishops appointed in secret by the Church's own Appointments Committee, which would contain a built-in majority of members chosen by the vacant diocese.	
Bishops appointed by a secret ballot of clergy and laity held at the Diocesan Synod or Conference of the vacant diocese, with a closed candidate list, which has been previously vetted by the House of Bishops.	
Bishops appointed by a secret ballot of clergy and laity held at the Diocesan Synod or Conference of the vacant diocese, with an open candidate list, but with the result subject to later agreement by the House of Bishops.	
Bishops appointed by a secret ballot of clergy and laity held at a Special Synod of all diocesan clergy and lay representatives from every parish! congregation in the vacant diocese., with an open candidate list and the House of Bishops having no veto on the election result.	

Your own Christian Beliefs?

AS—Agree Strongly   D—Disagree
A—Agree   DS—Disagree Strongly
N—Neutral

	AS	A	N	D	DS
Jesus is actually present in the consecrated bread and wine of the Eucharist.					
Sermons are for getting to grips with what the Bible teaches.					
We must come to religious Issues with an open mind.					
People full of the Holy Spirit want to sing and dance in church.					
Ditching the old Book of Common Prayer was a mistake.					
Ordaining women to the priesthood seriously breached Christian tradition.					
It's time we accepted homosexuality among nests and moved on.					
Robes and ceremonial help to create a worshipful atmosphere.					
If we fearlessly proclaimed the Word of God, we might see revival.					
The historical reliability of the Bible seems increasingly doubtful.					

	AS	A	N	D	DS
Our main task is to see non church people find a living faith in Jesus.					
The Church must take morecare of its historic buildings.					
Speaking in tongues and prophecy have a part in worship.					
We should encourage regular pilgrimagesto Walsingham and other shrines.					
Healings and other miracles should be part of normal church life.					

Laity: put a ring around your answer

Have you met your own bishop face to face at least once in—past year/ past2 years/ past 5 years?

Have you heard your own bishop preach or speak at least once in—past year/ past 2 years/ past 5 years?

AS—Agree Strongly   D—Disagree
A—Agree   DS—Disagree Strongly
N—Neutral

Clergy:

	AS	A	N	D	DS
I would consult a bishop about a spiritual matter					
I would consult a bishop about a personal matter.					
I would consult a bishop about a parish matter.					
I have been helped by consulting a bishop about a spiritual matter.					
I have been helped by consulting a bishop about a personal matter.					
I have been helped by consulting a bishop about a parish matter.					

Please use this space for any other comments you would like to make.

_____

_____

_____

_____

Bishops:

Please answer these questions on the enclosed blank sheet in whatever way you feel comfortable.

Any additional comments would be very much appreciated

A. What aspects of your episcopate did you find most satisfying?

B. What aspects of your episcopate did you find most frustrating?

REFERENCES

Adams, G.B. and Schuyler, R.L. (1935), *Constitutional History of England*, London, Jonathan Cape.

Addison, J.T. (1951), *The Episcopal Church in the United States 1789-1931*, New York, Charles Scribner's Sons.

Ayre, J. ed. (1845), *The Works of John Jewel, Bishop of Salisbury*, Cambridge, University Press for the Parker Society.

Alfeyev, H. (2002), *The Mystery of Faith—an Introduction to the Teaching and Spirituality of the Orthodox Church*, London, Darton, Longman and Todd.

Bamm, P. (1959), *The Kingdoms of Christ: the story of the early church*, London, Thames and Hudson.

Barnard, L.W. (1966), *The Apostolic Fathers and their Background*, Oxford, Basil Blackwell.

Barr, L. (2001), *Flodden*, London, Tempus Publishing.

Bauer, W. (1971), *Orthodoxy and Heresy in Earliest Christianity*, Philadelphia, Fortress Press.

Beckwith, R. (2003), *Elders in Every City: the origin and role of the ordained ministry*, Carlisle, Paternoster Press.

Bell, G.K.A. (1935), *Randall Davidson, Archbishop of Canterbury*, Oxford, University Press.

Benn, W.P. (2002), *Usher on Bishops—a Reforming Ecclesiology,* Sheffield, MENSA.

Bettenson, H. (1943), *Documents of the Christian Church,* Oxford, University Press.

Black, A. (1980), The Government of the Church, In Cumming, J. and Burns, P, *The Church Now—an enquiry into the present state of the Catholic Church in Britain and Ireland,* pp. 67-72, Dublin, Gill and Macmillan Ltd.

Blake, R. (1966), *Disraeli,* London, Eyre and Spottiswoode.

Blunt, A.W.F. (1925), *The Epistle of Paul to the Galatians,* Oxford, Clarendon Press.

Boddington, C. (2009), *Choosing Diocesan Bishops: the process,* London, Lambeth Palace.

Bogle, J. (2002), *South Bank Religion: the Diocese of Southwark 1959-1969,* London, Hatcham Press.

Bradley, I. (2003), *The Celtic Way,* London, Darton, Longmans and Todd.

Brierley, P. ed, (2005/6), *UK Christian Handbook: Religious Trends 5—the Future of the Church,* London, Christian Research.

Brown, R.L. (2006), *In Pursuit of a Welsh Episcopate: appointments to Welsh sees 1840-1905,* Cardiff, University of Wales Press.

Brown, R.L. (2007), *Evangelicals in the Church in Wales,* Welshpool, Tair Eglwys Press.

Browne, C.G. and Swallow, J.E. tr, (1894), *Select Orations of St. Gregory of Nazianzum,* Oxford, James Parker and Co. and New York, Christian Literature Co.

Bruce, F.F. (1988), *The New Testament Documents—are they reliable?* London/Grand Rapids. Inter Varsity Press/Wm. B. Eerdmans Publishing Co.

Burkett, D. (2002), *An Introduction to the New Testament and the Origins of Christianity,* Cambridge, University Press.

Burtchaell, J.T. (1992), *From Synagogue to Church,* Cambridge, University Press.

Butler, D. and Butler, G. (1994), *British Political Facts 1900-1994,* Basingstoke, Macmillan.

Cameron, E. (1991), *The European Reformation,* Oxford, Clarendon Press.

Cameron, S. ch. (1990), *Episcopal Ministry—Report of the Archbishops' Group on the Episcopate,* London, Church House Publishing.

Carpenter, S.C. (1954), *The Church in England 597-1688,* London, John Murray.

Carpenter, S.C. (1959), *Church and People 1789 to 1889,* London, SPCK.

Catechism of the Catholic Church (1992), London, Geoffrey Chapman.

Chadwick, H. tr. (1965), *Origen: Contra Celsum,* Cambridge, University Press.

Chadwick, O. (1990), *Michael Ramsey: a life,* Oxford, Clarendon Press.

Chadwick, P. ch. (2010), *Dioceses Commission Review Report No.2: Dioceses of Bradford, Ripon and Leeds and Wakefield,* London, Church House Publishing.

Church, L.F. (1949), *More about the Early Methodist People,* London, Epworth.

Church in Wales, (2010 edition), *Constitution of the Church in Wales,* Cardiff, Church in Wales Publications.

Clark, K. (1964), *The Gothic Revival,* Harmondsworth, Penguin.

Clark, M.T. tr, (1984). *St. Augustine of Hippo: selected writings,* London, SPCK.

Cooper, S.F. and Atterbury, P. (2001), Religion and Doubt, in Mackenzie, J. ed. *The Victorian Vision—Inventing New Britain,* pp. 125-145, London, V and A Publications.

Cormack, P. (1984), *English Cathedrals,* London, Artus Books.

Corrie, G.E. ed. (1844), *Sermons by Hugh Latimer—sometime Bishop of Worcester,* Cambridge, University Press for the Parker Society.

Coxe, A.C. (1886), *Fathers of the Third Century: Hippolytus, Cyprian, Caius, Novatian, Appendix,* New York, Christian Literature Publishing Co.

Cranfield, C.E.B. (1960), *I and II Peter and Jude,* London, SCM.

Cray, G. ch. (2004), *Mission Shaped Church,* Report of the Church of England Mission and Public Affairs Council, London, Church House Publishing.

Crossley, F.H. (1935), *English Abbeys,* London, Batsford Books.

Cundy, I. and Welby, J. (2000), Taking the Cat for a Walk? Can a Bishop order a Diocese? in Evans, G.R. and Percy, M. *Managing the Church?* pp. 25-48, Sheffield, Sheffield Academic Press.

Davies, J. (1993), *A History of Wales,* London, Allen Lane, The Penguin Press.

Davies, R. (1963), *Methodism,* Harmondsworth, Penguin.

Davies, W.D. and Allison, D.C. (1988) *The Gospel according to St. Matthew,* Edinburgh, T. and T. Clark.

Dawley, P.M. (1955), *John Whitgift and the Reformation,* London, Adam and Charles Black.

Deanesly, M. (1950), *A History of the Mediaeval Church 590-1500,* London, Methuen.

Deanesly, M. (1961), *The Pre-Conquest Church in England,* London, Adam and Charles Black.

Dickinson, J.D. (1979), *The Later Middle Ages—from the Norman Conquest to the eve of the Reformation,* New York, Barnes and Noble.

Dix, G. (1946), The Ministry in the Early Church. In K.E. Kirk, *The Apostolic Ministry,* pp. 185-303, London, Hodder and Stoughton.

Doe, N. (2002), *The Law of the Church in Wales,* Cardiff, University of Wales Press.

Donaldson, J. ed, (1880), *The Apostolical Constitutions,* Edinburgh, T. and T. Clark.

Duffield, G.E. (1964), *Thomas Cranmer*, Appleford, Sutton Courtenay Press.

Edwards, A.G. (1912), *Landmarks in the History of the Welsh Church*, London, John Murray.

Ehrman, B.D. (2003), *Lost Scriptures: books that did not make it into the New Testament*, Oxford, University Press.

Elton, G.R. (1991), *England under the Tudors*, London, Routledge.

Episcopal Church in Scotland, (1952), *Code of Canons of the Episcopal Church in Scotland*, Edinburgh, University Press.

Evans, D.G. (1989), *A History of Wales 1815-1906*, Cardiff, University of Wales Press.

Evans, D.G. (2000), *A History of Wales 1906-2000*, Cardiff, University of Wales Press.

Evans, E. (1985), *Daniel Rowland and the Great Evangelical Awakening in Wales*, London, Banner of Truth.

Evans, E.D. (1993), *A History of Wales 1660-1815*, Cardiff, University of Wales Press.

Evans, G.R. and Percy, M. (2000), *Managing the Church? order and organisation in a secular age*, Sheffield, Sheffield Academic Press.

Farmer, B.H. ed, (1983), *The Age of Bede*, London, Penguin Books.

Farrer, A.M. (1946), The Ministry in the New Testament, In K.E. Kirk, *The Apostolic Ministry*, pp. 113-182, London, Hodder and Stoughton.

Fellowship of Concerned Churchmen (2008), *Directory of Traditional Anglican and Episcopal Parishes*, www.anglicanchurches.net.

Fisher, D.J.V. (1973), *The Anglo-Saxon Age: c.400-1042*, London, Longman.

Fouyas, M. (1972), *Orthodoxy, Roman Catholicism and Anglicanism*, London, Oxford University Press.

Frend, W.H.C. (1991), *The Early Church: from the beginnings to 461*, London, SCM Press.

Frere, S.S. (1967), *Britannia*, London, Routledge and Kegan Paul.

Furlong, M. (2000). *The C. of E: the State it's in*, London, SPCK.

Gill R. and Burke, D. (1996), *Strategic Church Leadership*, London, SPCK.

Gillingham, J. (1984), The Early Middle Ages (1066-1290), In Morgan, K.O. ed. *Oxford Illustrated History of Britain*, pp. 104-165, Oxford, University Press.

Guelzo, A. (1994), *Towards the Reunion of Evangelical Christendom: the story of the Reformed Episcopal Church*, Philadelphia, University of Stanford Press.

Harnack, A. von, (1910), *The Constitution and Law of the Church in the First Two Centuries*, London, Williams and Norgate.

Harris, C. and Startup, R. (1999), *The Church in Wales: the sociology of a traditional institution*, Cardiff, University of Wales Press.

Hattersley, R. (2004), *The Edwardians*, London, Little Brown.

Hattersley, R. (2007), *Borrowed Time—the Story of Britain between the Wars*, London, Little, Brown.

Hebert, A.G. (1946), Ministerial Episcopacy, In K.E. Kirk, *The Apostolic Ministry*, London, Hodder and Stoughton.

Hinton, M. (1994), *The Anglican Parochial Clergy—A Celebration.* London, SCM Press.

Hooker, R. (1592), *The Laws of Ecclesiastical Polity*, 1875 edition, Oxford, Clarendon Press.

Howse, E.M. (1971), *Saints in Politics: the Clapham Sect and the growth of freedom*, London, George Allen and Unwin.

Iremonger, F.A. (1948), *William Temple, Archbishop of Canterbury: his life and letters*, Oxford University Press, London.

Jackson, B. tr. (1895), *St. Basil: Letters and Select Works*, New York, Christian Literature Publishing Co.

Jackson, R. (2002), *Hope for the Church—contemporary strategies for growth*, London, Church House Publishing.

Jacob, E.F. (1961), *The Fifteenth Century 1399-1485*, Oxford, Clarendon Press.

Jagger, P.J. (1982), *Clouded Witness: initiation in the Church of England 1850-75*, Allison Park, Pickwick Publications.

Jenkins, C. and Mackenzie, K.D. eds (1930), *Episcopacy Ancient and Modern*, London, SPCK.

Jenkins, P. (1992), *A History of Modern Wales 1536-1990*, Harlow, Longmans.

Johnson, P. (1974), *Queen Elizabeth I*, London, Futura Publications.

Jones, N. and Owen, M.E. (2003), Twelfth century Welsh hagiography: the *Gogynfeirdd* poems. In Cartwright, J. ed. *Celtic Hagiography and Saints' Cults*, pp. 45-76, Cardiff, University of Wales Press.

Jones, P. (2000), *The Governance of the Church in Wales*, Cardiff, Greenfach.

Keulemans, M. (2004), *Pennant Melangell—a case study in sacred place and pilgrimage*, unpublished MTh dissertation, University of Wales.

Kirk, J. (1989), *Patterns of Reform: continuity and change in the Reformation Kirk*, Edinburgh, T. and T. Clark.

Kirk, K.E. ed, (1946), *The Apostolic Ministry: essays on the history and the doctrine of episcopacy*, London, Hodder and Stoughton.

Kung, H. (1968), *The Church*, London, Search Press.

Lawson, J.P. (1843), *History of the Scottish Episcopal Church from the Revolution to the Present Time*, Edinburgh, Gillie and Bayley.

Lee, A.D. (2000), *Pagans and Christians in late Antiquity*, London and New York, Routledge.

Lienhard, J.T. (1984), *Ministry—Message of the Fathers of the Church*, Wilmington, Michael Glazier Inc.

Lightfoot, J.B. (1901), *The Christian Ministry*, New York, Macmillan and Co.

Linklater, E. (1968), *The Survival of Scotland*, London, Heinemann.

Linnell, C.L.S. ed. (1964), *The Diaries of Thomas Wilson DD*, London, S.P.C.K.

Lossky, Y. (1957), *Mystical Theology in the Eastern Church*, London.

Lynch, M. (1992), *Scotland—a new history*, London, Pimlico.

Lynn, J. and Jay, A. eds. (1986), *The Diaries of the Right Hon. James Hacker, vol.I*, London, BBC Publications.

MacCulloch, D. (1999), *Tudor Church Militant: Edward VI and the Protestant Reformation*, London, Allen Lane The Penguin Press.

Mackie, J.D, Lenman, B, and Parker, G. (1978), *A History of Scotland*, London, Penguin Books.

MacMullen, R. (1984), *Christianizing the Roman Empire A.D. 100-400*, New Haven and London, Yale University Press.

Maitland, F.W. (1955), *The Constitutional History of England*, Cambridge, University Press.

Malony, H.N. (1995), *The Psychology of Religion for Ministry*, New York and Mahwah, Paulist Press.

Marr, A. (2007), *A History of Modern Britain*, London, Macmillan.

Marshall, I.H. (1999), *The Pastoral Epistles*, Edinburgh, T. and T. Clark.

Marshall, P.V. (2005), A Note on the Role of North America in the Evolution of Anglicanism, *Anglican Theological Review*, Vol.87, No. 4, pp. 550-60.

Mayr-Harting, H. (1972), *The Coming of Christianity to Anglo-Saxon England*, London, Book Club Associates.

Melinsky, M.A.H. (1992), *The Shape of the Ministry*, Norwich, Canterbury Press.

Members of the English Church, tr (1843)., *The Homilies of St. John Chrysostem to the Philippians, Colossians and Thessalonians*, Oxford, John Henry Parker.

Menzies, A. ed. (1994), *The Ante-Nicene Fathers*, Peabody, Hendrickson Publishers.

Metzger, B.M. (1987), *The Canon of the New Testament*, Oxford, Clarendon Press.

Mierow, C.C. tr, (1963), *The Letters of St. Jerome*, Westminster, Maryland, Newman Press.

Moberly, G.H. (1887), *The Life of William of Wykeham*, Winchester, Warren and Sons.

Moorman, J.R.H. (1946), *Church Life in England in the 13th Century*, Cambridge, University Press.

Morgan, T. (2011), *Survey of Self-Supporting Ministers*, Oriel College Oxford and 1pf.co.uk.

Moorman, J.R.H. (1973), *A History of the Church in England*, London, Adam and Charles Black.

Murphy-O'Connor, C. (2004), *At the Heart of the World*, London, Darton, Longman and Todd.

Needham, N.R. (2000), *2000 Years of Christ's Power: the Age of the Early Church Fathers,s*, London, Grace Publications Trust.

Needham, N.R. (2002), *2000 Years of Christ's Power: the Middle Ages*, London, Grace Publications Trust.

Neil, C. and Willoughby, J.M. (1912), *The Tutorial Prayer Book*, London, Church Book Room Press.

Neill, S. (1977), *Anglicanism*, London, Mowbray and Co.

Osborne, C.E. (1903), *The Life of Father Dolling*, London, Edward Arnold.

Ottley, R.L. (1894), *Lancelot Andrewes*, London, Methuen.

Owen, F. (1954), *Tempestuous Journey: Lloyd George his life and times*, London, Hutchinson.

Parker, T.M. (1946), Feudal Episcopacy. In K.E. Kirk, *The Apostolic Ministry*, pp. 351-386, London, Hodder and Stoughton.

Pennington, A. and Bickley, P. (2007), *Coming off the Bench: the past, present and future of religious representation in the House of Lords*, London, Theos Think Tank.

Perry, B. ch. (2001), *Working with the Spirit: choosing diocesan bishops, GS 1405*, London, Church House Publishing.

Percival, H.R. ed. (1900), *The Seven Ecumenical Councils of the Undivided Church*, New York, Charles Scribner's Sons.

Petts, D. (2003), *Christianity in Roman Britain*, Stroud, Tempus Publishing.

Pevsner, N. *The Buildings of England*, Cheshire (1971), London 4 North (1998), Sussex (1965) and Worcestershire (1968), London, Penguin Books.

Pilling, J. ch. (2007), *Talent and Calling: Report of the Senior Church Appointments Review Group, GS 1650*, London, Church House Publishing.

Pollock, J. (1985), *Shaftesbury: the poor man's earl*, London, Hodder and Stoughton.

Podmore, C. (2001), The Choosing of Bishops in the Early Church and in the Church of England: a historical survey. In Perry, B. ch. *Working with the Spirit: choosing diocesan bishops, GS 1405*, pp. 113-142, London, Church House Publishing.

Powicke, M. (1962), *The Thirteenth Century, 1216-1307*, London, Oxford University Press.

Price, D.T.W. (1990), *A History of the Church in Wales in the 20th Century*, Cardiff, Church in Wales Publications.

Pritchard, R. (1991), *A History of the Episcopal Church*, Harrisburg, Moorehouse Publicity.

Purcell, W. (1969), *Fisher of Lambeth—a Portrait from Life,* London, Hodder and Stoughton.

Reid, D. (2010), Anglicans and Orthodox: the Cyprus Agreed Statement, *Journal of Anglican Studies, vol.8.2, November 2010, pp. 184-199.*

Richardson, A. (1959), *The Gospel according to St. John,* London, SCM Press.

Ridley, J. (1970), *Lord Palmerston,* London, Constable.

Riecke, B. (1964), *The Epistles of James, Peter and Jude,* New York. Doubleday.

Robertson, A. ed. (1892), *St. Athanasius: select writings and letters,* Oxford and New York, Parker and Co. and Christian Literature Publishing Co.

Robinson, J.A.T. (1952), *The Body—a Study in Pauline Theology,* Studies in Practical Theology, vol. XIV, London, SCM.

de Romestyn, H. and Duckworth, H.T.F. tr, (1896), *Some of the Principal Works of St. Ambrose,* Oxford and New York, James Parker and Christian Literature Publishing Co.

Ross, D. (2008), *Wales—History of a Nation,* New Lanark, Geddes Grosset.

Rupp, E.G. (1986), *Religion in England 1688-1791,* Oxford, Clarendon Press.

Salway, P. (1993), *The Oxford Illustrated History of Roman Britain,* London, Quality Paperbacks Direct.

Sandbrook, D. (2006), *White Heat—A History of Britain in the Swinging Sixties,* London, Little Brown.

Saul, N. (1997), *Richard II,* New Haven and London, Yale University Press.

Schama, S. (2000), *A History of Britain: at the edge of the world? 3000BC-AD1603,* London, BBC Worldwide.

Schama, S. (2002), *A History of Britain: the fate of empire 1776-2000,* London, BBC Worldwide.

Schnelle, U. (1998), *The History and Theology of the New Testament Writings*, London, SCM Press.

Schroedel, W.R. (1985), *A Commentary on the Letters of Ignatius of Antioch*, Philadelphia, Fortress Press.

Schweizer, E. (1982) *The Good News according to Matthew*, London, SPCK.

Scotland, N. (1995), *The Life and Work of John Bird Sumner*, Leominster, Gracewing.

Scottish Episcopal Church, (2005), *Ecclesiastical Law and the Code of Canons*, Edinburgh, General Synod Office.

Sherrin, N. ed. (1985), *Oxford Dictionary of Humorous Quotations*, Oxford and New York, Oxford University Press.

Smith, W. (1953), *An Economic Geography of Great Britain*, London, Methuen.

Smout, T.C. (1986), *A Century of the Scottish People 1830-1950*, London, Fontana.

Sordi, M. (1983), *The Christians and the Roman Empire*, London and Sydney, Croom Helm.

Souter, A. (1913), *The Text and Canon of the New Testament*, London, Duckworth.

Souter, A. tr, (1947), *Novum Testamentum Graecae*, Oxford, Clarendon Press.

Southern, R.W. (1992), *Robert Grosseteste: the Growth of the Mind in Mediaeval Europe*, Oxford, Clarendon Press.

Stewart, F. (1981), *Loretto One Fifty—the story of Loretto School from 1827 to 1977*, Edinburgh, William Blackwood and Sons.

Stott, J.R.W. (1990), *The Message of Acts*, Leicester, Inter Varsity Press.

Streeter, B.H. (1924), *The Four Gospels*, London and New York, Macmillan and Co.

Streeter, B.H. (1929), *The Primitive Church*, London, Macmillan and Co

Tenney, M.C. (1953), *New Testament Survey*, London, Inter-Varsity Press.

Thayer, J.P. (1896) reprinted 2000, *Greek-English Lexicon of the New Testament*, Peabody, Hendrickson Publishers.

Thiede, C.P. (1992), *The Heritage of the First Christians*, Oxford, Lion Publishing.

Thomson, J.A.F. (1993), *The Early Tudor Church and Society 1485-1529*, London and New York, Longman Group.

Todd, M. (2004), William Cowper of Galloway and the Puritan Episcopacy of Scotland, *Scottish Journal of Theology*, vol.57, no.3, pp. 300-312.

Trigg, J.W. (1983), *Origen—the Bible and Philosophy in the Third Century Church*, London, SCM Press.

Tugwell, S. (1989), *The Apostolic Fathers*, London and New York, Continuum.

Turton, D.W. (2003), *The Pastoral Care of the Clergy*, Unpublished Ph.D. thesis, University of Wales.

Wakeham, J. ch. (2000), *A House for the Future*, Report of the Royal Commission on the Reform of the House of Lords, Cmnd. 4534.

Walters, M. and Hanson, B. (1999), *Vacancies, Suspension and Reorganisation*, Watford, Church Society.

Ware, K. (1982), Patterns of Episcopacy in the Early Church and Today—an Orthodox view, In Moore, P. ed. *Bishops—But What Kind?* pp. 1-24, London, SPCK.

Watson, D. (1978), *I Believe in the Church*, London, Sydney, Auckland, Toronto, Hodder and Stoughton.

Welsby, P.A. (1984), *A History of the Church of England, 1945-80*, Oxford, University Press.

Welsh Churches Survey, (1995), *Challenge to Change*, Cardiff, British and Foreign Bible Society.

Williams, B. (1979), *The Work of Archbishop John Williams,* Abingdon, Sutton Courtenay Press.

Williamson, J. (1963), *Father Joe,* London, Hodder and Stoughton.

Willis, J.R. ed, (1966), *The Teachings of the Church Fathers,* New York, Herder and Herder

Wilson, W. tr. (1869), *The Writings of Clement of Alexandria,* Edinburgh, T. and T. Clark.

Wolffe, J. (2005), Lord Palmerston and Religion: A Reappraisal, *English Historical Review, vol. CXX, No.488, September 2005, pp. 907-936.*

Wright, N.T. (1992), *The New Testament and the People of God,* London, SPCK.

Zenos, A.C. and Hartrandft, C.D. eds, (1890) *Socrates, Sozomenus: Church Histories,* New York, Christian Literature Publishing Co.

INDEX

Lightning Source UK Ltd.
Milton Keynes UK
UKOW052258250112

186038UK00002B/2/P